The Canadian Contribution to a Comparative Law of Secession

Giacomo Delledonne · Giuseppe Martinico
Editors

The Canadian Contribution to a Comparative Law of Secession

Legacies of the Quebec Secession Reference

palgrave
macmillan

Editors
Giacomo Delledonne
Comparative Public Law
Sant'Anna School of Advanced Studies
Pisa, Italy

Giuseppe Martinico
Comparative Public Law
Sant'Anna School of Advanced Studies
Pisa, Italy

ISBN 978-3-030-03468-9 ISBN 978-3-030-03469-6 (eBook)
https://doi.org/10.1007/978-3-030-03469-6

Library of Congress Control Number: 2018960251

Cover design by Thomas Howey

This Palgrave Macmillan imprint is published by the registered company Springer Nature Switzerland AG
The registered company address is: Gewerbestrasse 11, 6330 Cham, Switzerland

Foreword

The Secession Reference Twenty Years Later

I remember quite vividly the night of the Quebec referendum in 1995. My mother and I were home in Orleans, just east of the Canadian national capital, watching the results broadcast live on television as the votes were tabulated, the yes and no sides exchanging leads back and forth. Even before the network announced the final tally—a razor-thin margin of 54,288 votes rejecting secession out of 4,671,008 valid ballots cast—the closeness of the vote and the emotions that accompanied it yielded only one certainty: the Canada I knew would change no matter the outcome.

We are still today living the consequences of the turbulent referendum campaign and its culminating vote. The strength of the support in Quebec for independence surprised Canadians in all corners of the land, and it has reawakened the country to the pressing challenge of internal reconciliation. And yet the secession referendum also reopened wounds that for many have yet to heal and perhaps never will, further deepening old fault lines that continue to divide Canadians.

The referendum result triggered a sequence of events that produced one of Canada's most well-known legal exports: the *Secession Reference*. Alongside the "living tree doctrine," the *Oakes* test, purposive interpretation and the Notwithstanding Clause, the *Secession Reference* has become what public law scholars around the world associate with Canada. The brilliance of the judgment doubles at once as its strength and weakness:

it gives something of a victory to all sides but it defers many questions for future resolution, some in the heat of the very moment when the choice between recognizing and refusing independence hangs in the balance. For some, this is a virtue of the judgment because it will catalyze democratic deliberation about the future of Quebec in Canada, including its implications for citizenship and borders, the national debt and the armed forces, commercial and economic relations, mobility and migration, currency and monetary policy, and Indigenous Peoples. For others, the *Reference* is a profound failure of jurisprudence because in fashioning a legal framework for a decidedly political question the Court fell short of specifying clear instructions for the circumstances in which they were needed most.

What strikes me as most fascinating about the *Reference* is neither whether the Supreme Court was right or wrong nor whether political actors are themselves right or wrong to find favor or fault in the judgment. I am most intrigued by the Supreme Court's view that provincial secession may proceed by simple formal amendment. The Court was careful to note that although a referendum has no "direct role or legal effect in our constitutional schedule, a referendum undoubtedly may provide a democratic method of ascertaining the views of the electorate on important political questions on a particular occasion." On the strength of a clear majority vote in favor of secession, Quebec political actors could point to the "expression of the democratic will of the people" to initiate a constitutional amendment. The Court stressed that any amendment arising out of these negotiations must respect the unwritten principles of the Canadian Constitution, including federalism, democracy, constitutionalism, the rule of law, and respect for minority rights.

But the Court's decision did not specify which of Canada's five amendment procedures must be used to formalize a provincial secession. It seems clear that neither the unilateral provincial amendment procedure nor the federal amendment procedure could be used to formalize a provincial secession, nor could the regional amendment procedure be used either. The debate therefore pits the general default multilateral procedure versus the unanimity procedure. Yet in a meaningful way, both of these may well be inappropriate, particularly in the case of Quebec, because the rules of constitutional amendment appear in the *Constitution Act, 1982*, which lacks both legal and sociological legitimacy for many in Quebec and well beyond its borders.

I was an undergraduate student at Yale University when the Court issued its *Reference*. In my capacity as Chair of the *Yale College Association of Canadian Students*, I convened a public forum featuring Justice John Major, then a sitting member of the Supreme Court of Canada, and Professor Jack Balkin, then and still today on the faculty at the Yale Law School. Justice Major and Professor Balkin had many enlightening exchanges that kept the audience captivated throughout the program, but one in particular touched on a simple but powerful contrast that may reveal something quite poignant about constitutional politics in Canada and the USA: the USA fought a Civil War over secession, losing quite literally hundreds of thousands of lives in battle, while Canada resolved its own secession crisis in Court.

Twenty years later, the 1998 *Secession Reference* continues to echo in Canadian law and politics. In April 2018, the Quebec Superior Court upheld the "Act respecting the exercise of the fundamental rights and prerogatives of the Québec people and the Québec State," a law adopted in Quebec in response to the *Reference*. The law recognizes that the "Québec people has the inalienable right to freely decide the political regime and legal status of Québec," a declaration some have interpreted as asserting the unilateral power to secede. The Superior Court rejected that reading of the law but still affirmed the law's broad declarations of Quebec's nationhood and self-determination. Perhaps this provocative law will continue to wind its way through the courts.

Much remains to be written about the *Secession Reference*, especially on its vicennial anniversary, which we mark this year in 2018. Professor Giuseppe Martinico and Dr. Giacomo Delledonne deserve great thanks from the community of public law for giving us the gift of this commemorative volume of reflections on the *Secession Reference* from scholars around the world. They have gathered a magnificent group of eminent and fresh voices, whose perspectives are as varied as they are rich. Whether interested in secession or federalism itself, or in larger questions of difference and diversity, or more generally in public law in times of pressure and change, this volume offers scholars an opportunity to look back on one of Canada's most important moments and the legal and political infrastructure that has bloomed in its aftermath, both in Canada and elsewhere in the world, including countries in Africa, Asia and Europe, as this volume reveals.

A word about Professor Martinico and Dr. Delledonne is appropriate if only by way of gratitude for all they have done and continue to do to enrich our study of public law. From their perch at the picturesque Scuola Superiore Sant'Anna in the Sant'Anna Legal Studies program, Professor Martinico and Dr. Delledonne have convened countless programs of integral importance to deepening the values of public law, they have published a mounting collection of papers on the great questions of our time, and they have seeded and sowed vibrant scholarly collaborations throughout the world. It is no exaggeration to say that comparative public law would not be what it is today without the excitement and creativity that their partnership has brought to the field.

Austin, USA

Richard Albert
William Stamps Farish
Professor of Law, The University
of Texas at Austin

Richard Albert is the William Stamps Farish Professor of Law at the University of Texas at Austin. He is currently completing a monograph on constitutional amendment, soon to be published by Oxford University Press. A graduate of Yale, Oxford and Harvard, he is a former law clerk to the Chief Justice of Canada.

Contents

Notes on Contributors

Dr. Erika Arban is an ARC Laureate Postdoctoral Fellow in Constitutional Law at Melbourne Law School. Her research focuses on comparative federalism, comparative constitutional law, and legal research methodology. Before joining the project, she lectured in Comparative Federalism at the University of Antwerp (Belgium) and in Public Law at the University of Ottawa (Canada). Erika received her Ph.D. at the University of Ottawa (Canada), where her doctoral thesis Italian Regionalism and the Federal Challenge was awarded the Governor General Gold Medal for the best thesis in the humanities. She also holds a LLM from the University of Arizona (USA) and a Bachelor in Law from the University of Trieste (Italy).

Roberto Castaldi is Associate Professor of Political Theory at the eCampus University since 2014. He is also Director of the Research Centre on Multi-Level Integration and Governance Processes created in November 2015 at the same University. He chairs the eCampus International Relations and Erasmus Committee. He cooperates with the Centre for Studies on Federalism (CSF) of Turin. For CSF, he is editor of the Bibliographical Bulletin on Federalism (www.federalism-bulletin.eu) and co-editor of the peer review open access journal *Perspectives on Federalism* (www.on-federalism.eu). In 2013, he co-founded the International Centre for European and Global Governance (CesUE—www.cesue.eu), first spin-off of the Dirpolis Institute of the Scuola Superiore Sant'Anna of Pisa. Since May 2014, he is "affiliated researcher" of DIRPOLIS (Law, Politics, Development) Institute of the Scuola Superiore Sant'Anna di Studi Universitari e di Perfezionamento di Pisa. He was academic coordinator of the Jean Monnet Network "MoreEU—More Europe to overcome the crisis" until March 2016. His research interests focus on the EU institutional development, federalism, nationalism, interdependence, globalization, and civilization processes.

Josep Maria Castellà Andreu is Professor of Constitutional Law at the Universitat de Barcelona where he teaches Spanish and comparative constitutional law. He has been member of the Venice Commission since 2014. He has written on comparative federalism in four different languages. He has been Visiting Professor or Fellow at the Università di Pisa (Italy), University of Ottawa, Université de Montréal and University of British Columbia (Canada), UNAM (Mexico), Université Catholique de Louvain (Belgium), Senshu University (Japan), Boston College (USA), Universidad de Chile, and Strathmore University (Kenya).

Luigi Crema is Researcher and Adjunct Professor at the Università degli Studi of Milan, where he teaches on such topics as the law of treaties, human rights in international investment arbitration, and settlement of international boundary disputes. His research interests focus on the foundations of international law and in particular on the law of treaties and international customary law. Crema's work has appeared in a variety of books and law reviews, including the *European Journal of International Law* and the *Italian Yearbook of International Law*. He was a 2011–2012 Fellow at NYU Law School's Jean Monnet Center for International and Regional Economic Law and Justice.

Giacomo Delledonne is currently Postdoctoral Researcher in Comparative Constitutional Law at Scuola Superiore Sant'Anna in Pisa. From 2015 to 2016, he conducted postdoctoral research at the Institute for European Studies of Université Saint-Louis in Brussels. In March 2014, he got a Ph.D. in Constitutional Law from Scuola Superiore Sant'Anna, where he also serves as STALS Editor (www.stals.sssup.it).

He was a visiting student in Paris (École Normale Supérieure de la rue d'Ulm), Heidelberg (Max Planck Institute for Comparative Public Law and International Law), and Montreal (Université de Montréal). He was Visiting Postdoctoral Fellow at the Faculty of Law and Political Sciences of the Pázmány Péter Catholic University in Budapest and guest researcher at the Institute for Legal Studies of the Hungarian Academy of Sciences (Autumn, 2014).

Since 2014, he has been one of the convenors of a research group of the International Association of Constitutional Law. He worked as trainee clerk at the Italian Constitutional Court under Justice Sabino Cassese (2010–2011).

He has written extensively in four languages (Italian, English, French, and Spanish). He published a monograph on *L'omogeneità costituzionale degli ordinamenti composti* (2017), which was awarded the 10th "Opera Prima—Sergio P. Panunzio Prize", organized by the Italian Association of Constitutional Law Scholars. He has co-edited, with Giuseppe Martinico and Leonardo Pierdominici, a collection of essays celebrating the sesquicentennial anniversary of the Canadian Constitution (*Il costituzionalismo canadese a 150 anni dalla Confederazione. Riflessioni comparatistiche*, 2017).

Jean-François Gaudreault-DesBiens is Dean of the Faculty of Law and Canada Research Chair in North American and Comparative Juridical and Cultural Identities. He previously taught at the faculties of law of the University of Toronto and of McGill University, in addition to having been visiting professor at various universities outside Canada (Aix-Marseille, Science Po, Case Western). His teaching and research interests are constitutional law (domestic and comparative), civil liberties, legal theory and epistemology, and the sociology of legal cultures. His work currently focuses on the legal treatment of religious claims in multicultural liberal societies, on the relations between the civil law and common law traditions in a globalized economy, and on the legal theory of federalism. Professor Gaudreault-DesBiens is a member of the Quebec and Ontario Bars. He furthermore acts as Canadian correspondent for the British journal *Public Law*.

Alastair MacIver is a Legal Adviser in the Legal Service of the Council of the European Union. He holds a Ph.D. from the European University Institute in Florence. He has previously held the posts of Lecturer at Tilburg University, The Netherlands and Michigan Grotius Research Scholar at the University of Michigan Law School.

Giuseppe Martinico is an Associate Professor of Comparative Public law at the Sant'Anna School of Advanced Studies, Pisa. Prior to joining the Sant'Anna School of Advanced Studies, he was García Pelayo

Fellow at the Centro de Estudios Políticos y Constitucionales (CEPC), Madrid, and Max Weber Fellow at the European University Institute, Florence. He is also affiliated to several international research centers (among others, the Centre for Judicial Cooperation of the European University Institute, Florence, and the Centre for Studies on Federalism, Turin-Moncalieri). There he has been carrying out international projects related to comparative federalism and subnational constitutionalism, and to the constitutional dimensions of EU law and international human rights law (especially the European Convention on Human Rights).

His research interests cover both comparative law and European law, fields in which he published extensively, including two monographs in English (one with Elgar and one with Routledge); he has published extensively in international peer-reviewed journals in three languages (English, Italian, and Spanish). His volumes have been reviewed in top-class reviews. As evidence of the impact of his research, his first monograph *L'Integrazione Silente* (Jovene, 2009) was quoted in the opinion given by Advocate General Dámaso Ruiz-Jarabo Colomer in the Umweltanwalt von Kärnten and Alpe Adria Energia SpA case decided by the Court of Justice of the European Union (C 205/08). More recently, he was also cited by Advocate General Cruz Villalon in his opinion on the Gauweiler (OMT) case and by Advocate General Tanchev in his opinion (ft 45) on Case C-541/16 European Commission v Kingdom of Denmark.

Professor Errol P. Mendes is a lawyer, author, and professor and has been an advisor to corporations, governments, civil society groups, and the United Nations. His teaching, research, and consulting interests include constitutional and human rights law, corporate law, global governance, public international law (including humanitarian and international criminal law), and international business and trade law. Professor Mendes completed his term as Director of the Human Rights Research and Education Centre on 30 June 2001 and returned to full-time teaching in the Common Law Section. He had been Director of the Centre since 1993. The Centre is the oldest university-based bilingual human rights research and education institution in Canada. As Director of the Centre, he was the project leader for human rights, governance, and justice projects in China, Thailand, Indonesia, Brazil, Peru, El Salvador, Sri Lanka, and India.

Matteo Monti is a Ph.D. student at the Scuola Superiore Sant'Anna Pisa where is conducting a research project on asymmetry and secession in three legal systems. Before joining the Scuola Sant'Anna, he got a degree in law from the University of Pisa.

Zoran Oklopcic is an Associate Professor at the Department of Law and Legal Studies at Carleton University. He earned his S.J.D. from the University of Toronto. He has been a MacCormick Visiting Fellow at the University of Edinburgh; a member of the junior faculty at Harvard Law School's Institute for Global Law and Policy in Doha, Qatar; and a Hauser Global Research Fellow at NYU School of Law.

Francesco Palermo is Professor for Comparative Public Law at the Faculty of Law at the University of Verona and Director of the Institute for Comparative Federalism at Eurac Research Bolzano/Bozen.

Dr. Asanga Welikala is Lecturer in Public Law at the School of Law, University of Edinburgh, and the Acting Director of the Edinburgh Centre for Constitutional Law. He is also a Research Associate of the Institute of Commonwealth Studies, University of London, and Research Fellow of the Centre for Policy Alternatives (CPA), Sri Lanka. Asanga's research interests lie in comparative constitutional law, applied constitutional theory, and commonwealth constitutional history. He teaches and supervises across the public law field in Edinburgh, at ordinary, honors, masters, and doctoral levels. Asanga has been involved in both sides of transnational influence on constitution-making: as a member of the Office of Constitutional Support, United Nations Assistance Mission for Iraq, in various international advisory capacities in other countries on constitutional and legal reform issues; and as an active civil society voice and an independent expert in the current constitution-making process in Sri Lanka.

Introduction: The Legacy of the *Reference Re Secession of Quebec*

Giacomo Delledonne and Giuseppe Martinico

Concept Behind the Book and Structure of the Volume

The aim of this collection of essays is to celebrate the 20th anniversary of the *Reference Re Secession of Quebec* (hereinafter *Quebec Secession Reference*), delivered by the Canadian Supreme Court in 1998.

The readers could wonder why two non-Canadian scholars have decided to engage in an enterprise like this. There are several reasons of course, let us recall just three of them. First of all, the recent revival of secessionist movements in Europe and elsewhere has definitely given new lifeblood to a long-standing debate (Webster 1833; Calhoun 1851) gathering the attention of scholars from all around the world. In some cases—the Catalan one perhaps being the most striking example—the secession strategy has been employed together with other arguments in order to present a broader identity question. This is nothing new; quite

G. Delledonne (✉) · G. Martinico
Sant'Anna School of Advanced Studies, Pisa, Italy
e-mail: giacomo.delledonne@santannapisa.it

G. Martinico
e-mail: giuseppe.martinico@santannapisa.it

G. Delledonne and G. Martinico (eds.), *The Canadian Contribution to a Comparative Law of Secession*,
https://doi.org/10.1007/978-3-030-03469-6_1

frequently secession has been invoked to address identity questions and indeed, as Mancini pointed out, "under prevailing circumstances, secessionist movements operate in the context of multinational states inhabited by autochthonous, territorially concentrated minorities which share a national or quasi-national identity" (Mancini 2012). In this, the Canadian Reference has represented a turning point thanks to the incredible effort made by the Supreme Court to frame secession from a legal point of view, by showing this way the added value of the legal dimension and the not exclusively political flavour of secession.

Second, this Reference contains incredible anti-populist potential, since, as we will see (Martinico in this volume), it resulted in giving a series of guidelines that are very useful to govern the relationship between referendum and representative democracy and because of its complex notion of democracy. This should not come as a surprise, since generally speaking Canada has been traditionally seen as a laboratory for comparative lawyers and this Reference does not represent an exception.

Third, secession—or, better said, the fear of secession—is a typical concern in federal orders and poses a formidable intellectual and political challenge to their stability. The Reference was a turning point in framing the internal balance of a multinational federation which is also a well-established constitutional democracy.

Structure of the Volume

In the light of these considerations, we gathered Canadian and non-Canadian scholars to celebrate such a milestone and to consider the influence that it has had after 20 years.

In order to do so, we have structured the book in three parts, mixing domestic, comparative and theoretical approaches to this landmark opinion. The collection of essays is opened by a foreword by *Richard Albert*, who makes some relevant points about the enduring influence of the Reference in Canada, paving the way for the first part of the volume.

In the first part, two Canadian scholars discuss the legacy of the Reference from a domestic perspective, exchanging thoughts in a sort of ideal dialogue, on one of the most questioned decisions ever of the Canadian Supreme Court.

Errol Mendes focuses on some of the key political and legal reasons that led the Court to issue its Reference in 1998. In so doing, his chapter looks into the intermingling of politics and law in the ruling itself and the legal attempts to entrench the outcome of the ruling in the Clarity Act, along with the subsequent backlash from Quebec. In Mendes' view, the political and legal factors underlying the *Quebec Secession Reference* may serve as cautionary signals for secessionist attempts in liberal democracies, like those which a number of European countries have faced in the last few years: in a nutshell, the Reference warns that process legitimacy is a critical issue for secessionist movements around the world.

Jean-François Gaudreault-DesBiens provides an overview of the main political and legal challenges which the Quebec independence movement is currently facing. His contribution revolves around three problems. First, it revisits the domestic legal framework applicable to a provincial secessionist attempt by virtue of the *Quebec Secession Reference*, which was a major game-changer in the debate over the potential secession of the overwhelmingly Francophone province. Second, it considers the potential impact of recent political events, e.g. the Scottish referendum in Autumn 2014, on the strategy of the Quebec independence movement. Third, it delves into an alleged new legal foundation for secession, i.e. the so-called right to decide, as distinct from the right to external self-determination. By emphasising the necessity of transparency throughout the process which may ultimately result in the secession of a constituent unit, the Reference contributes to shedding a critical light on the soundness of the alleged "right to decide".

In the second part, the influence of this Reference abroad is explored by asking non-Canadian scholars to reflect upon its influence in European and non-European contexts (Spain, Scotland, Eastern European countries, Ethiopia, Asia). The contributions are ordered on the basis of the greater or lesser proximity of each case study towards the *Quebec Secession Reference* and the Canadian scenario.

Constitutional orders in which a direct influence of the Reference is recognisable are considered first.

Josep Maria Castellà Andreu reviews the reception in Spain of the doctrine elaborated by the Supreme Court of Canada in its Reference. In Spain, both legal and political circles have developed a keen interest in the Reference of 1998 since the time it was issued. The existence of territorial tensions, the attempts at changing the constitutional status of the Basque Country and, above all, the secessionist crisis in Catalonia are among the main reasons for this glance at the Canadian case. In general terms, it is a laudatory, uncritical reception. At the same time, it often tends to be selective and partial, focusing exclusively on those aspects of the Reference which may provide support to the theses advanced by those who invoke it in the domestic debate. Sometimes, arguments drawn from the Reference of the Supreme Court are mixed up and confused with different ones from the Clarity Act. Catalan nationalism has used the Reference to delegitimise the Spanish response to secessionist demands.

Luigi Crema analyses the implications of the *Quebec Secession Reference* for public international law. International lawyers intervened in the proceedings which preceded the decision of the Canadian Supreme Court, and since 1998, the Reference has become a classic not only of constitutional but also of international legal literature. Most notably, the Canadian Reference was frequently cited in the written briefs submitted by the states that intervened in the proceedings of the 2010 Advisory Opinion of the International Court of Justice (ICJ) on Kosovo. The final section of Crema's chapter reflects on the legacy of the Canadian Reference and the Advisory Opinion of the ICJ in the light of present-day secession crises. Contemporary requests for secession resort to a number of arguments which were not mentioned either in Ottawa or at the Hague, such as the "right to decide", the principle of stability and the duty to negotiate between opposing factions.

Alastair MacIver analyses the influence of the Reference on the debate preceding and surrounding the Scottish independence referendum of 2014. The Reference influenced the framing of the referendum on three levels. First, the Supreme Court's response to Question 2 of the Reference shaped a normative concept of the "principle of constitutional tolerance" with significant implications for defining the relationship between a possible Scottish state and the European Union. Second, the Court's answer to Question 1 influenced those who sought to formulate a European legal response to a would-be Scottish "yes" vote in the light of a novel "fact of membership" approach to EU law. Finally, according to MacIver, the Reference also offers a way of resolving the procedural dilemma underlying Articles 48 and 49 of the Treaty on European Union.

Asanga Welikala considers the influence of the Reference as a case of migration of constitutional arguments within the Commonwealth. More particularly, he looks into the Sri Lankan debates about how to accommodate the political and territorial claims of the Tamil minority and putting an end to protracted ethnic conflict. The Reference has made an appearance in Sri Lankan constitutional discourse at two key moments: first, during the peace process facilitated by Norway and, second, in the recent *Chandrasoma v Senathiraja* judgement of the Sri Lankan Supreme Court which recognised the Tamils as a people entitled to a right to internal self-determination.

The subsequent chapters in the second part deal with cases of indirect, implicit or even weak influence of the *Quebec Secession Reference.*

Erika Arban explores the role of federalism, respect for minorities, constitutionalism and the rule of law, and democracy—the fundamental principles expounded by the Canadian Supreme Court in the Reference—in Ethiopia. The Ethiopian case is unique as its 1995 Constitution (three years before the Reference) is one of the few in the world which explicitly entrench a right to secession for all its Nations, Nationalities and Peoples. Arban argues that in spite of some relevant cultural and ideological differences, the Ethiopian Constitution and the Canadian Reference were both at the origin of the gradual departure from the idea of secession as a constitutional taboo. Furthermore, the secession procedure regulated by Article 39 of the Ethiopian Constitution actually responds to some of the substantial and procedural concerns raised by the Canadian Supreme Court in the Reference, showing a certain—although hidden—continuity.

Giacomo Delledonne and Matteo Monti analyse the impact of the Reference on the Italian constitutional order, looking at both the judgements of the Constitutional Court and the strategies and narratives of the political actors. In order to do so, they first focus on the weight of secessionist claims and threats in the drafting of the Constitution of the Italian Republic and the establishment of a peculiar regional system. After that, they consider the recent attempt to organise a secessionist referendum promoted by the regional legislature of Veneto, which was finally deemed unconstitutional by the Constitutional Court. The Quebec case is often cited in the political discourse—however, political actors almost exclusively focus on the necessity of a referendum. On the other hand, the argumentative strategy of the Constitutional Court—which excludes altogether the admissibility of secession under the Italian Constitution—reveals some limited similarities with the reasoning of its Canadian counterpart in 1998.

Zoran Oklopcic confronts the legacy of the *Quebec Secession Reference* from the vantage point of the "periphery" of the European Union, be it internal (Catalonia and Spain) or external (Kosovo and Montenegro). In so doing, he focuses on the Reference as an opportunity to re-examine what is generally meant by democracy. In this regard, the most important legacy of the Reference is not a broader understanding of democracy, but an opportunity to look at democratic constitutions from the perspective of institutional responsiveness. Oklopcic's chapter concludes by arguing that the *Quebec Secession Reference* should be viewed as an encouragement to approach our understanding of democracy more reflectively and systematically.

Finally, there are three general contributions adopting a broader perspective. A political theorist and a lawyer discuss the democratic theory behind that Reference. In the last chapter, a comparative constitutional law scholar studies the significance of the Reference in the emergence of a comparative constitutional law of secession.

The chapter written by *Roberto Castaldi* considers the actual and potential impact of the *Quebec Secession Reference* on the main political theory debates related to the issue of secession. These have to do, first, with legal ways of seceding and how they can be resorted to, especially within a federal system. Second, the decision-making processes linked to secession look intrinsically problematic, most notably because of the use of referendums. Third, the *Quebec Secession Reference* can provide some lessons for the process of withdrawal of the UK from the European Union after the Brexit referendum. Castaldi's contribution argues that the Reference sketches a rich and complex constitutional framework for Canada which can be extended to other federal democracies.

Giuseppe Martinico moves from the role of the *Quebec Secession Reference* in nurturing and enhancing the comparative visibility of the Canadian Constitution throughout the world; furthermore, the Reference hugely contributed to weakening views of secession as a constitutional taboo. In his chapter, Martinico considers the legal foundations underpinning the reasoning of the Supreme Court in 1998. First, he considers the emergence of an "exit-related conditionality", thereby meaning the necessity to preserve and respect the basic principles of the constitutional order throughout a secession process. This ultimately undermines the revolutionary potential of secession and ensures an axiological continuity between the old order and the possible new one. Second, he focuses on the complex, distinctive conception of democracy embraced by the Supreme Court in the Reference, which can challenge the constitutional counter-narrative currently advanced by a number of populist movements.

Finally, in his chapter, *Francesco Palermo* argues that a significant amount of law has been developed over the past 20 years in order to constitutionalise secession. In the light of this, the legacy of the *Quebec Secession Reference* has been remarkably influential and has permeated, implicitly or explicitly, several legal systems, especially through the activity of their top courts. However, the legal regulation of secessionist claims has so far been focusing almost exclusively on referendums. In so doing, it has also neglected the additional safeguards which should prevent referendums from being abusively turned in plebiscitary instruments. At the same time, the legal regulation of political phenomena, which is one of the chief missions of constitutionalism, is clearly also emerging with regard to secession, and several instruments are being or can be employed to achieve a more effective, legally guaranteed and democratic comparative constitutional law of secession. The chapter discusses five of them: the provision of quorums for the turnout and approval in a referendum on independence, the possibility to repeat referendums, the possibility of a nuanced deliberation with more than two options put to the vote, the involvement of actors and procedures other than the referendum vote and the provision of a "double-check" by the electorate. The *Quebec Secession Reference* greatly contributed to the trend towards establishing a set of rules for dealing with secessionist attempts.

We would like to thank wholeheartedly all the authors who have enthusiastically joined this project and contributed to making this book possible. Thanks to the diversity of viewpoints and methodological approaches in their essays, they testify to the enduring vitality of the Reference 20 years later. In prospective terms, we hope that this book will enrich the discussion about how to deal with secessionist claims in contemporary constitutional democracies.

References

Calhoun, John C. (1851), "A Discourse on the Constitution and Government of the United States", available at http://www.constitution.org/jcc/dcgus.htm.

Mancini, Susanna (2012), "Secession and Self-Determination", in Michel Rosenfeld and Sajó Andras (eds.), *The Oxford Handbook of Comparative Constitutional Law*, Oxford University Press, Oxford, 481–500.

Webster, Daniel (1833), "The Constitution Not a Compact Between Sovereign States: A Speech Delivered in the Senate of the United States, on the 16th of February, 1833, in Reply to Mr. Calhoun's Speech on the Bill 'Further to Provide for the Collection of Duties on Imports'", available at http://www.bostonleadershipbuilders.com/0speeches/1833_webster_constitution_not_a_compact.htm.

The Legacy of the Quebec Secession Reference Ruling in Canada and Internationally

Errol P. Mendes

The Challenge to the Rule of Law in Canada That Triggered the Reference to the Court

In the aftermath of the 1995 referendum on secession, there was so much anger among the secessionist leaders in Quebec that any court, let alone the Supreme Court of Canada, could contest the outcome of any decision by the majority of Quebecers to secede from Canada. They had taken this position soon after the Parti Quebecois won the provincial election in 1994. A June 1994 agreement by all the secessionist parties in Quebec's legislature declared that, after a positive vote in a referendum on secession, the National Assembly would proclaim the province a sovereign country after proposing to the rest of Canada a treaty on a new economic and political partnership. This was followed by the

E. P. Mendes (✉)
University of Ottawa, Ottawa, ON, Canada
e-mail: emendes@uottawa.ca

G. Delledonne and G. Martinico (eds.), *The Canadian Contribution to a Comparative Law of Secession*,
https://doi.org/10.1007/978-3-030-03469-6_2

introduction of Bill 1 on 7 September of 1995, titled "An Act respecting the future of Quebec." The bill essentially asserted that an offer of an economic and political partnership between a sovereign Quebec and Canada would be offered to the rest of Canada after a successful referendum but a unilateral declaration of independence would proceed regardless of the outcome of the offer.[1]

Before the referendum even took place, Quebec resident, Guy Bertrand, challenged the constitutionality of another draft bill, titled "An Act respecting the sovereignty of Quebec," tabled by the Premier of Quebec on 6 December 1994 which subsequently would become "Bill 1." Bertrand sought both a declaratory judgement and an injunction against the secession attempts. The secessionist government immediately challenged whether this action should even be heard in the courts, as the right to a unilateral declaration of independence would not be a justiciable matter for the Quebec courts. Their motion to dismiss was rebuffed by a Superior Court ruling by the presiding judge, Justice Lesage. He ruled that the court should hear the arguments presented by Guy Bertrand at the trial of the claims he had presented. What shocked the federal government were the key arguments the Attorney General of Quebec used to dismiss Bertrand's motion. These included the argument that Bertrand's action must be dismissed because Quebec's accession to sovereignty is basically a fundamental democratic process that is sanctioned by public international law and the Superior Court in Quebec had no jurisdiction over such matters. Constitutional experts outside Quebec, such as Mary Dawson (1999) and key ministers in the federal cabinet, were shocked that this line of reasoning by the Attorney General of Quebec amounted to "a direct assault on the jurisdiction of the courts in Quebec in these legal issues. This amounted to an assault on the rule of law itself" (p. 11).

While the Court ultimately refused to give the injunction to stop the referendum, Justice Lesage did rule that the Quebec government's actions seemed manifestly illegal and amounted to a repudiation of the Constitution and the Charter rights of the complainant and indeed other Quebecers.

The referendum was held on 30 October 1995. The confusing question put to Quebec voters, discussed below, resulted with a 50.58%

[1] See Dumberry (2006) for a detailed description of the events that led to the Supreme Court ruling.

vote for the "no" side and a very close 49.42% vote for the "yes" side. While there was a fear that the close vote would embolden the secessionist leaders to pursue the goal of secession by other means, there was also concern in the federal government and the rest of Canada not to do anything that would give credibility to the secessionists and so indirectly assist their efforts.

However, after the 1995 referendum, Bertrand continued his motion for a declaratory judgement and a permanent injunction. Again, the Quebec government sought to dismiss the actions and repeated its arguments in the motion brought by Bertrand that, while no new referendums were being planned, Quebec's right to secession was a democratic process supported by international law and the Court had no jurisdiction to hear the case. This position again enraged the federal government, who intervened in the case claiming that neither Canadian nor international law gave Quebec the right to unilateral independence. Another Superior Court judge who was assigned this motion, Justice Pidgeon, decided to allow the claim for a declaratory judgement and permanent injunction to be heard on its merits. The Quebec government decided not to appeal and then refused to take part in the action (Dumberry 2006).

History turned full circle in more recent times when, in August 2018, another person challenged a version of the original Bill 1. That bill, titled Bill 99, was passed in December 2000 in response to the federal *Clarity Act*, discussed below. A Quebec Superior Court would issue an inherently confusing ruling on the law. This time, the Quebec Court ruled that while the law was not unconstitutional, it did not give Quebec the right to a unilateral declaration of secession. This ruling was barely mentioned in the media in both Quebec and the rest of Canada.[2]

The Quebec secessionist leaders' assertion, repeated before and after the 1995 referendum in the courts of Quebec and elsewhere, that not even the courts in Quebec had any role in determining the legality of a unilateral declaration of independence led to the federal government deciding that this issue—critical to the very existence of Canada—had to be referred to the Supreme Court of Canada.

This author personally witnessed the indignant astonishment of key federal political leaders that the leaders in the Quebec government had

[2] See Hamilton (2018) for the report of the ruling in one of Canada's English language national newspapers but not mentioned elsewhere in print or television.

been sworn into uphold the rule of law and the constitutional order of the province. It seemed to be a complete abdication of the rule of law that these leaders would assert that not even their own courts had any say in what would impact enormously on the lives of every person living in the province. It was clearly the last straw for the federal government. Despite the need to stabilize the political fallout in Quebec and the rest of Canada from a very close referendum result, there was a clear duty on the government to seek the advice of the Supreme Court on the constitutional framework of any future attempts at secession by the then present government or those of future secessionist governments in Quebec.

This assertion, that the democratic rights of Quebecers as determined primarily by the secessionist leaders in Quebec and supported by their interpretation of international law would "trump" all other constitutional rights and duties, was considered by the federal cabinet as a flagrant attack on the rule of law in Canada.

What acerbated this sense of crisis by the federal government was the deceptive manner in which the referendum question was formulated, which brought into question critical foundational principles of the Canadian Constitution that the Court would ultimately use to decide the case.

The referendum question supposedly incorporated the agreement that the secessionist leaders in the National Assembly had signed but was little known outside secessionist circles. The question to be voted on 30 October 1994, was:

> *[Translation]*
> Do you agree that Quebec should become sovereign, after having made a formal offer to Canada for a new economic and political partnership, within the scope of the Bill Respecting the future of Quebec and of the agreement signed on June 12, 1995?

There was an immediate outcry from the federalist political leaders in Quebec who were not involved in the drafting. There was no consultation on the question with them or the federal government in Ottawa, even though it would be the key negotiating partner regarding the offer if the referendum had succeeded. Likewise, though the question had referred to a partnership with the rest of Canada, there had been no discussions and indeed no interest by any federal or provincial governments in negotiating such a partnership with an independent Quebec. Indeed, there was no framework existing under which such negotiations could take place to lead to a partnership with the rest of Canada (Came 2003).

Some strident critics of the wording of the question even suggested that it was designed to imply that some sort of agreement on a partnership had already been reached. Likewise, the reference to the agreement of 12 June 1995 could be mistaken by some voters that an agreement had been reached even though the reference was just to a political agreement between the secessionist parties in the Quebec National Assembly (Ruypers et al. 2005).

The reference procedure that the federal government initiated was aimed at securing what jurist Jean-Francois Gaudreault-DesBiens (1999) called a "grid" for analysing secessionist claims. He asserted that this grid was to be created in "the rather unusual setting of a liberal constitutional democracy where civil society exists, and where the rule of law prevails" (p. 794). However, it is the view of this author that given the reasons that led the federal government to seek the reference as described above, the "grid" that the federal government sought was to determine how a liberal democracy must react to a situation where secessionist leaders are seeking to undermine the rule of law in the entire country in the pursuit of their goals.

It was the particular history of what preceded the ruling that gives a special legacy to this use of the reference power. In many cases, the federal government usually sought a reference ruling relating to the interpretation of the constitution or the constitutionality of particular federal or provincial legislation, actual or potential. While a reference ruling from the Court is only advisory, given the authority and legitimacy of the Court such rulings are treated as binding as any other ordinary rulings addressed to the parties involved. On this occasion, the stage was being set for the Court not just presenting a challenge to the actions of the Quebec secessionist politicians. It was also the occasion to establish what permanent support structures should surround the constitution and the rule of law, and how these related to a broader view of federalism, the evolution of democracy in Canada and the rights of minorities in the context of controversial secessionist claims.

With that search for the support structure of these vital foundations of the Canadian constitutional and democratic order in mind, the federal cabinet acting as Governor-in-Council presented the following questions to the Court:

1. Under the Constitution of Canada, can the National Assembly, legislature or government of Quebec effect the secession of Quebec from Canada unilaterally?
2. Does international law give the National Assembly, legislature or government of Quebec the right to effect the secession of Quebec from Canada unilaterally? In this regard, is there a right to self-determination under international law that would give the National Assembly, legislature or government of Quebec the right to effect the secession of Quebec from Canada unilaterally?
3. In the event of a conflict between domestic and international law on the right of the National Assembly, legislature or government of Quebec to effect the secession of Quebec from Canada unilaterally, which would take precedence in Canada?

These three questions, and the preceding factual situation that led to the Supreme Court's ruling, are themselves a major international legacy. It could send a message to secessionists around the world that it would be unwise to follow the path the Quebec secessionist government took in challenging the application of the rule of law in the parent state and questioning the role of the courts in pursuing their goals.

When the hearing on the reference questions began, there were 15 government and interest groups intervenors. When Quebec refused to take part, the Court appointed an *amicus curiae* to argue for the secessionist arguments (Dumberry 2006).

The Ruling by the Court

On 20 August 1998, the Supreme Court issued its unanimous ruling. While to this day there is strict confidentiality on which judge or judges were the primary authors of this historic ruling of the Court, research done by this author has discovered it was most likely that the judge that had the most prior and continuing expertise and interest in the evolution of the history of Canadian society was likely one of the chief authors.

The Court first rejected the foundational position of the Quebec secessionist leaders, as argued by the *amicus curiae*, that it was beyond the jurisdiction of the Court to adjudicate on the political and democratic rights of Quebecers to determine their own future. The Court asserted that the reference questions as interpreted by the Court were strictly limited to aspects of the legal framework in which democratic decisions on attempts to secede are to be taken. Since the reference questions had to be interpreted as directed to legal issues, the Court was in a position to answer them.

The Court also rejected the argument that it could not determine the application of international law to the right of Quebec to unilaterally declare independence as a sovereign country as it was not an international tribunal. It also rejected the view that the issues were now moot or hypothetical given that the referendum had been decided and that no new ones were being planned. Having thus demolished this fundamental challenge by the secessionist leaders to the foundations of the rule of law in Canada, the Court then proceeded to examine how the attempt to achieve statehood as an independent entity was as much a legal act as it was a political one.

Turning to the first reference question, the Court dealt with the fact that the written part of the Canadian Constitution was silent on the issue of unilateral secession. The way in which the Court dealt with this gap in the Constitution's written text has established a historic foundation that would reverberate far beyond the actual ruling in the case. The Court was in effect surrounding the written part of the Constitution with what it would term its unwritten principles:

> The Constitution is more than a written text. It embraces the entire global system of rules and principles which govern the exercise of constitutional authority. A superficial reading of selected provisions of the written constitutional enactment, without more, may be misleading. It is necessary to make a more profound investigation of the underlying principles animating the whole of the Constitution, including the principles of federalism, democracy, constitutionalism and the rule of law, and respect for minorities. Those principles must inform our overall appreciation of the constitutional rights and obligations that would come into play in the event that a clear majority of Quebecers votes on a clear question in favour of secession. (*Reference Re Secession of Quebec*, 1998, paragraph 148)

Before elucidating on the listed unwritten principles, the Court ruled that, because unilateral secession would purport to alter the governance of the Canadian territory, it would be inconsistent with Canada's current constitutional arrangements. While the Court ruled that secession by Quebec would require an amendment to the Constitution, it refrained from stating which amending procedure would be required, no doubt because of the major political reaction that would be triggered. As Gaudreault-DesBiens (1999) argued, faced with the complexity of the task before it, the Court felt compelled to introduce these meta-principles to fill the constitutional void and serve "both a legal/epistemological purpose, e.g., reintroducing complexity into the juridical analysis, and a political purpose, e.g., influencing perceptions about the usefulness as well as the limits of the Canadian Constitution with respect to a possible Quebec secession" (p. 826).

The Court could have stated its view that since unilateral secession was unconstitutional, it was unnecessary to answer the other questions. This author suggests that the Court's desire to continue and focus on how the unwritten principles can offer a "grid" for secession attempts relates to establishing a legitimate foundation for potential future attempts at secession in Canada. The Court perhaps also wanted to provide a teachable lesson on the value of legitimacy for secessionists in other parts of the world.

Focusing on the unwritten principle of democracy, the Court ruled that there must be a clear expression by Quebecers of their desire to pursue secession. This democracy criterion is also linked to what the Court states is the need for a clear expression of a clear majority on a clear question to pursue secession. In addition, the Court reinforced the procedural aspects of this democracy principle by stating that the referendum result must be free of ambiguity in terms of both the question asked and the support it achieves. The Court was careful not to specify what would constitute a clear question or a clear majority, leaving those massively contentious criteria to a "political evaluation" given it is the political actors that have the information and expertise to make the appropriate judgement. While the Court did not seem to exclude the 50% plus one favoured by the secessionist leaders in Quebec, it rightfully did not endorse it either. Given the well-publicized backlash against the wording of the question, this author has little doubt that the reference to a "clear question" was designed to bring into question the legitimacy of the tortured wording of the 1995 referendum question.

By this carefully crafted analysis of the unwritten principle of democracy, the Court is alluding to the lack of democratic legitimacy in the way the Quebec secessionist government designed the referendum question. At its worst, the framing of the question was aimed at manipulating voters into supporting secession or, at its best, was so vague that it confused the voters on the critical choice before them.

The Court's focus on the legitimacy of how the secession question was framed could also be one of the international legacies of the ruling. There is a striking contrast between the 1995 Quebec referendum wording and the wording of the Scottish referendum on independence in 2013. That wording was the result of hard negotiations by the UK Government, the Scottish Parliament and the review of the independent Scottish Electoral Commission. While those supporting secession had promoted wording equating secession to maximum devolution or other wording that made outright secession seem less disruptive, the UK government, which had agreed to the referendum process, insisted on a clear choice being given to the people of Scotland.

After the Scottish Electoral Commission determined that even the simpler "Do you agree that Scotland should be an independent country?" could be a leading question eliciting a positive response, the Scottish Parliament agreed to the much more neutral "Should Scotland be an independent country?" wording. Unlike the severe critique of the framing of the Quebec 1995 referendum question, there were no concerns raised by anyone in the 2014 Scottish Independence referendum (Waters 2016).

This ruling on the "clear question" should be noted as a precedent that the legitimacy in the process of secession could involve both the substantive democratic rights of a minority to secede within a multinational society and, as importantly, the need for transparency in the referendum process, especially regarding how the secession question should be worded.

If such process legitimacy issues are in order, the Court then issued its monumental ruling that may have shocked many national governments around the world, especially the liberal democratic societies that were or are presently facing secessionist demands:

> [T]he democratic principle, and so an expression of the democratic will of the people of a province carries weight, in that it would confer legitimacy on the efforts of the government of Quebec to initiate the Constitution's amendment process in order to secede by constitutional means. … The federalism principle, in conjunction with the democratic principle, dictates that the clear repudiation of the existing constitutional order and the clear expression of the desire to pursue secession by the population of a province would give rise to a reciprocal obligation on all parties to Confederation to negotiate constitutional changes to respond to that desire. (*Reference Re Secession of Quebec*, 1998, paragraphs 87–88)

The Court looked at the detailed history of how Canadian Confederation had evolved in order to require the imposition of this duty to negotiate the manner in which secession can be legitimately achieved after the secessionists have achieved a clear majority on a clear referendum question. Dumberry (2006) and others have pointed out that the duty to negotiate was not supported by any authority and there was not really a satisfactory account of its justification (p. 429; Usher 1999; Haljan 1998: 208–210), while others have lauded the Court for coming up with this constitutional innovation (Newman 1999: 83–89; Gaudreault-DesBiens 1999: 828–838).

One potential international legacy of the Canadian Court's ruling on these points is whether the Court's endorsement of the duty to negotiate obligation that flows out of the democracy meta-principle could be a powerful precedent in other multinational or multi-ethnic democratic societies, whether federal or not. This author faced this aspect of the legacy of the ruling while on a conflict resolution mission to Sri Lanka at the height of the secessionist movement by the Tamil population in that country. Several high-level officials in the authoritarian, but still marginally democratic, government rebuked the Canadian Supreme Court (and this author for supporting the ruling) in conversation for potentially offering constitutional ammunition to the moderate secessionist leaders seeking a non-violent way out of the conflict in that country. In the view of these Sri Lankan officials, even the existence of a theoretical duty to negotiate was an incentive to seek secession leading to the break-up of the country and so was unacceptable. Sadly, history has shown that the failure to agree to any form of effective negotiation with secessionists and even moderate elements seeking greater autonomy for the Tamil majority in Sri Lanka resulted in mass violence and atrocities by both sides to the conflict and a military suppression of the secessionists that caused tens of thousands of lives (Wickremesekara 2016).

However, what is not generally understood by would-be secessionists around the world who may laud the Canadian Supreme Court for pointing a legitimate path to secession is that the Court imbued the duty to negotiate with very large constraints. The duty to negotiate would require participation in the negotiations by all relevant governments and minorities in the national or territorial state within the framework of the constitution of the country and the rule of law. In the context of Canadian Confederation, the Court recognized this would not be an easy task and could well end in considerable upheaval and uncertainty and may not end in a successfully negotiated secession:

> Negotiations following a referendum vote in favour of seeking secession would inevitably address a wide range of issues, many of great import. After 131 years of Confederation, there exists, inevitably, a high level of integration in economic, political and social institutions across Canada. The vision of those who brought about Confederation was to create a unified country, not a loose alliance of autonomous provinces. Accordingly, while there are regional economic interests, which sometimes coincide with provincial boundaries, there are also national interests and enterprises (both public and private) that would face potential dismemberment. There is a national economy and a national debt. Arguments were raised before us regarding boundary issues. There are linguistic and cultural minorities, including aboriginal peoples, unevenly distributed across the country who look to the Constitution of Canada for the protection of their rights. Of course, secession would give rise to many issues of great complexity and difficulty. These would have to be resolved within the overall framework of the rule of law, thereby assuring Canadians resident in Quebec and elsewhere a measure of stability in what would likely be a period of considerable upheaval and uncertainty. Nobody seriously suggests that our national existence, seamless in so many aspects, could be effortlessly separated along what are now the provincial boundaries of Quebec. (*Reference Re Secession of Quebec*, 1998, paragraph 96)

Through these statements, the Court is integrating into the essential legitimacy of the secession process asserted by the Quebec secessionists the unwritten principles of federalism, constitutionalism and the rule of law, along with the rights of linguistic and cultural minorities and the constitutional rights of indigenous peoples.

What this means in terms of the duty to negotiate is that after a successful referendum, the secessionist leaders would have to negotiate in good faith "to address the interests of the federal government, of Quebec and the other provinces, and other participants, as well as the rights of all Canadians both within and outside Quebec" (*Reference Re Secession of Quebec*, 1998, paragraph 92).

These rights of all Canadians could include a host of groups adamantly opposed to the claims of the Quebec secessionists. This would include the Anglophone minority in the province and the large indigenous communities in many parts of Quebec who had voted overwhelmingly against secession. The federal government would also have a fiduciary duty to consult the indigenous peoples of Quebec where secession would impact their treaty and Aboriginal rights. A lesser obligation on the federal government would be a duty to take into account the rights of the linguistic and other minorities in Quebec.[3]

However, the Court warned that these most likely adversarial parties to the negotiations could not negotiate "in such a way as to amount to an absolute denial of Quebec's rights" (*Reference Re Secession of Quebec*, 1998, paragraph 93), neither could the secessionist leaders assert a similar absolute denial of the other parties' rights. The reality of present-day Quebec would present huge obstacles to the attitude that the architects of the 1995 referendum had demonstrated before and after the vote, namely that only the will and interests of the majority who voted in favour would prevail. The Court did not exclude the probability that such extremely difficult negotiations could fail.

Like the determination of what would constitute a legitimately clear question and what would be a clear majority, the Court threw this required duty to negotiate into the political realm and would not assert a "supervisory role over the political aspects of constitutional negotiations" (*Reference Re Secession of Quebec*, 1998, paragrpah 100). Leading constitutional expert Patrick Monahan (1999), as well as other jurists, points out that in any future secession referendum, the Court may have to intervene if the negotiations are not consistent with the unwritten principles discussed above and would undermine the legitimacy of the whole process (p. 96; Dumberry 2006: 430).

Indeed, the Court warned that failure to adhere to the identified constitutional framework of the negotiations could have important ramifications on whether the international community would recognize the asserted new state. With this part of the ruling, the Court seemed to acknowledge the role that international law and practice would have on the outcome of a successful secession referendum. It then turned to the second question, on whether international law gave Quebec the right to effect secession from Canada and whether the asserted right of self-determination under international law gave the right to effect the secession of Quebec from Canada unilaterally.

[3]See Gaudreault-DesBiens (1999: 827–28) for support on this key duty to negotiate obligation.

International Law and the Right to Unilateral Declaration of Independence

Turning to the second question put to the Court by the federal government, the Court again started its analysis by stating that international law did not give a definite positive or negative answer on the unilateral right of secession. Instead, that right would depend on the right of self-determination, which has been widely recognized under international law. However, its application has been consistently held to be exercised "within the framework of existing sovereign states and consistently with the maintenance of the territorial integrity of those [sovereign] states" (*Reference Re Secession of Quebec*, 1998, paragrpah 122). The Court is asserting that in a liberal democratic sovereign state like Canada, the Quebec secessionists must frame their claims within the national political, economic, social and cultural environment in which their claims were made:

> While the International Covenant on Economic, Social and Cultural Rights and the International Covenant on Civil and Political Rights do not specifically refer to the protection of territorial integrity, they both define the ambit of the right to self-determination in terms that are normally attainable within the framework of an existing state. There is no necessary incompatibility between the maintenance of the territorial integrity of existing states, including Canada, and the right of a "people" to achieve a full measure of self-determination. A state whose government represents the whole of the people or peoples resident within its territory, on a basis of equality and without discrimination, and respects the principles of self-determination in its own internal arrangements, is entitled to the protection under international law of its territorial integrity. (*Reference Re Secession of Quebec*, 1998, paragrpah 130)

This author asserts that this part of the ruling is another of the key international legacies of the Court's ruling. The Court is giving its internationally authoritative status to the assertion that, for most liberal democracies, self-determination should be regarded primarily as an internal right for existing states or greater internal autonomy rather than an external right to secession and independence.

The Court then makes the exception where there may well be a right to external self-determination in most extreme cases, such as in claims of colonial peoples or where a people is subject to alien subjugation, dominance or exploitation. A final situation is where a people is blocked from a meaningful form of exercising self-determination internally. It became clear that the Court was setting the stage for concluding that these exceptional circumstances for transforming an internal right to self-determination to one that is an external right leading to secession could not possibly apply to Quebec:

> The population of Quebec cannot plausibly be said to be denied access to government. Quebecers occupy prominent positions within the government of Canada. Residents of the province freely make political choices and pursue economic, social and cultural development within Quebec, across Canada, and throughout the world. The population of Quebec is equitably represented in legislative, executive and judicial institutions. In short, to reflect the phraseology of the international documents that address the right to self-determination of peoples, Canada is a 'sovereign and independent state conducting itself in compliance with the principle of equal rights and self-determination of peoples and thus possessed of a government representing the whole people belonging to the territory without distinction'. (*Reference Re Secession of Quebec*, 1998, paragraph 136)

The Court also downplayed the faint hope of the Quebec secessionists that the failure to get Quebec's signature on the Constitution repatriated from the UK in 1982 was proof of being unable to pursue the right of self-determination within Canada. The Court clearly rules that this omission did not come anywhere within the scope of "exceptional circumstances" permitting external forms of self-determination:

> The continuing failure to reach agreement on amendments to the Constitution, while a matter of concern, does not amount to a denial of self-determination. In the absence of amendments to the Canadian Constitution, we must look at the constitutional arrangements presently in effect, and we cannot conclude under current circumstances that those arrangements place Quebecers in a disadvantaged position within the scope of the international law rule. (*Reference Re Secession of Quebec*, 1998, paragraph 137)

This part of the ruling is one of the more ambiguous international legacies of the Court's ruling. When would a failure to incorporate key aspirations of a people asserting the right of self-determination override the other aspects where the autonomy of the people is respected? For example, would failure to respect or give the language of the minority people equal status in the local or national institutions be one such exceptional circumstance that could legitimately trigger a right to external self-determination? There are examples in recent international history that suppressing the language of minority peoples has led to claims of external self-determination and the right to secession. Again, the suppression of the language of the Tamil minority in Sri Lanka is just one such example that resulted in claims to the right to secede, due in large part to language discrimination in education and other national institutions and agencies (DeVotta 2004).

Having answered the first and second questions in the reference in the negative, the Court ruled that it was not necessary to answer the third question put by the federal government to the Court. Finally, the Court also dispensed with the argument of the *amicus curiae* relating to the right of Quebec to effect de facto secession, even if it did not have the right to unilateral secession under Canadian or international law. This argument was based on the contested international law concepts of effectivity and the related issues concerning the establishment of sovereignty based on recognition by other states.

The Court ruled that these contested concepts have "no constitutional or legal status in the sense that it did not provide an *ex ante* explanation or justification for an act" (*Reference Re Secession of Quebec*, 1998, paragraph 107). In other words, the Court asserted that the concept of effectivity refers to a factual situation and not one of law. It seemed according to the Court to be an asserted political concept that only comes into effect after the law of the territorial state has been broken, but secession has still managed to succeed. The Court rightly points out that this concept would seem contrary to the Canadian notion of the rule of law. However, the Court did acknowledge that if a people did establish a new state, albeit illegally and was effectively in control of is territory, then if there was sufficient recognition of the new state by other states then "legal consequences would flow from political facts" (*Reference Re Secession of Quebec*, 1998, paragrpah 142).

The Court seemed to caution future Quebec secessionists if they were ever to consider this unconstitutional avenue to sovereignty based on effectivity and the declaratory principle of state recognition. The Court raised the possibility that, in such a situation, politically it could be argued there is more than a single people in the territory of province by posing the question whether the people of Quebec would "encompass the entirety of the provincial population or just a portion thereof"

(*Reference Re Secession of Quebec*, 1998, paragrpah 125). Given their opposition to secession, it is certain that the indigenous Cree, Mohawk and Inuit peoples of Quebec would be a major hurdle to Quebec being declared a sovereign state on the basis of the principle of effectivity and recognition by other states. Their opposition would also trigger the issue of whether a separate Quebec would itself be subject to partition based on the desire of the indigenous populations to remain in Canada.[4]

Despite such potentially insurmountable hurdles to Quebec secessionists obtaining sovereignty through the effectivity doctrine and the declaratory theory of state recognition, the Court warns that such a process would still require proving the legitimacy of the secession process established by the Quebec secessionists. While recognition of de facto states by other states has been a matter of sovereign discretion, the Court is of the view that there is greater attention being paid to what it terms "legal norms." These include whether secession was achieved in accordance with the foundational legal norms of the larger territorial state from which separation is being pursued.

Dumberry (2006) and others have asserted that these conclusions are controversial statements by the Court that may not be supported by state practice where recognition is essentially a discretionary political act that does not necessarily include respect for the legal norms of the parent territorial state. Dumberry points, as an example, to the recognition of Croatia and Slovenia which was done in clear contravention of the Yugoslavian constitutional norms (pp. 441–442).

Such a rebuke to the Court may well be warranted in cases such as the new states of the Balkans, which were created in the midst of a severe civil war. However, it is suggested that when constituent parts of functioning Western liberal democracies are pursuing secession, the legitimacy of the process of secession will indeed be taken into account, at least by the traditional allies of such liberal democracies.

The Federal Government's Response to the Court's Historic Ruling: The *Clarity Act*

This historic ruling of Canada's top court was a catalyst for the federal government to introduce legislation in advance of any future attempt by the secessionist leaders in Quebec to attempt to design another

[4] See Dumberry (2006: 443–446) for the discussion of this issue and the relevance of the international law principle of *uti possidetis juris*.

referendum in the hope of a third-time success. The federal government passed a law in Parliament titled, "An Act to Give Effect to the Requirement for Clarity as Set Out in the Opinion of the Supreme Court of Canada in the Quebec Secession Reference."[5] Also called the "*Clarity Act*," it established the Canadian government's focus on what circumstances would oblige the Canadian government to negotiate secession of Quebec. The key circumstances would focus on the clarity of any future referendum question and second, the role of Parliament in determining what is a "clear expression" of the will by Quebecers to secede.

Regarding the clarity of any future referendum question, the *Clarity Act* (2000) described two aspects of the wording that would prevent a duty to negotiate and so prevent a province ceasing to be a part of Canada:

a. A referendum question that merely focuses on a mandate to negotiate without soliciting a direct expression of the will of the population of that province on whether the province should cease to be part of Canada; or
b. A referendum question that envisages other possibilities in addition to the secession of the province from Canada, such as economic or political arrangements with Canada, that obscure a direct expression of the will of the population of that province on whether the province should cease to be part of Canada [paragraph 1(4)].

It is clear that this was a direct attack on the confusing wording used in the 1995 referendum. However, the *Clarity Act* went even further. The Canadian House of Commons would also take into account, in deciding on whether the question provided clarity, the views of other partners in Canadian Confederation. These would include all political parties in the legislature of the province proposing the referendum wording and any formal statements or resolutions by other provincial or territorial governments or legislatures. The views of the Canadian Senate and similar input by representatives of the Aboriginal peoples of Canada and any other

[5] See An Act to give effect to the requirement for clarity as set out in the opinion of the Supreme Court of Canada in the Quebec Secession Reference [Clarity Act] (2000) for the full text.

views the House of Commons considers relevant would also be taken into account.

These additional requirements on the wording of any future referendum question were again a rebuke to the secessionist leaders in Quebec that had not consulted anyone outside their colleagues in the other secessionist parties in the legislature when designing the wording of the 1995 referendum question. However, it is not an illegitimate inquiry to question whether the *Clarity Act* overreached by requiring more than the other parties in the Quebec National Assembly, the federal government, indigenous peoples and minorities in Quebec to be consulted on the wording of the referendum.

If the wording of the referendum question satisfied the hurdles put forward by the *Clarity Act* (2000), then, according to the Act, in the aftermath of a referendum, the House of Commons would still have to determine whether "there has been a clear expression of a will by a clear majority of the population of that province that the province cease to be part of Canada" [paragraph 1(3)]. A failure to demonstrate such a clear majority would prevent any negotiations with Quebec on secession.

The passing of the *Clarity Act* by the federal government was the result of an urgently needed response to the manipulation of the wording of the 1995 referendum question that could have resulted in the break-up of the Canadian state (see Dion et al. 2000, for discussion). The drafters had to be careful to not overreach what the Court had laid down in terms of what would constitute a clear question and a clear majority.

Indeed, the Court itself was careful to impliedly acknowledge that it had reached the limits of what its interpretation of Canada's constitutional law and history had to offer in terms of providing the legal framework of secession. The Court passed the duty regarding who would define what a clear question and a clear majority are to the politicians, stating that "it will be for the political actors to determine what constitutes 'a clear majority on a clear question' in the circumstances under which a future referendum vote may be taken" (*Reference Re Secession of Quebec*, 1998, paragraph 153). The reference to "political actors" would have to be more than just the secessionist leaders if the rebuke to those same leaders is taken into account in how the Court framed what would be unacceptable wording of the referendum question.

Many, perhaps most, Quebec jurists along with the Parti Quebecois asserted that a clear majority must mean 50 plus one per cent (Dumberry

2006: 448).[6] Finally, the *Clarity Act* lays down what would be perhaps the most unattainable hurdle that a successful negotiation on secession would require an amendment to the Constitution under the formula that requires unanimity of all provinces and the Government of Canada.

There was, and still today is, a significant backlash by Quebec elites and those beyond the secessionist ranks to the *Clarity Act*, who view it as a straitjacket on any attempt by Quebec to secede and of necessity severely undermining the powers of the National Assembly to determine what would be a clear question and a clear majority. One leading jurist argued that the "clear question on a clear majority" requirement of the Act imposes a double veto to the House of Commons on any negotiations and could not be said to be in conformity with the spirit of the ruling by the Supreme Court on the legal framework of legitimate secession.[7]

It was not surprising, however, that jurists outside Quebec have tended to regard the *Clarity Act* as a necessary follow-up to the Supreme Court's ruling. Monahan (2000: 1) went further and criticized the federal government for not defining what a clear majority would be.

Conclusion: The Legacy of the Quebec Secession Ruling on Liberal Democracies

Stéphane Dion, as a leading Canadian constitutional and political studies academic (who later to become a Canadian minister of intergovernmental affairs and environment), asserted that secession would be difficult to achieve in well-established democracies. Writing soon after the 1995 referendum, Dion (1996) argued that to have a successful majority in favour of secession, the population of the region seeking to secede must have a fear of the parent state and confidence of the viability of the secessionist group's project. He asserted that confidence in secession is unlikely to succeed when fear about the existing parent state and union is low.

According to Dion, this critical perception of fear manifests itself when a minority fears that its cultural, economic, or political situation

[6] See Brun and Tremblay (1990) for the argument that not only the 50% plus one was a clear majority but also that the entire *Clarity Act* was unconstitutional.

[7] See Pellet, cited in Dumberry (2006, footnote 170) for a discussion of the double veto.

will deteriorate within the political union. Dion argued, somewhat prematurely, that neither Scotland nor other parts of Western Europe are likely to successfully secede based on these drivers of possible secession in liberal democracies.

Dion asserted that conflicting perceptions of fear and confidence will tend to deprive the secessionists in Quebec from getting majority support when the stark choice between staying and leaving Canada is put before the electorate. The Supreme Court itself reinforced Dion's thesis when it asserted that there could hardly be fear of oppression in the parent Canadian state given that the highest offices of the country were held by Quebec and that the province had substantial autonomy within the Canadian state.

The ruling of the Supreme Court could have reinforced the other key perception of those sympathetic to an independent Quebec posited by Dion for successful referendums on secession to succeed, namely the ability to demonstrate confidence in the secessionist project. After any successful referendum on secession of Quebec, the Court asserted that the secessionist leaders will be unable to act unilaterally even if they presented a clear question in the referendum and obtained a clear majority. The secessionist project will still present huge challenges in the required negotiations which must respect the four unwritten and foundational principles of the Canadian Constitution. As the Court concluded, there would be no likelihood of success even if negotiations were to go ahead.

With the widespread acceptance of the Supreme Court's ruling both within Quebec and across Canada, it would be difficult in the future for secessionist leaders in Quebec to ignore the legal framework for a legitimate secession process established by the Court. If such leaders did decide to ignore this legal framework, as the Court ruling indicated and most experts agree, there would be few if any foreign states that would recognize the existence of an independent Quebec within its existing boundaries, especially if Canada refused to recognize the secession as legitimate (e.g., Crawford 1998).

Given these huge legitimacy obstacles to any future attempted secession by secessionist leaders in Quebec, could there be an incentive on the part of these leaders to ignore the legal framework established by the Court? Would they be tempted to attempt what would be considered an illegal unilateral declaration of independence in violation of the foundational constitutional norms of Canada? While the Canadian Constitution rests on the principles found in its preamble of peace, order and good government, it is not beyond the realm of possibility that failure by any secessionist groups in Canada, be it in Quebec or elsewhere in the Canadian federation, could trigger retaliatory and even potentially illiberal actions by the Canadian state.

The actions of the secession leaders in Catalonia, Spain, could be the paradigm example of what could happen if there is a flagrant violation of a liberal democracy's constitutional norms. As one writer has noted, a failure by the secessionists to follow the pre-existing legal and constitutional framework of the Spanish Constitution and indeed aspects of the political and legal framework in Catalonia led to significant deficiencies in liberalism and democracy in actions not only by the secession leaders in Catalonia but also by the authoritarian responses by the Spanish government:

> Whereas Catalan secessionists broke the law in many occasions and intended to build new constitutional structures without having clear majorities favouring unilateral independence (for instance, violating parliamentary rules and procedures, passing unconstitutional laws and resolutions, disobeying the Spanish Constitutional Court repeatedly, providing the creation of a Catalan Supreme Court composed by new judges appointed by the political branches without qualified enough majorities to facilitate the legal transition), Spanish unionists showed lack of accommodation of peaceful and persistent democratic claims and severe and disproportionate coercion against self-determination and secession performances and actions (for example, avoiding the negotiation of any secession referendum or qualified procedure to secede, denying more fiscal autonomy for Catalonia and limiting its fiscal autonomy under a constitutional clause that merely establishes the fiscal golden rule, disproportionate use of police force to prevent the voting in the illegal referendum of 1 October 2017, severely judging many secessionist leaders for the high crime of rebellion and harshly imprisoning several of them before trial). (Bossacoma Busquets 2018)

Given the precedent from the disastrous secessionist attempts in Spain, the less disruptive but extremely challenging path to a peaceful, orderly and good governance secession framework laid down by the Canadian Supreme Court may well be more attractive to other secessionist groups in liberal democracies. Adapting and adopting the legal framework laid down by the Court to the particular nation's constitution and legal framework may be attractive to national governments facing secessionist groups. This would include not overreacting to unilateral attempts to secede.

There should also be a recognition by these same national governments that the reason why Canada has immensely benefited from this historic ruling is because over its one hundred and fifty years as an independent country, the national government has also strived to lessen the fear of the majority francophone population of Quebec that its cultural, economic or political situation will deteriorate within the political union of Canada. For this and other reasons discussed in this article, the ruling by the Supreme Court of Canada in the Quebec Secession Reference should also be viewed as a vital authoritative precedent for liberal democracies around the world facing secessionist challenges.

References

An Act to Give Effect to the Requirement for Clarity as Set Out in the Opinion of the Supreme Court of Canada in the Quebec Secession Reference, S.C. (2000), c. 26.

Bossacoma Busquets, P. (2018), "Obstacles and Passages to Secession in Liberal-Democratic Contexts: Lessons from Catalonia", in *Political Theory Working Paper*, 20, 1–24, retrieved from http://hdl.handle.net/10230/34424.

Brun, H. and Tremblay G. (1990), *Droit Constitutionnel*, 2nd ed., Éditions Yvon Blais, Cowansville.

Came, B. (2003), Referendum Question Unveiled, *Canadian Encyclopedia*, retrieved from http://www.thecanadianencyclopedia.ca/en/article/referendum-question-unveiled/.

Crawford, J. (1998), "State Practice and International Law in Relation to Secession", in *British Yearbook of International Law*, 69 (1), 85–117.

Dawson, M. (1999), "Reflections on the Opinion of the Supreme Court of Canada in the Quebec Secession Reference", in *National Journal of Constitutional Law*, 11 (1), 5–48.

DeVotta, N. (2004), *Blowback: Linguistic Nationalism, Institutional Decay, and Ethnic Conflict in Sri Lanka*, Stanford University Press, Stanford, CA.

Dion, S. (1996), "Why Is Secession Difficult in Well-Established Democracies? Lessons from Quebec", in *British Journal of Political Science*, 26 (2), 269–283.

Dion, S., Gibson, G., Claude, R., Facal, J. and Monahan, P. (2000), "The Clarity Act Debate in the House of Commons", in *Canadian Parliamentary Review*, 23 (2), 20–30.

Dumberry, P. (2006), "Lessons Learned from the *Quebec Secession Reference* Before the Supreme Court of Canada", in M.G. Kohen (ed.), *Secession:*

International Law Perspectives, Cambridge University Press, New York, pp. 416–452.

Gaudreault-DesBiens, J.-F. (1999), "The Quebec Secession Reference and the Judicial Arbitration of Conflicting Narratives About Law, Democracy, and Identity", in *Vermont Law Review*, 23 (4), 793–843.

Haljan, D.P. (1998), "Negotiating Québec Secession", in *Revue belge de droit international*, 31 (1), 190–216.

Hamilton, G. (2018, April 19), "Court Upholds Quebec Law on Self-Determination But Says It Doesn't Give Unilateral Right to Secede", *National Post*, http://nationalpost.com/news/canada/court-upholds-quebec-law-on-self-determination.

Monahan, P.J. (1999), "The Public Policy Role of the Supreme Court of Canada in the Secession Reference", in *National Journal of Constitutional Law*, 11 (1), 65–105.

Monahan, P.J. (2000), "Doing the Rules: An Assessment of the Federal Clarity Act in Light of the Quebec Secession Reference", in *C.D. Howe Institute Commentary*, 135, 1–39.

Newman, W.J. (1999), *The Quebec Secession Reference: The Rule of Law and the Position of the Attorney General of Canada*, York University, Toronto.

Reference Re Secession of Quebec, [1998] 2 SCR 217, 161 DLR (4th) 385.

Ruypers, J., Austin, M., Carter, P. and Murphy, T.G. (2005), *Canadian and World Politics*, Emond Montgomery Publication, Toronto.

Usher, D. (1999), "The New Constitutional Duty to Negotiate", in *Policy Options*, 41–44.

Waters, T.W. (2016), "For Freedom Alone: Secession After the Scottish Referendum", in *Nationalities Papers*, 44 (1), 124–143.

Wickremesekara, C. (2016), *The Tamil Secessionist War in Sri Lanka*, Routledge, New York.

The Law and Politics of Secession: From the Political Contingency of Secession to a "Right to Decide"? Can Lessons Be Learned from the Quebec Case?

Jean-François Gaudreault-DesBiens

Introduction

Quebec's secessionist movement is one of the oldest of the sort in any democratic country. Yet, it has not been in such a dire state for decades. Both past strategies and recent internal struggles can account for this situation, but the legal framework for secession that has been put in place in Canada since 1998 has also contributed to it.

Dean of Law, Université de Montréal. This article is an updated English version of the following article published in Spanish: Gaudreault-DesBiens (2016). This Spanish article was itself a longer, and more elaborated version of the following one, published in Italy: Gaudreault-DesBiens (2014).

J.-F. Gaudreault-DesBiens (✉)
Université de Montréal, Montreal, QC, Canada
e-mail: jf.gaudreault-desbiens@umontreal.ca

G. Delledonne and G. Martinico (eds.), *The Canadian Contribution to a Comparative Law of Secession*,
https://doi.org/10.1007/978-3-030-03469-6_3

In spite of these evolutions, the situation in Quebec continues to raise interest in other parts of the world, particularly in plurinational democratic states such as the UK, Spain or Belgium, which have also had to wrestle with secessionist dynamics for decades. Comparisons between Quebec, Scotland, Catalonia, the Basque Country or the Belgian Flanders have almost become a cottage industry. Yet, social, economic, political and legal differences abound between these regions, even if they all share a minority or minorized status within a larger federal or decentralized polity.

Of all secessionist challenges, the ones that typically tend to draw the most attention in Quebec are those that take place in Scotland and in Catalonia. Catalonia is close to Quebec in that its national language is a minority one in Spain, as is French in Canada, but unlike French, Catalan has little reach outside of Catalonia. Secessionist movements in both regions rely on strong cultural nationalist assumptions, even though Catalonia's significant place in Spanish economy allows it to credibly add an economic layer to its secessionist claims. On the other hand, Quebec and Catalonia have significantly different legal regimes, Quebec's secessionist wishes being grasped by a legal regime largely anchored in the common law tradition. In that, it is much closer to Scotland than it is to Catalonia.

Conversely, Quebec secessionists' quest for independence has been intensely scrutinized in both Scotland and Catalonia. Actually, Quebec is invoked as much as an anti-model than as a model, and very often, the complexities of that province's situation are obscured in passing.

That being said, the primary focus of this paper is not comparative; it rather seeks to provide its readers with an overview of some of the main political and legal hurdles currently faced by the Quebec independence movement. It may be that some lessons can be drawn for secessionist parties in other parts of the world; I will leave to the judgement of my readers. However, the fact remains that Quebec's contested quest towards independence has inspired to a large extent many significant political and legal developments in the manner of addressing secessionist claims. Be it only for that, it is worth re-examining it.

I will first revisit the domestic legal framework applicable to a provincial secession attempt since the seminal 1998 opinion of the Supreme Court of Canada in *Reference re Secession of Quebec*,[1] which was a

[1] Reference re Secession of Quebec, [1998] 2 S.C.R. 217 (hereinafter called the "Quebec Secession Reference").

major game-changer in the debate over Quebec's potential secession (1), notably by refusing to characterize an act of secession as purely legal or political (2), by emphasizing the need for clarity both in the process and the outcome of referendums on secession (3), and by triggering legislative reactions which largely amount to symbolic politics (4). I will then examine the potential impact of Scotland's recent referendum process on the strategy of the Quebec secessionist movement (5), and recent political events that have revealed deep rifts within Quebec's nationalist movement, and that may have significantly reduced its appeal in key parts of the electorate (6). Last, I will look at an alleged new legal foundation for secession, i.e. a so-called right to decide distinct from the right to external self-determination (7).

The 1998 Secession Reference as a Game-Changer

In order to better understand the domestic legal framework applicable to Quebec's potential secession, two preliminary observations must be made.

Firstly, *as a matter of principle*, referendums entail no legal effect in Canadian constitutional law. This flows from the principle of parliamentary supremacy, which Canada inherited from the UK. Under this principle, no legislature, be it federal or provincial, may abdicate its legislative powers in favour of another body, even if that body is the "people".[2] The outcome of a referendum is thus merely consultative and, consequently, it does not bind any legislator; the British constitutional tradition clearly favours the sovereignty of parliament over that of the people.

Secondly, prior to the enactment of the *Constitution Act, 1982*,[3] the constitution of Canada did not contain any formal amending procedure; amendments were then governed by other legal and conventional rules.[4] It now contains such a procedure, but no provision expressly addresses the hypothesis of a provincial secession. This is worth noting, since the constitutional changes that led to the integration of amending procedures in the constitution took place *after* the first Quebec referendum on

[2] In Re Initiative and Referendum Act, [1919] A.C. 935 (J.C.P.C.).

[3] Constitution Act, 1982, which constitutes Schedule B of the Canada Act, 1982 (U.K.), 1982, c. 11.

[4] Re: Resolution to amend the Constitution, [1981] 1 S.C.R. 753.

secession in 1980. Thus, even if the amendments brought about by the *Constitution Act, 1982* (over Quebec's objections) were largely triggered by the turmoil that surrounded this first referendum, it was not deemed appropriate to include a "secession clause" in the constitution, perhaps for fear of legitimizing *ex ante* secession attempts. As a result of this, no clear and transparent legal framework was in place when the second referendum on secession was held in 1995, which led to a near-death experience for Canada.

It is against this legal backdrop that post-1995 legal evolutions must be assessed. The most important certainly lies in the Supreme Court of Canada's advisory opinion in *Reference re Secession of Quebec*,[5] which arguably represents the Court's most significant contribution to contemporary global jurisprudence. It is beyond the scope of this comment to provide an in-depth analysis of this opinion; it shall therefore suffice to identify a few highlights, which all point to the conclusion that the Court then integrated into the Canadian constitution a judicially elaborated secession clause, albeit an imperfect one.

Secession as a Political and Legal Fact

One is the rejection of a long-standing secessionist claim that the alleged silence of the Canadian constitution regarding the secession of a province meant that it did not preclude a province from seceding, and that, as a result, secession was a purely political act located outside the law's ambit. In other words, this claim was somehow based on the idea that the secession of a province could not be characterized as an "ordinary" amendment of the constitution, because of the magnitude of the changes involved. The Supreme Court held instead that the secession of a province clearly required a formal constitutional amendment, while declining to specify which amending formula would be applicable.[6] Should Quebec ever opt for secession, this finding could prove a thorny issue, in addition to having tremendous consequences on the concrete feasibility of secession under domestic law. Even assuming that the negotiating teams of the governments involved in post-referendum discussions,

[5] *Supra*, note 1. On this opinion, see, inter alia Gaudreault-DesBiens (1999: 24).

[6] Quebec Secession Reference, *supra*, note 1, at paragraph 84. It is to be noted that the Court alluded to the possibility of adjudicating on the issue of the amending formula should a positive vote on Quebec's sovereignty occur.

which would involve at least the federal and Quebec governments, agree on the modalities of secession, the constitution's amending procedure would require the ratification of such agreement not only by the federal Parliament and the Quebec National Assembly, but also by the legislative assemblies of all provinces affected. This is where the identification of the relevant amending procedure becomes critically important. On the one hand, there is the so-called general amending formula, requiring the consent of the federal Parliament and "of the legislative assemblies of at least two-thirds of the provinces that have, in the aggregate, according to the then latest general census, at least fifty per cent of the population of all the provinces"[7]; on the other hand, there is the unanimity procedure that generally applies to the amendment of the country's foundational institutions.[8] Opinions differ as to which procedure would be applicable. However, even though both are quite demanding in terms of the degree of provincial assent required, the second one renders extremely difficult, if not impossible outright, substantial modifications. This is already the case when political actors are not facing a crisis such as that which would arise as a result of a provincial vote for secession. In the context of a major unity crisis, and even though the executive power tightly controls the legislative power whenever the government involved is a majority government, there is always a risk of deliberations going out of control and legislatures rebelling. This is to some extent what happened when the Meech Lake accord, which would have recognized Quebec as a "distinct society", collapsed in 1990. This agreement had been prompted by a desire to induce Quebec to sign the 1982 Constitution, which, while legally applicable to the province, had never, and still has not, been accepted by its successive governments. This Quebec-centred focus triggered a "why not me?" syndrome among other provinces and groups such as Aboriginal peoples, which soon formulated their own particular constitutional claims. In other words, asymmetrical arrangements risk creating ripple effects that may lead to their ultimate failure. Thus, while elite accommodation strategies involving executive actors may succeed, they sometimes risk being overturned by legislative assemblies if elected representatives feel that popular support for them is insufficient or vanishing. After the 1995 Quebec referendum,

[7] Constitution Act, 1982, s. 38.

[8] Constitution Act, 1982, id., s. 41.

another hurdle was even added to the internal procedure that must be followed in the federal Parliament for the consideration of multilateral constitutional amendments (such as those that would be required in the case of secession): no federal minister may table a motion authorizing such an amendment if a majority of provinces has not consented to it, and this majority must include Quebec, Ontario, British Columbia and at least two Atlantic and two Prairie provinces.[9] This regional veto statute could further complicate the constitutional amendment process that should theoretically "crown" a successful secession attempt from a domestic legal standpoint.

Should any legislative blockade happen after successful post-referendum negotiations between the Canadian and Quebec governments, the constitutional process necessary to give a legal form to the outcome of the negotiations would be stalled, thereby increasing the risk of a unilateral declaration of independence by Quebec, in which case the ultimate arbiter would in all likelihood be the international community. This would raise doubt as to the relevance, at this stage, of Canadian domestic law, since the Supreme Court stated in the *Secession Reference* that a vote in favour of secession emanating from the democratically expressed will of the people could not be ignored. In this respect, the rejection of an approach solely based on a legalistic and formalistic conception of constitutional normativity constitutes another highlight of the *Secession Reference*. This rejection is implemented through the Court's reliance on unwritten constitutional principles that constitute the intellectual and normative superstructure of the country's constitution and whose role is to "(…) inform and sustain the constitutional text (…)".[10] Although they cannot prevail over "clear" constitutional provisions, these principles may be used to fill gaps or to construe ambiguities. Most importantly, as opposed to mere constitutional conventions, the Supreme Court acknowledges their legal status, which entails that they can give rise, alone or together, to general or specific obligations imposed upon constitutional actors. In other words, neither governments nor courts can ignore them.[11]

The Supreme Court's departure from a strictly positivist reading of the Canadian constitution allows it to elaborate tools from which to

[9] Act Respecting Constitutional Amendments, S.C. 1996, c. 1.

[10] Quebec Secession Reference, *supra*, note 1, at paragraph 49.

[11] Id., at paragraph 54.

better grasp a potential provincial secession attempt. In the case at bar, the unwritten principles that were deemed relevant were federalism, democracy, constitutionalism and the rule of law, and, lastly, the protection of minorities. Although the Court drew various conclusions from these principles, examining them in depth would prove beyond the scope of this article. I will thus focus on the two most important ones, which are in my view the founding stones of the legal framework currently applicable for the secession of a Canadian province. They lie in the "discovery" of a duty to negotiate in some circumstances and in a requirement of clarity, albeit itself rather vague.

Of Clarity and Democracy

The *Secession Reference*'s main constitutional novelty probably resides in the Supreme Court's finding, primarily on the basis of the unwritten principles of democracy and the rule of law, of a constitutional duty "to engage in constitutional discussions in order to acknowledge and address democratic expressions of a desire for change in other provinces".[12] This duty is the logical consequence of the right conferred on federal actors to initiate, but not to realize unilaterally, constitutional change. However, to arise, this duty must be preceded by a "democratic expression of a desire for change". At this stage, the Court expressly links legality with legitimacy, as the evaluation of the democratic character of an expression is conditional upon its political legitimacy, hence the requirement of a "clear expression by the people of Quebec of their will to secede (…)".[13] A clear expression is equated by the Court to a *clear majority*, which must be assessed qualitatively, i.e. as referring to both the numerical majority and the wording of the question on which the population is upon to vote, which must be free of ambiguity.[14] It must be recalled here that this clarity requirement was judicially devised in a political context where two referenda had already been held before the Supreme Court handed its opinion in the *Secession Reference*. It is certainly not irrelevant, at this stage, to cite the text of the referenda questions that were then asked (Table 1).

[12] Id., at paragraph 69.

[13] Id., at paragraph 87.

[14] Ibid.

Table 1 Texts of 1980 and 1995 referendum

1980 Referendum	*1995 Referendum*
The Government of Quebec has made public its proposal to negotiate a new agreement with the rest of Canada, based on the equality of nations; this agreement would enable Quebec to acquire the exclusive power to make its laws, levy its taxes and establish relations abroad—in other words, sovereignty—and at the same time to maintain with Canada an economic association including a common currency; any change in political status resulting from these negotiations will only be implemented with popular approval through another referendum; on these terms, do you give the Government of Quebec the mandate to negotiate the proposed agreement between Quebec and Canada?	Do you agree that Quebec should become sovereign after having made a formal offer to Canada for a new economic and political partnership within the scope of the bill respecting the future of Quebec and of the agreement signed on June 12, 1995?

The Court might indeed have had these questions in mind when it framed its clear question/clear majority threshold in the *Secession Reference*, and held that the presence of a clear majority on a clear question about secession would trigger the application of the constitutional obligation "to negotiate constitutional changes to *respond* to that desire".[15] This "response" would imply "acknowledg[ing] and respect[ing] that expression of democratic will by entering into negotiation and conducting them in accordance with the underlying constitutional principles already discussed".[16] The Court makes clear that this duty to negotiate cannot be construed as meaning that the federal government and the other provinces are under an obligation "to accede to the secession of Quebec, subject only to negotiation of the logistical details of secession".[17] Moreover, in spite of its constitutional nature, the duty to negotiate would be non-justiciable, its enforcement being left to political actors. Failure by them to agree on the terms of secession, and, subsequently, on whether or not they have behaved in a manner

[15] Id., at paragraph 88 (italics are mine).

[16] Ibid.

[17] Id., at paragraph 90.

that satisfies the duty to negotiate would lead to a situation of constitutional anomia, to say the least, and would in all likelihood exhaust the resources of domestic law, a possibility that the Court expressly acknowledged.[18] Thus, an orderly provincial secession in the Canadian context would presuppose respect for democracy and the rule of law; yet, it is quite possible that at some stage, and absent an agreement on the terms of secession, the domestic rule of law could eventually be superseded by the international rule of law.[19]

Given its *ex ante* dimension, as opposed to the so-called duty to negotiate's *ex post facto* application, it is no surprise that it is the requirement of clarity that has made the most lasting impression since the release of the Supreme Court's opinion in the *Secession Reference*. The alleged lack of clarity of the referendum questions of 1980 and 1995 had been central in the debates that then took place, at least on the federalist side. Indeed, in a context where the preferred option of Quebecers has always been, and remains, a renewed version of federalism, more decentralized and flirting with a genuine confederation (as improbable as this hypothesis may currently seem), any question alluding to maintaining some form of ties with Canada is hardly without ambiguity. To wit, the 1995 question referred to Quebec becoming sovereign—note the absence of the words independence or secession—"after having made a formal offer to Canada for a new economic and political partnership within the scope of the bill respecting the future of Quebec and of the agreement signed on June 12, 1995?" The bill respecting the future of Quebec, never enacted into law given the defeat of the secessionist option, provided that following a "yes" vote, the province's National Assembly would be "empowered to proclaim the sovereignty of Quebec", while being bound to propose the partnership referred to in the referendum question. The partnership would have included "joint political institutions", and more precisely a Council, a Secretariat, an Assembly and a Tribunal for the resolution of disputes. Moreover, the treaty establishing the partnership would have "ensured that the partnership ha[d] the authority to act" with respect to customs union, free movement of goods, individuals, services and capital, monetary policy, labour mobility and citizenship. The sovereignty of Quebec would have been declared after the conclusion

[18] Id., at paragraph 103.

[19] For a recent analysis of the international legal dimensions of secession, see Dugard (2013).

of an agreement on the partnership treaty. However, and most importantly, the bill set a one-year period after the referendum for reaching an agreement on that treaty.[20] Absent such an agreement, the National Assembly would have been empowered to make a unilateral declaration of sovereignty.

Was the 1995 question "clear"? Yes, to the extent that a careful reading of the bill could indeed lead one to understand that the ultimate outcome of the process *would* be a declaration of independence, with a partnership or not. No, to the extent that it induced the population to believe, notably through its preamble, that a partnership would almost be inevitable given the long-standing entanglement of Quebec and Canadian economies and institutions. A further problem was that the question merely *referred* to the documents clarifying that the ultimate outcome of a "yes" vote would be the secession of the province—there was of course no guarantee that voters had read these documents. In a way, absolute sovereignty, i.e. sovereignty without any partnership, was almost presented as a derivative and last resort option. Voters could hardly ignore that it was in the cards, especially after a referendum campaign in which the federalist side construed this question as leading to independence, but they could also be led to believe that the partnership was an equally important component.

Interestingly, if not ironically, a recent book of interviews with major political actors of the 1995 referendum reveals that the two main leaders of the "yes" camp, former Premier Jacques Parizeau and then Bloc québécois leader Lucien Bouchard, had very different views of what would happen following a "yes" vote. Parizeau had independence as its main goal, with or without partnership. For his part, Bouchard preferred a new partnership akin to the European Union; moreover, he believed that a second referendum would be needed so as to confirm Quebec's

[20] Many questioned, during the referendum campaign, the realism of a one-year deadline for concluding such an agreement in the context of the secession of a constituent part of a full-fledged sovereign state such as Canada. Albeit not involving the secession of a constituent part of a "state", the laborious process characterizing the implementation of the UK's "Brexit" decision seems to indicate, *ex post facto*, that those who criticized the one-year deadline envisaged by the Quebec government in 1995 were right. In spite of the fact that the vote in favour of Brexit took place on June 23, 2016, and that the UK's intention to withdraw from the European Union was formally notified on March 29, 2017, an agreement on the conditions of Brexit has yet to be reached between the parties at the time of writing (end of August 2018).

new constitutional status (Hébert and Lapierre 2014: 33–34).[21] This could easily be construed as evidence of the lack of clarity of the question posed in 1995.

The Legislative Sparring Following the Secession Reference

The *Secession Reference*'s insistence on clarity was picked up by the federal Parliament when it enacted in 2000 the *Clarity Act*,[22] in which it provides its own interpretation of the Reference's clarity requirements, emboldened as it was to do so by the Supreme Court's view that the referendum process would not be judicially monitored.

In a nutshell, this Act imposes upon the House of Commons the obligation to consider, within a certain delay, any question tabled in a provincial legislative assembly "relating to the secession of that province from Canada" and to determine whether or not it is clear.[23] In order to do so, it must examine "whether the question would result in a clear expression of the will of the population of a province on whether the province should cease to be part of Canada and become an independent state".[24] In a clear reference to prior referendum questions, the Act posits that

> (…) a clear expression of the will of the population of a province that the province cease to be part of Canada could not result from (*a*) a referendum question that merely focuses on a mandate to negotiate without soliciting a direct expression of the will of the population of that province on whether the province should cease to be part of Canada; or (*b*) a referendum question that envisages other possibilities in addition to the secession of the province from Canada, such as economic or political arrangements with Canada, that obscure a direct expression of the will of the population of that province on whether the province should cease to be part of Canada.[25]

[21] Hébert and Lapierre (2014: 33–34).

[22] Clarity Act, S.C. 2000, c. 26.

[23] Id., paragraph 1 (1).

[24] Id., paragraph 1 (3).

[25] Id., paragraph 1 (4).

The *Clarity Act* then establishes a regime for determining whether, after a referendum, there was a clear majority in favour of the province's secession, this being a precondition for the federal government to enter into negotiations with the secessionist province. The Act therefore sets out a two-step evaluation, first of the referendum question's clarity after it has been tabled, then of the clarity of the majority in favour of secession after the referendum was held. It is relevant to observe here that long before the enactment of this Act, the federal government had participated in the two Quebec referenda even if it did not have a say in the elaboration of the question and if the entire process was conducted under Quebec law. Even in 1992, when a pan-Canadian referendum was held on the Charlottetown Accord—a major project of constitutional reform—the referendum on the territory of Quebec was governed by provincial law while it was conducted under federal law in all other provinces and territories. It is thus no surprise that the enactment of the *Clarity Act* was greeted with outrage in Quebec's nationalist circles, because it represented the first time the federal government ever affirmed a right to influence the referendum process itself rather than the mere referendum results. Of course, this influence is indirect in the sense that the *Clarity Act* does not apply to the National Assembly of Quebec; the government of that province may ask whatever question it wants, but it runs the risk of being rebutted ab initio by the House of Commons if it is not clear enough. However, it does lay out the federal government's position on a critical component of the referendum process prior to the referendum itself, i.e. the question, and actually precludes the government from entering into negotiations with a secessionist province if the House of Commons has not determined that both the referendum question and the majority vote to secede were clear. However, under this regime, the federal government could be taken hostage by the House which, in a time of crisis, could actually block any determination of the clarity of the question or the majority, thereby acting in bad faith and placing the federal government at risk of not fulfilling its constitutional obligation to negotiate even in a situation arguably giving rise to such an obligation.

Reacting to the federal *Clarity Act*, the Quebec National Assembly soon adopted, under the helm of Premier Lucien Bouchard's secessionist government,[26] an *Act Respecting the Fundamental Rights and*

[26]Bouchard had become leader of the Parti québécois after the resignation of Premier Jacques Parizeau following the defeat of the secessionist option. Since the PQ was still in power, Bouchard succeeded Parizeau as Premier of the province.

Prerogatives of the Québec People and the Québec State,[27] which sought inter alia to reaffirm the Quebec people's right to self-determination[28] and that of its political institutions to "determine alone the mode of exercise of its right to choose the political regime and legal status of Quebec".[29] It also posited that in case of a referendum, "the winning option is the option that obtains a majority of the valid votes cast, namely 50% of the valid votes cast plus one".[30] It is to be noted that although a certain nationalist elite and most of the media were extremely critical of the *Clarity Act* and supportive of the *Act Respecting the Fundamental Rights and Prerogatives of the Québec People and the Québec State*, the population of the province did not mobilize against the federal initiative, which eventually led to the resignation of Premier Bouchard.

Since this legislative sparring of the early 2000s, the domestic legal framework for secession has not changed: the *Secession Reference* remains its centrepiece while the *Clarity Act* and the *Act Respecting the Fundamental Rights and Prerogatives of the Québec People and the Québec State* still frame what the federal and Quebec governments could respectively do should Quebec seek to secede from Canada.[31] But neither may reasonably pretend to have resolved all the dilemmas raised by the clarity of the referendum question and of the majority to be obtained. Saying that something is "clear" implies a prior interpretation and represents an act of authority seeking to end a debate (van de Kerchove 1988: 291): however, it should be stressed that the *Secession Reference* does not vest

[27] S.Q., 2000, c. 46, s. 2.

[28] Id., s. 1–2.

[29] Id., s. 3.

[30] Id., s. 4.

[31] A constitutional challenge to the *Act Respecting the Fundamental Rights and Prerogatives of the Québec People and the Québec* was recently rejected by the Quebec Superior Court, after the main provisions of the Act were "read down" by the Court, essentially as not evincing the provincial legislature's intent to establish a framework that could be used as a justification for a unilateral secession: *Henderson* c. *Procureure générale du Québec*, 2018 QCCS 1586. Although Henderson has decided to appeal that decision, both the federal and Quebec governments declared themselves happy with it. The Superior Court's decision has been vigorously criticized by Professor Maxime Saint-Hilaire in a series of seven blogs: https://blogueaquidedroit.wordpress.com/2018/06/17/affaire-henderson-de-contestation-de-la-loi-99-sur-les-droits-fondamentaux-du-peuple-et-de-letat-du-quebec-vers-un-controle-judiciaire-de-constitutionnalite-sans-droit-constitutionnel-bille-6/.

any political actor involved, voluntarily or not, in a provincial referendum on secession with absolute authority over either the process or the outcome. Actually, clarity can better be evaluated in context; obviously, the question and the outcome of the vote are critically important issues, but other variables may impact on this evaluation. For example, what did political actors say during the debate? From this perspective, these statutes clearly exemplify what could be characterized as political legislation.

The Impact of the Scottish Referendum Process

The ideal situation is arguably that which was arrived at by Westminster and Edinburgh in the case of Scotland, i.e. an agreement on the question and the majority, as well as a shared commitment to an orderly process should the answer be positive. Through prior cooperation, they created a significant political precedent for other referenda on secession. However, this precedent is not so easily transposable in the Canadian context. Indeed, as was noted earlier, Quebec alone determined the rules of the game in the past two referenda on Quebec secession, which did not prevent the federal government from participating in the debate once it was launched. And since then, Quebec has always denied the federal government any legitimacy to mingle with the process. On the other hand, post-*Clarity Act* Canada increasingly tends to take the high moral ground and to depict Quebec secessionism as a monolithically backwards movement so as to deny it any form of legitimacy, which inevitably precludes acknowledging, through a pre-referendum agreement, that this option is legitimate and could even win, and that Canada would somehow have to take stock of it, in addition to having an interest in making the transition as smooth as possible. Finally, in order for the hypothesis of a bilateral pre-referendum agreement to materialize, both the *Clarity Act* and the *Act Respecting the Fundamental Rights and Prerogatives of the Québec People and the Québec State* would arguably have to be amended in some respects, which would likely provoke vigorous debates. Ultimately, it may well be that while the population, both in Quebec and elsewhere in Canada, could lend their support to a Scotland-style solution, the weight of the current antagonistic tradition could prevent it from being implemented in the political realm.

But the population's expectations about clarity will not vanish overnight, which might prove a problem for the Quebec secessionist movement. As was seen, the first two referendum questions were not unambiguous, as both referred, directly or indirectly, to the possibility of a renewed partnership between Quebec and Canada. The reason they were formulated as such by avowedly secessionist governments is simple: they knew very well that Quebecers overwhelmingly preferred renewed federalism or a EU-like agreement over outright separation from Canada. But the strategy of toning down the secessionist option in view of luring a majority of people to vote "yes" in referenda may have been counterproductive in the long run, as Quebec independence was never really presented as the best option, even when considering the inconveniences potentially associated with it. The most mainstream proponent of secession, i.e. the Parti Québécois, never dared to directly argue that Quebec's cultural and linguistic blossoming—the primordial justification of the secessionist movement—offset the various costs associated with independence, as high as they may be. It instead tried to assuage fears about these costs by hiding, or even denying, their existence. This was, and remains, a significant domestic hurdle for the movement. However, there may be further obstacles ahead, especially at the international level. In addition to the fact that there has not been a successful secession attempt in the past decades in an economically advanced, democratic Western state—the break-up of Czechoslovakia was more akin to an implosion—the process in Scotland may have raised the bar in terms of the international community's expectations concerning secession. And this might be cause for concern for Quebec secessionists, as it might indeed force them to tangibly abide by the principle of clarity, thereby reducing, at least in the short term, their chances of ever winning a referendum. At the same time, it is always hard to anticipate what the international community would have done had Scots clearly voted in favour of independence. In this respect, neither secessionists nor federalists can rely on the outcome of the Scottish process to buttress any argument raising the question of the international recognition of an independent Quebec in a future debate.

That being said, while the legal framework potentially applicable to a unilateral secession of Quebec does raise numerous hurdles, there exists a variable that arguably better explains the bluesy mood of Quebec secessionists today, i.e. the deepening of the rift within nationalist ranks as to what Quebec is, or should become.

The Woes of Quebec Nationalism

Quebec nationalism is old; it has emerged in a context where the province's French-speaking majority was marginalized both in Canada as a whole and in the province's economic sphere. This precarious situation, combined with the unique linguistic and religious characteristics of that group, led to the development of a nationalism that revolved around the defence of the majority's cultural, political and economic interests. It was, in a nutshell, an ethnic nationalism. As of the 1960s, Quebec society underwent rapid modernization, became secularized, and the provincial government was vested with the responsibility of promoting the distinct identity of the Quebec people. French-speaking Quebecers' longstanding reference to their "French-Canadian" identity was abandoned and replaced by the affirmation of a Quebec identity, the idea being that French-speaking Quebecers had to be masters in their own house and that a nationalism of affirmation had to prevail over the nationalism of survival they once espoused. Politically and legally, it led to the implementation of public policies consistently informed by methodological nationalism (see Wimmer and Glick Schiller 2002: 301), which, in turn, has fed a logic of possessive individualism (see Macpherson 2010 [1962]). This logic had led to envisaging constitutional competences as objects of property that must be relentlessly acquired. In this process, jurisdictional conflicts, even minor ones, systematically become vested with a significant identity value that helps elevate them to the status of national fetishes. This dynamic has arguably, and perhaps paradoxically, contributed to undermining Quebec secessionism's appeal in the population. This can be attributed to what I would metaphorically call "the crying wolf syndrome". It is indeed fair to surmise that the systemic identitization of all potential objects of constitutional jurisdiction—which I have called elsewhere a manifestation of constitutional fetishism (Gaudreault-DesBiens 2009a: 301)—induces a dynamic of trivialization of most, if not all objects of jurisdiction, as a result of which all lose their salience, even when the population could arguably mobilize against them. In other words, a constitutional fatigue is susceptible of ensuing from the constant reiteration of arguments premised upon a mythology of systematic victimization.

That said, the identity redefinition described above did not come without aporias. Indeed, the shift from a non-territorialized French-Canadian ethnic identity dispersed throughout the federation but with its largest concentration in Quebec, to a territorialized Quebec-centred political identity primarily defined by language raised the question of what to do with all those Quebec residents who were not of French descent or who were not even French speakers. Did they qualify as Quebecers? The overwhelming answer given within mainstream nationalist/secessionist circles from the 1960s to the 1990s was "yes". Yet, these citizens were asked to accept the primacy of French as the common public language and, eventually, Quebec's sole official language, subject to the constitutional rights of the English-speaking minority. In a federation with two official languages (French and English), one of them (English) being significantly dominant, such a demand was no small feat.

This very cursory glance at the reinvention of Quebec nationalism reveals a tension that runs deep into that nationalism: How can it pretend to be "civic", and thus theoretically inclusive of all citizens if, at the same time, it practically promotes a cultural and political agenda that mirrors the majority's experience, thereby essentially seeking to advance the latter's interests and self-representation? Beyond illustrating the relative artificiality of the ethnic/civil dichotomy, this question raises an important point with respect to secession: since nationalism and secessionism are generally intertwined—and nowhere is it truer than in Quebec—how can a secessionist project informed by what may be perceived as a cosmetic conception of civic nationalism appeal to all citizens? In this respect, the civic conception of the Quebec nation, which had been adopted by the province's main secessionist party, the Parti Québécois, had essentially focused on the French language as the common public language of the province. After the initial shock provoked by the adoption of the *Charter of the French Language* in 1977,[32] a fragile, but real, modus vivendi had emerged, and if Anglophones and Allophones largely resisted the appeal of secessionist sirens, they nevertheless felt increasingly included in Quebec's mainstream. In the meantime, the demography in the province was changing with immigration. More precisely, immigration from French-speaking countries was viewed as a means to ensure the blossoming of that language in Quebec. However, these immigrants did not only come with French in

[32] The Charter of the French Language, R.S.Q. c. C-11, made French the sole official language of the province, limited to use of languages other than French in advertising and forced all to send children to French schools, subject to the vested rights of English-speaking Canadians.

their luggage, but also brought other things as well, one of them being religion.

In 2007, a fierce debate erupted over the "reasonable accommodation" of religion by courts of law.[33] In a nutshell, this doctrine, which was adopted by the Supreme Court of Canada, provides that when a facially neutral rule indirectly infringes one's equality rights or freedom of religion, the victim can ask for an individual accommodation which must be granted unless the organization from which the accommodation is requested demonstrates that granting it would cause undue hardship. While the doctrine had been applied for many years without problem to various sorts of claimants, including pregnant women and physically handicapped persons, a series of cases involving religious accommodations drew the attention of media and politicians, and the so-called reasonable accommodation crisis began, which ultimately led to the creation by the government of an inquiry commission co-chaired by sociologist Gérard Bouchard and philosopher Charles Taylor, who tabled an important report confirming that there was no tangible problem with religious accommodation, calling what had happened a "perception crisis".[34] At the same time, they noticed the resilience of the French-speaking majority's cultural insecurity and the possible (over)reactions to which it could lead. The process that led to the Bouchard-Taylor report somehow pacified the debate, but the report itself was for the most part shelved by the Liberal government then in power.

What is interesting is that while the 2007 debate was largely fuelled by the media and some politicians, the underlying insecurity of the French-speaking majority had already been appropriated by neoconservative intellectuals[35]—all nationalists and most of them secessionists—who essentially argued that the civic turn of Quebec nationalism resulted from the caving-in of the political and intellectual elite to the ideals of Canadian multiculturalism, the latter being associated with a federal ploy designed to drown the national community formed by Quebec into the Canadian multicultural melting pot. This intellectual posture, which Maclure labels as "romantic-conservative", essentially holds that "the

[33] For a socio-legal analysis of this debate, see Gaudreault-DesBiens (2009b: 151).

[34] Commission de consultation sur les pratiques d'accommodement reliées aux différences culturelles (2008).

[35] For recent formulations of their theses, see, inter alia: Bock-Côté (2012) and Beauchemin and Beaudoin (2010), C5.

'historical majority' (Quebecers of French-Canadian origins) somehow lost its political empowerment and assertiveness as it opened up to plurality" (Maclure 2011: 137).

The 2007 episode had clearly revealed the resilience of a form of identity ticklishness within Quebec's French-Canadian majority. The secessionist Parti Québécois tried to capitalize on it after having gained power in 2012. In 2013, it tabled a project of "Charter of values" which formally became a "Charter of secularism" when a bill seeking to give it effect was tabled in the National Assembly.[36] In essence, it sought to impose a very strong form of secularism, largely inspired by the French conception of *laïcité*. Its centrepiece was a blanket ban on ostensible religious signs worn by employees from the public sector and from organizations subsidized by the government. Formally, all ostensible religious signs were banned, including "large crosses". The problem is that in a heavily secularized society, where the influence of the Catholic Church, once a major sociopolitical actor, is now marginal at best, few people, if any, wear "large crosses". But a good number of Muslim women wear hijabs. Thus, in practice, this secularism charter would have had a disproportionate impact on religious minorities.

Interestingly, the government's justifications for this project evolved during the course of the debate; it began with generic, facially neutral, normative justifications, but it slowly shifted towards value judgements made about individual beliefs and behaviours, and it culminated with blatantly anti-Muslim discourses not directly emanating from the government itself but tolerated by the government when coming from some of its very prominent supporters.

First, the project was defended on the basis of secularism, and the ensuing need to create a perfectly "neutral" space where the people's freedom of conscience would not be troubled by religious signs, the wearing of such signs being associated with proselytization. It was then defended on the basis of an alleged need to protect the equality of women, that equality being apparently threatened by religious diktats; in this context, women wearing religious signs were often depicted as victims of false consciousness. Last, it was justified as a means to defend

[36] Charter affirming the values of State secularism and religious neutrality and of equality between women and men, and providing a framework for accommodation requests, Bill 60, 40th Legislature, first Session, National Assembly, Quebec Official Publisher, 2013.

"Quebec values"—including secularism and gender equality—against the external threat of Islamism.

Although some members of the government may have genuinely believed in the need for a muscular approach to secularism, the primary impetus for the adoption of this project was arguably to mobilize the government's secessionist electoral base and to instrumentalize the cultural insecurity of the French-Canadian majority in view of obtaining the parliamentary majority it had failed to get a year before. The strategy was to create a kind of "us" versus "them" polarization, or, if one prefers, a Schmittian enemy/friend dichotomy (see Mancini 2014: 111). The polls showing strong support for its charter project among the French-speaking electorate, the Parti Québécois government called an election for March 2014, in which it was routed by the federalist Liberal Party. What happened was that the Liberal Party campaigned on the ambiguous position of the Parti Québécois on secession, which frightened the electorate, including segments of it that were generally supportive of the government's policies. From that perspective, the election of 2014 clearly shows that outside hard-line secessionist circles, the idea of secession tends to be seen as a non-realistic dream or, worse, as a repulsive one. But the charter of secularism's consequences appears even more catastrophic for Quebec's secessionist movement, as it has revealed deep and possibly irreconcilable divisions within that movement as to what type of society an independent Quebec should become. In this sense, the cleavage between "romantic-conservative" and pluralist nationalists that the charter project amplified has only accelerated the implosion of the Parti Québécois as the main torchbearer of the independence idea and strengthened other smaller parties which have begun reclaiming the leftist and pluralist values that were for a long time part and parcel of the Parti québécois' own political programme. Beyond this internal wrangle, the worst outcome of this episode for the secessionist movement arguably lies in the rupture of communication with minority groups within the province. Historically, in spite of moderate electorate success among these groups, the Parti Québécois had made serious efforts in legitimizing its option vis-à-vis these groups. Most of these efforts are now fuming ruins, as some of these groups were directly victimized by the charter project. Muslims were among its primary targets, even though many of them had embraced the cause of Quebec independence because of their affinities with the province's French-speaking majority—French-speaking nationals from Maghreb countries constitute a significant proportion of immigrants to Quebec.

In short, the re-emergence of ethnic nationalism and its embrace by the Parti Québécois, as evinced by the now defunct secularism charter that it tabled when it formed the government, may have inflicted a near fatal blow to the cause it promotes. What is all the more striking here is that it is a largely self-inflicted blow.

Democracy, Transparency and the "Right" to Decide[37]

Faced with what increasingly looks like a political and legal dead end, a segment of Quebec's secessionist movement seems inclined to consider previously discarded and more radical paths towards independence. Such was the case of *Option nationale*, a very small yet surprisingly influential political party that supported the view that a mere election should be enough to trigger a secession process. That party recently merged with a marginally stronger one, *Québec solidaire*, which tends, however, to prioritize left-wing policies over independence, and which advocates a more moderate approach as to how to achieve independence. Thus, hard-line positions are increasingly marginal, as mainstream secessionist parties seem keenly aware of the necessity of a referendum for increasing the likelihood of an international recognition of a unilateral declaration of independence. In other words, they somehow accept, albeit reluctantly, the Supreme Court of Canada's view that neither Canadian domestic law nor international law vest Quebec with a *legal* right to unilaterally secede that would be based on the right to external self-determination.

It is in that context, and in the wake of equivalent debates in Catalonia,[38] that an alleged "right to decide", purportedly distinct from the already recognized right to self-determination,[39] has increasingly been invoked, but never as strongly or frequently as in Catalonia. There is a

[37]This Section Expands an Argument Initially Iterated in Gaudreault-DesBiens (2015: 17).

[38]The "right to decide" argument could gain traction in Scotland as well if it were faced with a reaction in Westminster akin to that of the Spanish government vis-à-vis Catalonia. This hypothesis might not be as far-fetched as one would think. Indeed, in light of the imminence of Brexit, the Scottish government has alluded to the possibility of holding a second referendum on independence prior to the end of the negotiations between the UK and the E.U. However, Westminster's reaction to such declaration was that it would refuse to cooperate with the Scottish government, contrary to what it did in 2015. See Stewart et al. (2017).

[39]Or, alternatively, as a significant expansion of what normally is associated to "the right to self-determination".

good reason explaining that discrepancy: Canada has never denied Quebec the possibility of holding a referendum on independence. In this respect, the Spanish government's refusal to entertain the idea that Catalans could express their views on the constitutional status of their community is difficult to understand from a Canadian perspective, irrespective of the merits of both secessionist and unionist positions. However, contrary to the thesis defended by some secessionists in both Quebec and Catalonia, such an expression could hardly proceed from a legal "right to decide" and entail formal normative effects on that basis.

Admittedly, the expression of the views of a political community on its constitutional status in the context of a democratic debate to which all interested stakeholders, including the central state, are invited to participate remains very relevant from the standpoint of democracy. This was acknowledged by the Canadian government through its participation in two referendums where the possible secession of Quebec was on the agenda. It was also recognized by the Supreme Court of Canada in its 1998 advisory opinion, in which the Court underscored, on the basis of the constitutional principle of democracy, that an expression of a desire to change a province's constitutional status could give rise to a duty to negotiate imposed upon all parties affected, even if this change could ultimately lead to secession. However, being solely an obligation of means, this duty to negotiate would not guarantee any particular outcome. In other words, there is no assurance that a negotiation would lead to results meeting the population's expectations, as they might have been at the time of the vote. Moreover, any modification of a province's constitutional status flowing from such a negotiation would have to be effected through a formal constitutional amendment. Indeed, the democratic principle which provides the foundation for the duty to negotiate cannot obscure another important principle, i.e. the rule of law. And if negotiations were to fail and a unilateral declaration of independence ensued, that declaration would be illegal under domestic law. If any justification for the province's "exit" ever existed, it would have to be found in international law. However, the right to external self-determination recognized under international law does not apply to the situation of a province such as Quebec, which cannot seriously be depicted as being submitted to some sort of foreign domination. It is thus clear that the framework established by the Supreme Court of Canada in the Secession Reference can in no way be construed as supporting "a straightforward inference to be drawn from democratic principles of a constitutional right to secede[.]" (Mancini 2008: 553). This is where the alleged existence of a *legal* right to decide comes into the equation.

However, seeking to legally ground a unilateral declaration of independence on such a presumed right could prove extremely perilous. Yet, in the *Act Respecting the Fundamental Rights and Prerogatives of the Québec People and the Québec State*,[40] the Quebec National Assembly somehow alluded to such a "right". Indeed, in response to the federal Parliament's *Clarity Act*, the National Assembly formally stated that "[t]he right of the Québec people to self-determination is founded in fact and in law",[41] that it "has the inalienable right to freely decide the political regime and legal status of Québec",[42] and that, "acting through its own political institutions", it "shall determine alone the mode of exercise of its right to choose the political regime and legal status of Quebec".[43] One could construe this type of declaratory legislation as a mere manifestation of legislative bravado, but that would be taking too lightly a discourse that seeks to operate a semantic shift into the very concept of "right", i.e. by transforming what may at best be a moral right into a legal one.[44] Such a semantic shift is likely to increase confusion as to what positive law really says concerning peoples' right to self-determination, which remains the juridical standard recognized under international law, and to provide a false sense of security to voters, as it induces them to assume an ex ante right the existence of which has yet to be demonstrated.[45] The fact is that positive international law cannot be construed as recognizing an absolute "right" to secession that would be grounded on a generic "right" to decide. It is precisely that type of "right", which has very little to do with a right recognizable by a legitimate legal order, that Quebec's 2000 legislation sought to protect while absolutizing it in passing. Interestingly, such an affirmation of a "right to decide", if that

[40] *Supra*, note 25.

[41] Id., s. 1.

[42] Id., s. 2.

[43] Id., s. 3.

[44] As mentioned earlier, *supra*, note 31, a recent decision of the Quebec Superior Court "read down" this provision, construing it as not implying the affirmation of a legal right to external self-determination, a conclusion that is, in this author's view, debatable.

[45] The semantic ambiguity of the right to decide as it is used in Catalonia has been documented and analysed in Sierra and Olivas (2013).

right is understood as entailing positive legal consequences, pushes the secessionist discourse a step further. As two Canadian authors recently observed, the difficulty experienced by small nations integrated into broader democratic states to resort to the external right to self-determination to legally ground a secession attempt had for some time led many nationalists or secessionists to shift their discourse from an ex ante legal justification for such an attempt to an *ex post facto* one founded on the principle of effectiveness (Bérard and Beaulac 2015: 250, note 13). However, the invocation of a "right to decide" distinct from the right to external self-determination somehow represents a departure from the effectiveness argument and a return to a form of ex ante justification.[46]

According to its most recent promoters (see, e.g., Turp 2013; Turp and Sanjaume-Calvet 2016), and there are several in Catalonia (see, e.g., Lopez 2015: 28), this "right" to decide would find its main legal origin in the International Court of Justice's 2010 advisory opinion in the case of Kosovo's unilateral declaration of independence. Reference is actually made to some statements made by the Court in its opinion, such as the following: (1) the scope of the principle of state territorial integrity would be limited to interstate relations,[47] (2) no international law rule would prohibit unilateral declarations of independence,[48] unless such declarations are accompanied by significant violations of jus cogens norms[49] (3) opinions differ regarding "whether, outside the context of non-self-governing territories and peoples subject to alien subjugation, domination and exploitation, the international law of self-determination confers upon part of the population of an existing State a right to separate from that State",[50] or (4) the authors of Kosovo's unilateral declaration of independence were not bound by the constitutional framework

[46] It bears noting that in its opinion on Catalonia's Declaration of Sovereignty and of the People of Catalonia's Right to Decide, the Spanish Constitutional Court construed this alleged "right to decide" as currently existing within the structures of the Spanish state, i.e. as susceptible of actualization through the exercise of the right to internal self-determination. See Tribunal Constitucional (2014) Sentencia 42/2014, de 25 de marzo de 2014, on line: http://hj.tribunalconstitucional.es/fr/Resolucion/Show/23861, paragraph 2.

[47] Accordance with International Law of the Unilateral Declaration of Independence in respect of Kosovo, Advisory Opinion, I.C.J. Reports 2010, 403, §80.

[48] Id., §79.

[49] Id., §82.

[50] Ibid.

to which they were submitted under domestic law.[51] The promoters of a legal "right to decide" read in such statements a foundation that confirms the juridical nature of that alleged "right".

Even leaving aside the arguable lightness of some ICJ statements in its Kosovo opinion, interpreting it as grounding a "right", i.e. a valid claim, to decide would seem dubious, with all due respect, and this for at least three reasons. Firstly, such an interpretation universalizes the scope of statements made in relation to a case that arose out of a very specific factual context, i.e. that of a state born after a bloody war. At the same time, it decontextualizes the said statements and leaves aside most needed nuances. Secondly, it obscures the fact that the ICJ refuses to decide "debates regarding the extent of the right of self-determination and the existence of any right of 'remedial secession', however, [which] concern the right to separate from a State".[52] Thirdly, and most importantly, such an interpretation wilfully ignores the difference between an ex ante positive right to do something and the inference, as the case may be, of legal consequences from a factual situation the existence of which is independent from the exercise of a prior positive right to create it. Recall here that the ICJ distinguishes the question raised in the Kosovo case from that submitted to the Supreme Court of Canada in the 1998 *Secession Reference*. The ICJ indeed observes in its opinion that the Supreme Court "inquired whether there was a right to 'effect secession', and whether there was a rule of international law which conferred a positive entitlement on any of the organs named", while the ICJ had been asked by the General Assembly "whether the declaration of independence was 'in accordance with' international law", which amounted to asking whether or not the applicable international law prohibited the declaration of independence".[53] The Court thus mentions that it is not asked to decide whether Kosovo had a positive right to unilaterally declare its independence, nor "*a fortiori*, (...) whether international law generally confers an entitlement on entities situated within a State unilaterally to break away from it".[54] It even adds that "it is entirely possible

[51] Id., §120.

[52] Id., §83.

[53] Id., §56.

[54] Ibid.

for a particular act — such as a unilateral declaration of independence — not to be in violation of international law without necessarily constituting the exercise of a right conferred by it".[55]

The broadest (and most generous) possible interpretation that can be made of these comments by the ICJ is that the law may sometimes, *ex post facto*, draw some legal consequences from a factual situation it is bound to grasp, but the existence of which is not dependent upon the exercise of a prior positive right allegedly recognized under international law. The non-violation of the international legal order does not create rights per se, a fortiori the right to ignore or, worse, violate a domestic legal order. In other words, nothing in the Kosovo opinion supports the recognition of a right to decide, in a strict juridical sense, which would be independent from the right to self-determination. This is particularly true if the alleged right to decide is construed as leaving open *all* options, including unilateral secession—a view that would reflect what Mancini (2008: 573) calls the "choice theory". Moreover, as John Dugard (himself a former ad hoc judge of the International Court) observes, state practice provides no foundation for the argument that the applicability of the right to self-determination is not a necessary condition to the creation of a new state (Dugard 2013: 270).

If no general and absolute legal right to decide exists under international law, constantly affirming its existence nonetheless represents a politically efficient discursive strategy.[56] Yet, it is a misleading one. Actually, it would be more accurate to say that it is efficient *because* it is misleading. Indeed, to speak of a "right" to decide has a somewhat

[55] Ibid.

[56] In the context of the 2017 "referendum crisis" in Catalonia, a report sponsored by the Catalan government and authored by eminent scholars cautiously argued in favour of the existence of a right to decide on the basis of international law, European law, as well as international and European practice. These scholars shied away, however, from conflating that right to decide with a right to external self-determination, focusing instead on the right to a democratic process. Yet, some of the conclusions reached by the authors—for example, that European law recognized the existence of a right to decide, and that there were indications in European treaties and in the recent practice of European states that such states would react positively to a new European state candidacy to join the Union—were blatantly contradicted by the practice of European states after Madrid imposed its rule on Catalonia to prevent the holding of a referendum on independence, which points, as we will see later, to the particular stakes raised by secession claims affecting "major powers". See Levrat et al. (2017).

performative effect, to the extent that it is susceptible to instilling in the mind of those who will eventually "decide" the belief that their secessionist act is beforehand consonant with international law. The confusion cleverly entertained between a legally recognized right and a right that can at best aspire at being characterized as a "moral" one reflects a cosmetic political move that seeks to assuage the fears of citizens who could otherwise have doubts as to the serenity of the aftermath of a "decision" in favour of secession. This is true for Quebecers, but arguably also for Catalans, Basques, Scots or Flemish.

Recall here that one of the most significant aspects of the Supreme Court of Canada's opinion in the Secession Reference revolves around the requirements that it imposes as to the quality of the process that is deemed to lead to the democratic expression of a will that would trigger a duty to negotiate. By requiring that both the question posed during the referendum and the majority obtained in favour of the change proposed be clear, the Court emphasizes the need for transparency in the process that may result in the secession of a province. It thus reminds its audience of the fact that expressing an opinion is a qualitatively different gesture from making a decision. A decision implies a choice the consequences of which must be reasonably ascertainable and the terms of which must be formulated in the clearest manner possible. The intensity of this clarity requirement, which is applicable at all steps of the process, arguably grows depending on the importance and the irreversibility of the choice to be made. From that perspective, it is far from clear that a mere election (or plebiscitary election), even if it is depicted as a quasi-referendum by some political parties, would meet this clarity requirement. Indeed, even when a particular question becomes the main theme of an election, pre-existing political cleavages or incidental stakes may influence its outcome; and even when the question of secession is front and centre in the debate, it is not necessarily posed in terms that are absolutely clear. Even if a pro-secession party manages to make this question the main theme of the election campaign, some voters may still support that option merely for the sake of pressuring the central government to respond to their claims, without actually desiring a full-fledged secession. Secession thus becomes a trump used to alter a power relation. In this context, the "answer" given in the election can hardly be characterized as clear. What happens after in the process may also cause problems. For instance, a newly elected secessionist government could seek to instrumentalize for its own political purposes the debate with the central government that its election will trigger, and to concretely seek to undermine any negotiation susceptible to lead to a political status that is lesser than that of an independent state, which would be viewed as a dilution of the secessionist project itself. In such circumstances, it is probably not so difficult to exploit and exacerbate the feeling of victimization in the population and to induce it to support, through a referendum or otherwise, a project of unilateral declaration of independence. Thus, the process launched by an election turned into a plebiscite or referendum will almost inevitably lead, if the secessionist parties win, to a formal secessionist action. In other words, the political dynamic at play risks making it irreversible. This is arguably what Jacques Parizeau, who was Quebec's secessionist Premier at the time of the 1995 referendum, had in mind when he said that after a "yes" vote in favour of the secessionist option, Quebecers would have been trapped like lobsters in a cage. Bearing that hypothesis in mind and returning to the "right" to decide which would seemingly justify such a strategy, it is not illegitimate to ask oneself the following question: The right to decide what, after all?

The problem is that this type of strategy is often defended in the name of democracy. Granted, references to the people's democratically expressed will are often little more than mantra-like incantations, but one must nevertheless acknowledge that nationalist lyricism sometimes compensates for the lack of transparency of the process in the context of which that will is expressed. This is why the imposition of precise juridical criteria seeking to frame political processes is desirable, particularly in view of ensuring a process that is both transparent and less susceptible of instrumentalization.[57] Unfortunately, invoking a vague "right" to decide which has no legal foundation raises more problems rather than it leads to solutions.

The point here is not to say that states, which are historically contingent political communities, can never be dissolved, notwithstanding arguments to the contrary, be they grounded or not upon explicit constitutional provisions. Rather, it merely seeks to specify that save scarce exceptions, there is no such thing as a positive right to dissolve them. This is true even in federal states constituted after an aggregative process. Indeed, once these entities have created a federation, the federation becomes a legal order distinct from them, which is vested with certain sovereign jurisdictions that are constitutionally protected (Schmitt 1993: 513).

[57] On secession clauses, see Mancini (2008), Weinstock (2001), and Sunstein (2001).

Now, it is one thing to say that there is no positive right to dissolve a state through a secessionist gesture, particularly a unilateral declaration of independence, but it is quite another to say that secession is outright impossible. As the ICJ notes in its Kosovo opinion, such a declaration would not in and of itself constitute a violation of the international legal order even if it does constitute a violation of the domestic legal order of the state affected by that declaration. Accordingly, international law could eventually, *ex post facto*, draw legal consequences from the new factual situation in which the secessionist entity would find itself. However, the international recognition of the new state could not be taken for granted. As was recently argued by Catherine Maia (2018: 46–50), even when all the preconditions for the recognition of a new state are met, recognition remains a unilateral and discretionary decision. This means that there is no such thing as an obligation of recognition under international law, and that a state can exist without the recognition of other states if it meets the preconditions for statehood. However, and this is important, when such preconditions are not met, states are under an obligation *not* to recognize the emergent state. In practice, as was noted by Milena Sterio (2010: 137), one cannot ignore the fact that the success of any secessionist project is to a large extent determined by the reaction of states that can reasonably be characterized as "major powers". In this respect, it is often hard to identify the interest that major powers would have in condoning the dissolution of an advanced democracy such as Canada. The same observation arguably applies to countries such as the UK, Belgium or Spain.

Examining the case of France vis-à-vis Quebec may prove interesting in that regard. Considering its cultural and linguistic affinities with Quebec as well as Canada's sovereignty, France has long applied to Quebec's situation a policy of "non-intervention, non-indifference", which has predictably given rise to expectations, in secessionist circles, that should Quebec secede, France would immediately recognize the new state and pressure other states to do the same. In a nutshell, it was the gamble that the Quebec government was ready to make in 1995 (Hébert and Lapierre 2014: 53).

It could have happened and it could still happen, for sure. But this hypothesis assumes that France would have been, or would currently be ready to take the risk of making uncomfortable close European partners faced with their own secessionist movements. And this leaves aside the domestic problem posed by Corsica. So this begs the question: beyond all the nice diplomatic discourse extolling the virtues of the cultural proximity between France and Quebec, would the former really be ready to disregard the concerns of its European partners and wholeheartedly support a unilateral declaration of independence by the latter? Given the weight of realpolitik in international affairs as well as France's historic defence of the notion of *raison d'État*, one can legitimately raise doubts about it. Although Canada is not a member of the European Union while Spain is, France's relatively indifferent reaction towards Madrid's thwarting of Catalonia's efforts to hold a referendum on independence in 2017 tends to support that view. What France as well as other major powers could do, however, would be to pressure the Canadian government to not unduly stall negotiations after a clear secessionist vote in a referendum, as it could foster instability. Indeed, while great powers like stability, and thus tend to be opposed to secessionist projects emanating from regions of developed democracies, they might reach a point where concerns for stability could induce them to support democratically supported secessionist projects if not respecting a clear vote in favour of secession is likely to lead to instability. But all this, it must be noted, takes place *ex post facto* and does not depend, or rely, on an ex ante right.

Ultimately, we are back to square one, so to say: small, but not dominated or otherwise persecuted nations such as Quebec or Catalonia can hardly claim a generic legal "right" to decide, that would be distinct from the right to external self-determination recognized under international law in exceptional circumstances. It may very well be that an international legal regime governing the conditions of exercise of the right to external self-determination by sub-states nations incorporated in democratic states is warranted. Such a regime, one might surmise, would draw legal consequences from the principle of democracy and would better take stock of questions pertaining to political legitimacy, so as to reduce the negative impact of ultra-dogmatic and formalist responses to secessionist challenges such as those displayed by Madrid in the Catalonia case, or by France in respect of Corsica.[58]

But it does not exist yet, and affirming the contrary, based on an overstretched interpretation of the ICJ's Kosovo opinion, is at best misleading, for absent circumstances potentially justifying the exercise of the

[58] See that country's constitutional council decision in: Décision sur le Statut de la Corse, Conseil constitutionnel français, décision n° 91-290, 9 mai 1991, JO 14 mai 1991: 6350.

qualified right to external self-determination, the recognition of secessionist ventures remains a question of effectiveness, with the additional hurdles that come with it.

And contrary to what some proponents of the "right to decide" have argued, merely relying on the democratic principle cannot transform what is perhaps a moral right into a legal one. Moreover, the Supreme Court of Canada's qualified finding that a clear majority on a clear question on independence could trigger a duty to negotiate, cannot be so easily universalized so as to be taken as evidence that a generic, legal "right to decide" now supplements the external right to self-determination recognized in exceptional circumstances under international law (Turp 2016). As difficult as it may be since it is dependent on a mutual will to compromise, elaborating domestic institutional and symbolic solutions to the reconciliation of nationalisms should remain the first choice of any sub-state autonomist movement evolving in the context of a broader state which also characterizes as a stable democracy.[59]

Conclusion

I have sought in this text to draw attention to the main legal and political hurdles that the secessionist movement in Quebec currently faces. While these hurdles will be difficult to overcome, it would be premature to announce the death of the patient, for as long as there will be a "small nation" distinguished from the rest of North America by its "deep diversity" (Taylor 1992: 179, 212–213), nationalism will play a role in the politics of this nation. And secession will always be a reasonable option in the eyes of many. Indeed, many Quebecers genuinely feel as if they were in a form of "internal exile" within Canada (Laforest and Roy 2014), given the rejection by Quebec of the current constitutional order. Political developments at the federal level in the past ten years or so may not help either: the former Conservative government's right-wing policies tended to be at odds with Quebecers' values. The current Liberal government led by Justin Trudeau is much closer to their values, subject perhaps to its emphasis on multiculturalism, but, while it remains popular, it has clearly rejected the possibility of opening constitutional talks with Quebec. Thus, Quebec's estrangement from Canada could grow in

[59] On accommodation strategies and secessionist crises, see Basta (2017).

light of a majority nationalism[60] feeding either on a conservative values agenda, or, alternatively, on liberal Charter of rights-worshipping multiculturalism perceived as obscuring or ignoring the concerns of a majority of Quebecers.

Counting of the youth's disaffection towards secessionism may not be a reliable strategy either. The 2014 provincial election showed that today's young voters do not tend to prioritize Quebec independence over other issues even if their sense of belonging to Canada seems rather thin. The fact that they are more concerned with human rights, environmental issues and work-life balance and that they are more cosmopolitan than their forebears does not mean either that their connection to Canada qualitatively increases. Many of them are agnostic at best when it comes to their Canadian identity. Thus, counting on the new generations to evacuate the threat of secession might be presumptuous. It is therefore much premature to write the obituary of Quebec's secessionist movement.

Yet, recent debates over secularism and the feeling of exclusion, if not outright rejection, that many minority groups have experienced, shed light on a deeper problem facing not only Quebec's, but possibly all nationalist/secessionist movements whose political programme primarily revolves around cultural/linguistic claims. This problem lies in the additional costs incurred by minority groups, particularly recent immigrants, if they want to be recognized as genuinely part of the "Us" rather than being relegated to the "Them" group in societies where nationalism or secessionism functionally serve as promotion tools for the particular *cultural* interests of the majority. These costs may significantly delay, and even hinder, these groups' embrace of nationalist/secessionist narratives. If one looks at the situation in Quebec, the very requirement of adopting a minority language in the broader Canadian context, however legitimate and acceptable that demand may be, is in and of itself an added cost that other sub-state communities, such as Scotland, do not have to impose on their newcomers since the common public language is the same as that of the global polity, regional accents aside. Language represents in a way an additional entry cost, but the revival of ethno-nationalism arguably adds a further layer of costs. For example, in Quebec, it is one thing to demand from minority groups that they learn and use French in the so-called public sphere, it is quite another to ask them to identify

[60] On majoritarian nationalism, see Gagnon et al. (2007).

with a narrative emphasizing the mistreatment of the French-Canadian majority between the British conquest of New France in 1759 and today, and heralding the victory of secularism over religious obscurantism as of the 1960s, especially if the conception of secularism that is promoted enshrines prejudices about particular types of religious behaviour. Demanding that minority or immigrant groups adhere to such a thicker identity drastically increases the "transaction costs" they incur if they want to be tangibly considered and thus included as genuine Quebecers. This type of move is inevitably susceptible of deterring them from appropriating and internalizing nationalist or secessionist narratives, and more concretely renders any secessionist project suspect. In a context where, as in Quebec, most of the population's growth comes from immigration, the recent political developments in this province certainly cast a shadow over the long-term viability of the secessionist project. If the secessionist song once had an upbeat tempo, it has now morphed into a blues. To wit, in the recent 2018 provincial election, the historic proponent of Quebec secession, the Parti québécois, decided to put the question of independence on the back burner in its electoral platform—it eventually obtained 17% of the votes. For its part, Québec solidaire, the only party which promised that, if elected, some form of process that would lead to independence—a constituent assembly—would be launched, got a mere 16% of the votes. Together, the non-secessionist parties, the Quebec Liberal Party and the victorious Coalition Avenir Québec got the support of about 62% of voters.

References

Basta, Karlo (2017), "The State Between Minority and Majority Nationalism: Decentralization, Symbolic Recognition, and Secessionist Crises in Spain and Canada", in *Publius: The Journal of Federalism*, 48 (1), 51–75.

Beauchemin, Jacques and Beaudoin, Louise (2010), "Le pluralisme comme incantation", in *Le Devoir*, February 13, 2010, available at https://www.ledevoir.com/opinion/idees/283016/le-pluralisme-comme-incantation.

Bérard, Frédéric and Beaulac, Stéphane (2015), *Droit à l'indépendance. Québec, Monténégro, Kosovo, Écosse, Catalogne*, XYZ éditeur, Montréal. A Shorter Version of Their Book Has Recently Been Published in English: Bérard, Frédéric and Beaulac, Stéphane (2017), *The Law of Independence. Quebec, Montenegro, Kosovo, Scotland, Catalonia*, LexisNexis, Toronto.

Bock-Côté, Mathieu (2012), *Fin de cycle. Aux origines du malaise politique québécois*, Boréal, Montréal.

Commission de consultation sur les pratiques d'accommodement reliées aux différences culturelles (2008), *Fonder l'avenir. Le temps de la conciliation*, in G. Bouchard and C. Taylor (co-chairs). Commission de consultation sur les pratiques d'accommodement reliées aux différences culturelles, Québec.

Dugard, John (2013), *The Secession of States and Their Recognition in the Wake of Kosovo*, Nijhoff, Leiden.

Gagnon, Alain-G, Lecours, André and Nootens, Geneviève eds. (2007), *Les nationalismes majoritaires contemporains: identité, mémoire, pouvoir*, Les Éditions Québec Amérique, Montréal.

Gaudreault-DesBiens, Jean-François (1999), "The Quebec Secession Reference and the Judicial Arbitration of Conflicting Narratives About Law, Democracy and Identity", in *Vermont Law Review*, 24, 792–843.

Gaudreault-DesBiens, Jean-François (2009a), "The Fetishism of Formal Law and the Fate of Constitutional Patriotism in Communities of Comfort: A Canadian Perspective", in John Erik Fossum, Paul Magnette, and Johanne Poirier (eds.), *Ties That Bind: Accommodating Diversity in Canada and the European Union*, P.I.E. Peter Lang, Brussels, Bern and Berlin, 301–330.

Gaudreault-DesBiens, Jean-François (2009b), "Religious Challenges to the Secularized Identity of an Insecure Polity: A Tentative Sociology of Québec's Reasonable Accommodation Debate", in Ralph Grillo, Prakash Shah, André J. Hoekema, et al. (eds.), *Legal Practice and Cultural Diversity*, Ashgate, London, 151–274.

Gaudreault-DesBiens, Jean-François (2014), "Secession Blues: Some Legal and Political Challenges Facing the Quebec Independence Movement", in *Percorsi Costituzionali*, 3, 765–786.

Gaudreault-DesBiens, Jean-François (2015), "¿Un derecho 'legal' a decidir?", in *La Vanguardia*, August 8, 2015, available at https://www.lavanguardia.com/opinion/articulos/20150808/54434791655/un-derecho-legal-de-cidir-jean-francois-gaudreault-desbiens.html.

Gaudreault-DesBiens, Jean-François (2016), "Algunos de los desafíos legales y políticos que debe afrontar el movimiento de independencia de Quebec", in *Teoría y Realidad Constitucional*, 37, 135–162.

Hébert, Chantal and Lapierre, Jean (2014), *Confessions post-référendaires. Les acteurs politiques de 1995 et le scénario d'un oui*, Éditions de l'Homme, Montréal.

Laforest, Guy and Roy, Jean-Olivier (2014), *Un Québec exilé dans la fédération: Essai d'histoire intellectuelle et de pensée politique*, Les Éditions Québec Amérique, Montréal.

Levrat, Nicolas, Antunes, Sandrina, Tusseau, Guillaume and Williams, Paul (2017), *Catalonia's Legitimate Right to Decide. Paths to Self-Determination*, Generalitat de Catalunya, Barcelona.

Lopez, Jaume (2015), "A Right to Decide? On the Normative Basis of a Political Principle and Its Application in the Catalan Case", in Klaus-Jurgen Nagel, and Stephan Rixen (eds.), *Catalonia in Spain and Europe: Is There a Way to Independence?* Nomos, Baden-Baden, 27–40.

Maclure, Jocelyn (2011), "Quebec's Culture War: Two Conceptions of Quebec Identity", in Stephan Gervais, Christopher Kirkey, and Jarrett Rudy (eds.), *Quebec Questions: Quebec Studies for the Twenty-First Century*, Oxford University Press, Oxford, 137–148.

Macpherson, Crawford Brough (2010 [1962]), *The Political Theory of Possessive Individualism: Hobbes to Locke*, Oxford University Press, Oxford.

Maia, Catherine (2018), "Les critères de l'obligation de non-reconnaissance du statut d'État à des entités contestées", in Thierry Garcia (ed.), *La reconnaissance du statut d'État à des entités contestées. Approches de droits international, régional et interne*, Pedone, 43–58.

Mancini, Susanna (2008), "Rethinking the Boundaries of Democrrativc Secession: Liberalism, Nationalism, and the Right of Minorities to Self-Determination", in *International Journal of Constitutional Law*, 6 (3–4), 553–584.

Mancini, Susanna (2014), "The Tempting of Europe, the Political Seduction of the Cross: A Schmittian Reading of Christianity and Islam in European Constitutionalism", in Susanna Mancini and Michel Rosenfeld (eds.), *Constitutional Secularism in an Age of Religious Revival*, Oxford University Press, Oxford, 111–135.

Schmitt, Carl (1993), *Théorie de la constitution*, Presses Universitaires de France, Paris.

Sierra, Sonia and Olivas, Jose Javier (2013), "On the 'Right to Decide'", London School of Economics, Euro Crisis in the Press: The Politics of Public Discourse in Europe, December 6, 2013, available at http://blogs.lse.ac.uk/eurocrisispress/2013/12/06/on-the-right-to-decide/.

Sterio, Milena (2010), "On the Right to External Self-Determination: 'Selfistans', Secession and the Great Powers' Rule", in *Minnesota Journal of International Law*, 19, 137–176.

Stewart, Heather, Walker, Peter and Carrell, Severin (2017), "Theresa May Rejects Nicola Sturgeon's Demands", in *The Guardian*, March 16, 2017, available at https://www.theguardian.com/politics/2017/mar/16/theresa-may-rejects-nicola-sturgeons-scottish-referendum-demand.

Sunstein, Cass R. (2001), "Should Constitutions Protect the Right to Secede? A Reply to Weinstock", in *Journal of Political Philosophy*, 9, 350–355.

Taylor, Charles (1992), "Convergences et divergences à propos des valeurs entre le Québec et le Canada", in Charles Taylor (ed.), *Rapprocher les solitudes. Écrits sur le fédéralisme et le nationalisme au Canada*, Presses de l'Université Laval, Québec, 179–214.

Turp, Daniel (2013), "Le droit de décider du peuple catalan", December 10, 2013, available at http://danielturpqc.org/upload/2013findoc/Turp-_Le_droit_de_decider_du_Parlement_catalan_10_decembre_2013_Version_finale.pdf.

Turp, Daniel (2016), "Conclusion", in Daniel Turp and Marc Sanjaume-Calvet (eds.), *The Emergence of a Democratic Right to Self-Determination in Europe*, Centre Maurits Coppieters, Brussels, 264–271.

Turp, Daniel and Sanjaume-Calvet, Marc eds. (2016), *The Emergence of a Democratic Right to Self-Determination in Europe*, Centre Maurits Coppieters, Brussels.

van de Kerchove, Michel (1988), "Le sens clair d'un texte: argument de raison ou d'autorité?", in Guy Haarsher, Léon Ingber, and Raymond Vander Elst (eds.), *Arguments d'autorité et arguments de raison en droit*, Éditions Némésis, Brussels, 291–315.

Weinstock, Daniel (2001), "Constitutionalizing the Right to Secede", in *The Journal of Political Philosophy*, 9, 182–203.

Wimmer, Andreas and Glick Schiller, Nina (2002), "Methodological Nationalism and Beyond: Nation-State Building, Migration and the Social Sciences", in *Global Networks*, 4, 301–334.

The Reception in Spain of the Reference of the Supreme Court of Canada on the Secession of Quebec

Josep Maria Castellà Andreu

Interest in Spain for the Reference of the Supreme Court

The Reference of the Supreme Court of Canada (SCC) on the unilateral secession of Quebec, issued on 20 August 1998,[1] has elicited great interest in Spain from the first moment. Such interest transcends the realm of academia, reaching the society at large, politics and even case law. Evidence for that is the translation and publication of the Reference already in 1998 (Chacón and Ruiz Robledo 1998:

[1] *Reference Re Secession of Quebec*, [1998] 2 S.C.R. 217.

J. M. Castellà Andreu (✉)
Department of Constitutional Law,
Universitat de Barcelona, Barcelona, Spain
e-mail: castella@ub.edu

G. Delledonne and G. Martinico (eds.), *The Canadian Contribution to a Comparative Law of Secession*,
https://doi.org/10.1007/978-3-030-03469-6_4

129 et seq.). The press, too, reported extensively on the ruling, publishing opinion pieces authored by scholars specialized in Canadian federalism.[2]

The existence in Spain of persistent political–constitutional conflicts between centre and periphery, above all with the Basque Country and Catalonia, explains to a large extent this particular interest, which transcends the justified, but abstract constitutional interest for the Reference shown by Constitutional Law scholars all over the world. Furthermore, the publication of the Reference in Canada took place at a time when Spain was witnessing the intensification of political demands for greater autonomy and asymmetry from the different "nationalities" (the Pact of Estella between the Basque nationalist parties, and the Declaration of Barcelona issued by the main nationalist parties in the Basque Country, Catalonia and Galicia), coinciding with the twentieth anniversary of the approval of the Spanish Constitution and the starting point of the assumption of autonomy by these nationalities.

[2]Fossas, Enric, "Una decisión ejemplar", *El País*, 3 September 1998. The Autonomous University of Barcelona professor provided an assessment of the Reference which set the tone of what eventually became the majority opinion on the ruling among Spanish Constitutional Law scholars. Thus, he began the article by showing his admiration for the decision: "Canada never ceases to surprise and amaze for its political forms. The judgment (sentencia, sic) issued by the Supreme Court on August 20 represents a new display this country's capacity to address its 'national question' peacefully and democratically through a political debate presided by tolerance and fairness." Fossas underscores how jurists will "find a small treatise on Constitutional Law in the reflections laid out by the Court on federalism, democracy, constitutionalism, rule of law, and respect for minority rights. Reading is absolutely advisable and it will certainly contribute to ensuring that these legal and political concepts, subjected today to confusion and trivialization, keep meaning something." Contrary to opinions that reduce the Reference to a condemnation of secession, he sees the ruling as a "Solomonic decision that attempts to articulate the principle of constitutionality, which demands the subjection of all powers to the Constitution, with the democratic principle, which 'would demand that considerable weight be given to a clear expression by the people of Quebec of their will to secede from Canada.'" Finally, Fossas concludes that the main lesson from the ruling lies in "the Court's abstention from imposing concrete solutions and in the proclamation of a constitutional obligation to negotiate by means of a process 'which would require the reconciliation of various rights and obligations by negotiation between two legitimate majorities.' In short, a model decision because it opts for dialogue, negotiation, consensus, compromise, and agreement. In other words, for constitutionalism, democracy, and federalism."

From that point onwards, more than a few Constitutional Law scholars and political scientists have alluded to the Canadian Reference, together with politicians and journalists. There has been no shortage either in Spanish publications of contributions on the issue from noted Canadian jurists. In the first years, the quotations to the Reference were above all scholarly. Citations to the Reference multiplied after the outbreak of the Catalan secessionist crisis in September 2012, in an attempt to find guidance in Comparative Law on how to address the situation from a constitutional point of view (section "Reception of the Reference by the Constitutional Doctrine: "New Paradigm" on the Treatment of Secession by Constitutional Law"). This moment also marks the point of intensification of partial interpretations and of attempts at appropriating the doctrine of the SCC by the competing political and constitutional positions on how to reach a solution to the Catalan crisis. Or the use of such doctrine as a weapon against the opposing party, charged with not following its positions. This may be seen not only in legal academia, but also in the institutional stances in the Basque Country and Catalonia and in documents prepared by civil society organizations and by bodies created to justify political options in favour of the right to decide. They provided the groundwork for Basque nationalists first and, later, for their Catalan counterparts to develop legal and political proposals that allegedly codified the doctrine of the SCC on secession (section "Use of the Canadian Reference by Basque and Catalan Nationalism in Their Respective Sovereigntist Processes"). Finally, the tipping point of the reception in Spain of the Canadian doctrine was marked by the explicit reference in the Constitutional Court judgement 42/2014 on a resolution of the Parliament of Catalonia on sovereignty and the right to decide of the Catalan people (section "The Invocation of the Reference of the SCC by the Constitutional Court in Judgement 42/2014"). Since then, as the secessionist discourse has grown increasingly radical—unilateralism, disobedience of the Catalan authorities to the constitutional order—Canadian mentions from the pro-independence camp have diminished, replaced by other models of secession.

It is important to clarify from the beginning that the allusions in Spain to the doctrine of the Supreme Court tend to be favourable, although they are often superficial or very generic (even distorted, for example, by calling it *sentencia*, ignoring the kind of procedure that originates the decision and defines its effects, or the fundamental traits of Canadian constitutionalism from which stems the Reference of 1998). Beyond this general consensus in highlighting it as the "model" to be known and followed, a legal document such as an advisory opinion, together with its content, because of its extension, complexity and nuances, is likely to lead to diverse and contradictory interpretations. The discrepancies among them arise in more than a few occasions as a result of reading the Reference from a Spanish mindset trying to read what happened in Canada with Hispanic eyes. Because of that, some aspects are underscored, while setting aside or omitting others. As a result, the correctness and rigour of the interpretation are often sacrificed in the interest of the author's thesis or the political position for which they advocate, with the aim of associating it with the Canadian position, used as an argument of authority.

This partial reading of the doctrine of the SCC on the unilateral right to secession by a member entity of the State or Federation by Spanish academia (and political actors) contributes to a frequent confusion or mixture of two different levels: on the one hand, the content of the Supreme Court 1998 Reference and, on the other hand, the legislation passed in 2000 by the Canadian Parliament (the *Clarity Act*, Act C-20), promoted by the Canadian Federal Government and, more precisely, by the then minister of Intergovernmental Affairs, Stéphane Dion, as the legal concretion of the Reference. To this should be added the response of the National Assembly of Quebec in 2001 (*Loi sur l'exercice des droits fondamentaux et des prérogatives du peuple québécois et de l'État du Québec*, Loi 99), less well known in Spain, which followed the approval of the federal Clarity Act. Before us, there are two mutually contradictory concretions of the Reference of the Supreme Court, which attempt to answer to questions left open by the advisory opinion (in order to remain within the proper boundaries of a judicial ruling of this kind, so as not to supplant the competent legislator) or to set certain criteria on who is to decide on them: what is the required majority for a sovereignty option in a future referendum in order to be a "clear majority," and the supervision of the drafting of the question to ensure that it is also "clear," and apt to lead to negotiations, as well as their scope and requirements. Although we shall subsequently focus on the "naked" content of the 1998 decision, it is necessary to point out that the reading of the Reference in Spain has often been accompanied by or based on one of the two legislative developments: on the "constitutionalist" side (that is, those who support the 1978 Constitution), by the Clarity Act as a model, on the secessionist camp, by the same interpretation as that of the National Assembly of Quebec.

Reception of the Reference by the Constitutional Doctrine: "New Paradigm" on the Treatment of Secession by Constitutional Law

In order to review the impact of the Reference of the Supreme Court of Canada on Spanish Constitutional doctrine, we shall distinguish between two subsequent stages: the first one, between 1999 and 2012, before the outbreak of the Catalan crisis; the second one, from 2012 to the present. To this, it is important to add the publication in Spain of scholarly works on the issue by Canadian authors. It has been above all over the last six years that the doctrine of the Supreme Court on secession has received greater attention in Spain. The reason for that is to be found in the doctrinal attempt to find references in Comparative Law with which to address the events in Catalonia. Before 2012, the references' value resided in themselves, that is, they highlighted the style of argumentation (through general principles of the Constitution, not specific dispositions), the relevance of the Court's ruling (the establishment of a legal framework for the secession of a province in accordance with the Constitution, which is to be respected at all times), its fundamental conclusions (there is no room for unilateral secession under the Canadian Constitution, and the case of Quebec does not fulfil the criteria envisaged by International Law), as well as the consequences stemming from a majority will for independence in a given territory: the need to negotiate. These reflections came mostly from authors well acquainted with Canadian federalism or scholars working on federalism in general. By contrast, in the second stage explicit comparisons with the case of Spain have become more prominent and, along with them, quite often, but not always, more or less biased or *pro domo sua* interpretations by the authors who put them forward.

López Basaguren has brilliantly summarized the implications of the Canadian Reference for the Constitutional approach to secession in Comparative Law: the 1998 Reference opens a "new paradigm in the way democratic systems address secessionist aspirations from territories that are part of a State, especially in federal systems and in those with territorial autonomy." The new paradigm would find continuity later in Scotland and would stand in contrast with the "traditional paradigm embodied by the US and its Civil War" (López Basaguren 2013: 90). For this Basque professor, the construction by the SCC has "great importance, in that, as Sujit Choudhry pointed out, 'it provides a narrative which warns about the limits of constitutional design and their capacity to address the threat of illegal secession from minority nations'" (ibidem: 92). This new paradigm stems, in his view, from the following premise: "the acceptance of the fact that there is no such thing as a 'right to decide', understood as the right to unilaterally determine the legal status of a territory or community within a State, or to secession in order to become a new independent State. It is possible to seek the recognition of the 'right to decide' in these terms, but one may not demand its indisputable acceptance and, consequently, the right to exercise it even beyond the scope of legality" (ibidem: 100). Spanish Constitutional Law scholars, concludes López Basaguren, "must address the answers provided by the systems that form this new constitutional paradigm, with the aim of analyzing whether the Spanish system is consistent with similar parameters or if, by contrast, those answers cannot fit in it, and what are the reasons-the constitutional arguments- that justify taking a different approach in a way that is solidly based on democratic principles. Otherwise, the democratic legitimacy of the answers provided will be seriously affected; that is, the democratic legitimacy of the Spanish constitutional system will be gravely damaged" (ibidem: 91). Thus, the author confirms that the response of the Canadian Court is a "model" for the Spanish case (and other contemporary ones), but, at the same time, he addresses the scope of application and the limits of Comparative Law: in our view, such a comparison between these two constitutional systems is possible because they both have in common a consolidated democracy, with a stable rule of law, and a constitutional order that guarantees political autonomy for its nationalities (which is not the case in other secessions that have taken place in different contexts over the last twenty years). Furthermore, comparing does not mean "uncritically assuming" the Canadian system, but rather the need to adequately justify the differences in order to turn away from the new paradigm.[3] Indeed, the Canadian paradigm must be compared with what has happened subsequently, considering particularly the responses provided by the Constitutional Courts of Italy and Germany, as well as that of Spain, to similar questions, but with significant differences in the conclusions.

As explained above, in a first stage, Spanish Constitutional scholars glossed the content of the Reference and considered its meaning in the

[3]As pointed out by Biglino Campos (2016: 453), the need for a clear majority to a clear question "has already become part of the constitutional patrimony in the field of secession."

context of Canadian Constitutional Law and the impact of its teachings for the future of Canadian federalism and, therefore, for constitutionalism in general. Ruiz Robledo and Chacón highlight, first, the creation of a "legal duty of cooperation between the parties" in order to proceed to the secession of Quebec and, secondly, how the "internal architecture of the Canadian Constitution, the combination of its written letter and the principles that define it, all with identical legal force, lead to a judicial decision that returns to the law its role of social peacemaker." Lastly, they underscore the clarity of Court's exposition and its self-restraint, which leads it to "refraining from imposing concrete solutions that are incumbent upon the citizens' representatives." Because of that, these experts of Canadian Constitutional Law conclude that it is an "Advisory opinion that is worth reading and from which one may derive useful conclusions for composite States with problems of national integration" (Ruiz Robledo and Chacón 1999: 282, 283). In this first stage, the commentaries of López Aguilar (1998: 519 et seq.; 1999: 7 et seq.),[4] Pérez Tremps (2004)[5] and Sáiz Arnáiz (2007: 33 et seq.) stand out.[6]

Some Catalan political scientists underscored the advisory opinion's acknowledgement of the legitimacy of a decision of Quebec in a self-determination referendum, which would compel the Canadian government to open political negotiations. Their interpretation of the Reference is shaped by the perspective of plurinational federalism.[7]

The Catalan secessionist crisis, which begins in September 2012, brings the Canadian decision, together with the Clarity Act to the

[4] The author, while thanking the Court for its efforts and the substantial contributions, points out a shortcoming: from the "perspective of democratic theory, not all of the implications and suggestions that have been considered have been addressed fully or fairly" (López Aguilar 1999: 34).

[5] The author underscores not only the rigour and the legal skill of the Canadian decision, but also the balanced position (*equidistancia*) between the debated positions (Pérez Tremps 2004: 32–33).

[6] The author holds the advisory opinion as an "exemplary" judicial ruling, which has become an "unavoidable universal benchmark" in the debate on secession because of its "convincing and thorough arguments" (Sáiz Arnáiz 2007: 46).

[7] Requejo highlights the fact that the Reference supports the legitimacy of the "peoples" in a plurinational federation to start a constitutional change which may lead to secession, as long as certain conditions are met. Thus, the Court gives legitimacy to the right of self-determination from a federal, rather than a nationalist, standpoint. In doing so, it creates a "new form of constitutionalism" in which the right to self-determination represents an expression of the collective freedom of national groups (2003: 121–122). See also Caminal (2002: 117–118, footnote 157).

centre of the debate among Spanish Constitutional Law scholars, without clarifying which contributions correspond to each of them.[8]

As shown above, attempts to apply to Spain the Canadian solution have taken priority. It is precisely because of it that oftentimes certain parts of the doctrine of the SCC are chosen that suit better the defence of a given position in the Spanish debate, thereby sacrificing in more than a few occasions the full, authentic meaning of this doctrine. The Reference is invoked both in press articles[9] and in scientific publications.

Some texts propose the implementation in Spain of the doctrine of the SCC, even if authors disagree among them when underscoring its teachings. For some, what is most relevant is the obligation to negotiate if a majority of a nationality might be in favour of secession. This would be a consequence of the recognition in both constitutional systems of principles such as the democratic principle (Aja 2014: 367).[10] For others,

[8]López Basaguren warns of a "mechanistic interpretation" put forward by many in Spain regarding the Clarity Act. The author correctly distinguishes between what he calls "the clarity theory," laid out by the SCC, and the "Clarity Act", which is an interpretation of the former "that is debatable and which has indeed been debated" (by the National Assembly of Quebec, for example) (2016: 165–166). Calonge also draws a distinction between the Reference of the SCC and its legislative concretion, both at a federal level and by the Assembly of Quebec (2013: 117 et seq.). The author rejects simplistic readings of the Canadian case and shows a certain skepticism on whether the situation in Quebec has been resolved (ibidem 2013: 123).

[9]We would like to highlight, given the relevance of its author and the influence it has had on the Spanish public debate, the article by Francisco Rubio Llorente, "Un referéndum para Cataluña," *El País*, 8 October 2012. In this article, Professor Rubio invoked the decision of the SCC as a suitable solution to the Catalan case. More precisely, he calls for a referendum to "find out the reality and strength" of the desire for independence in a territorialized minority, before a constitutional reform. In disagreement with the Reference, according to Rubio a clear question "need not be a single one." In fact, it is the Clarity Act that specifies this aspect. See also the article by Agustín Ruiz Robledo, "El federalismo de la reconciliación," *El País*, 9 August 2017. With the perspective provided by the events in Catalonia over these years, the lesson the author draws from the Canadian experience is the necessity of a combined use by the Government of the State of legal and political instruments to oppose the independence of Catalonia.

[10]According to this author, "[f]rom any standpoint, either legal or political, in order to solve grave political conflicts that affect the unity of the State it seems preferable to refer to the guidance of the Canadian Supreme Court, based on the principles of democracy and federalism, through a political negotiation for both the definition of a possible vote (the referendum envisaged in Article 92 of the Spanish Constitution may be valid if its terms

what is decisive is that there is no “right” of the citizens to be consulted on constitutional matters, while at the same time they deny that, either in Canada or in Spain, the residents of an autonomous territory suffer a situation of discrimination that justifies invoking the norms of international law on secession; or that the failure of constitutional (in Canada) or statutory reforms (in Spain-Catalonia) means that their respective citizens do not enjoy “internal self-determination” or autonomy (Ferreres Comella 2016: 466, 470).

In our opinion, the comparison between Canada and Spain is fully justified: in both cases, the constitutions are written, rigid and superior norms (which is not the case in the UK). Observing the Canadian (and British) experience leads to the conclusion that a unilateral secession against the constitutional order is rejected, while guarantees and precautions are in order with regard to holding a referendum on secession. However, at the same time, the differences between both cases are obvious (different histories, legal systems and foundations of their respective Constitutional orders), as are the difficulties of importing automatically foreign solutions (Castellà Andreu 2014: 462–467).[11] Among the differences, it has been stated that the existence of explicitly limited constitutional powers in the Spanish Constitutional system leads to having to choose between inaction and constitutional reform in order to introduce the right to secession, with no room for “third ways” like the one offered by the SCC (Aláez Corral 2015: 149–150).[12]

Lastly, further evidence for the interest generated by the Reference of the SCC in Spain has been the translation and/or publication of texts by noted Canadian authors. This is what happened right after the SCC decision was issued, with Woehrling (1999: 405 et seq.).[13] It is also worth

have been agreed upon beforehand) and the specification of its effects” (Aja 2014: 367). It should be borne in mind that the SCC also mentions the principles of constitutionality, rule of law and respect for minorities. See also Ruiz-Rico (2016: 331).

[11] See also Tudela Aranda (2016: 494).

[12] In his opinion, supported by the case law of the Constitutional Court, “A mere appeal to the democratic principle in the terms of the Supreme Court of Canada is not sufficient to develop this third way in Spain through interpretation, given that the normative consequences of such principle are determined by the Spanish Constitution itself, and they do not include the attribution to the territorial entities of powers or faculties not envisaged by our legal system” (Alaez 2015: 149–150).

[13] Later Woehrling (2006: 146–148).

mentioning the compilation in a volume of several writings by Dion, political scientist at the University of Montreal, but above all intellectual father of the Clarity Act, as minister of Intergovernmental Affairs of the Government of Canada (2005).[14] Essays have been published thereafter by, among others, Laforest (2013: 348), and lately by Guénette and Gagnon (2017: 13 et seq.)[15] and Gaudreault-DesBiens (2016: 135 et seq.).

Use of the Canadian Reference by Basque and Catalan Nationalism in Their Respective Sovereigntist Processes

From the decade of 2000, several intents to change the autonomic State have taken place, with proposals of confederalist or secessionist thesis based on the "right to decide." First came Basque nationalism (2004–2008) and later its Catalan counterpart (independence process, since 2012), which has led to unilateral rupturist proposals that sideline the legal order. As Solozábal reminds us, both nationalisms have observed with great interest the experience of Quebec. In their proposals, they have attempted to include aspects present in the Reference of the SCC like holding a self-determination referendum or the need to negotiate

[14]The book includes a speech by Dion given in Ottawa on 20 August 1998, "Declaration as a reaction to the decision of the Supreme Court" (ibidem: 351–355). Later, Dion has intervened on several occasions in the Spanish territorial debate, offering his point of view on how the Clarity Act has decisively contributed to the fact that no more referendums have been held in Quebec since 1995. See Dion (2013).

[15]These authors compare the treatment given by the central governments of Canada and Spain, and underscore the "intolerance" and "intransigence" of the Spanish government "regarding autonomist and pro-independence Catalans," while, at the same time pointing out, as regards the judgement, "the teachings of the Supreme Court of Canada could inform and provide with arguments autonomist and pro-independence Catalans"; namely: "by imposing the need to act in good faith and with respect for constitutional principles, as well as the obligation to negotiate the secession in response to the expression of a clear majority in favour of it, the Supreme Court laid out cardinal principles that may provide strong arguments in Catalonia regarding to the exercise of democracy" (ibidem: 26–27. UQAM political scientist A. Gagnon received the 2006 Vilaseca Price of the Institute of Autonomic Studies of the Government of Catalonia for his *Au-delà de la nation unificatrice: Plaidoyer pour le fédéralisme multinational*, 2007).

with the central State.[16] Other aspects of the Reference, however, have been ignored: this is what happened regarding the requirement of a clear question (in the proposals of a popular consultation both in the Basque Country in 2008 and in Catalonia in 2014) and of a broad majority to approve it (in the cases mentioned above as well as in the self-determination referendum of 1 October 2017, envisaged by the Catalan Law 19/2017, of September 6th). In the Catalan case, subjection to the principles of constitutionality and rule of law were also omitted in Laws 19 and 20/2017, on the referendum and on the legal transition to the Catalan Republic, both of which assert their primacy over the Constitution and the Statute of Autonomy of Catalonia.

In the Basque Country, the initiative of statutory reform presented by President Ibarretxe in 2003 had been preceded by proposals from groups of the pro-independence and pacifist milieu such as Elkarri. They underscore the teachings of the Canadian case for the Basque situation: "the decision[17] opens up paths for Quebec and Ottawa, allowing the development of new initiatives to break the deadlock through negotiation. It has reassuring consequences: (1) secession cannot be addressed as something criminal, but instead in legal and political terms; (2) it compels both parties to return to the field of negotiation. This obligation to negotiate reassures the community and fosters the exercise of democracy" (Elkarri 2002: 114).[18] The reform project of the Basque Statute put forward by Ibarretxe (known as the Ibarretxe Plan) sought to establish a confederal relation between the Basque Country and the State, based on bilateral negotiation. In 2008, he proposed a popular consultation on the right to decide of the Basque Country. The Congress of Deputies rejected the first proposal in 2005,[19] while the Constitutional Court rejected

[16] Juan José Solozábal, "Los independentistas de Quebec," *El Imparcial*, 25 June 2014.

[17] *Sentencia*, in the original version of the text.

[18] This volume includes the writings of Quebecois Constitutional Law scholars Pelletier, Turp and Woehrling.

[19] In his speech before Congress, Ibarretxe mentioned, among others, the case of Quebec: "... we propose modern legal and political instruments, not from the 19th century, but rather from the 21st century, in order to develop the right to decide and the obligation to reach an agreement, as it is being proposed nowadays in advanced societies like Canada, Quebec, Ireland, Flanders, Wallonia, etc." (1 February 2005). See http://paralalibertad.org/discurso-de-juan-jose-ibarretxe-en-el-congreso-el-122005/ (retrieved 9 August 2018).

the second one (STC 103/2008)[20] on the grounds that it exceeded the scope of constitutional framework.[21]

The Canadian experience has also been present in the Catalan independence process and, more precisely, the 1998 Reference of the SCC. Let us take a look at three examples of the first stage of the process (2013–2014) as an example of it. First, in January 2013, the recently opened Legislature of the Catalan Parliament passed a resolution on the sovereign character of the Catalan people and on the right to decide (Resolution 5/X, of 23 January 2013). This resolution was challenged by the Madrid government before the Constitutional Court, as we shall see in the next section. What matters now is to highlight how there was an attempt from constitutional milieus close to the sovereignty movement to justify its consistency with the Constitution by invoking the Canadian case.[22] Second, the Advisory Council for the National Transition, created by the Government of the *Generalitat* to advise on, among other issues, the possibilities or paths to exercise the right to decide, mentions the lack of a requirement of a qualified majority in its first report: "a comparative study shows that the absolutely general rule, accepted as a good practice by the Council of Europe, is that of the non-requirement of a minimum turnout and a simple majority of cast ballots. These rules are consistent with the demands of the democratic principle and ensure clarity in the interpretation and implementation of the results. Requiring, by contrast, special or reinforced majorities represents a notable exception to the democratic principle and may furthermore lead to complex and problematic situations" (2013: 184). In the tenth Report the Advisory Council differentiates the form that used Spanish authorities regarding Catalan case from Scottish or Quebecer by their national authorities

[20]Among the claims of the Basque Parliament before the Constitutional Court, the Clarity Act is mentioned as a similar case to what the Basque popular consultation would represent, whose "… starting point is not the right to self-determination, but rather a context which demands solutions, like the one represented by the Canadian Clarity Act, that address the problem of structural minorities within a sovereign political community" (see Case History (5c) STC 103/2008).

[21]According to the Constitutional Court, there is room for the right to self-determination in the Spanish legal order, as long as the Constitution is reformed. According to Fernández Manjón and Torrado, this is the reason why a Clarity Act is not necessary in Spain, as it is in Canada (2009: 283).

[22]Thus, Vintró mentions twice the 1998 Reference of the SCC (2013).

(2014: 10).[23] Finally, Quebec was explicitly mentioned in the resolution passed by the Parliament of Catalonia by which it was decided to submit before Congress a proposal of *ley orgánica* (parliamentary bill) to delegate to the *Generalitat* the powers to call a referendum on the political future of Catalonia (which corresponds with an attempt to hold a mutually agreed upon referendum): "Calling a vote must be regarded as a normal scenario, fully comparable with countries with a democratic tradition and character, as is the case of Canada or Great Britain, which, faced with demands from a national community attached to a territory which is clearly defined both politically and administratively (Quebec and Scotland, respectively), consider that the best form of expression for this collective will is a referendum." The democratic principle and the principle of legality are mentioned thereafter.[24]

As the secessionist process has advanced and radicalizing its leadership (together with the reaction of the State, consequently), nationalism's foreign references have changed. Quebec and the Reference of the SCC are not as frequently invoked, and instead of them appear Kosovo, Slovenia or the Baltic republics. The strategy of the promoters of the project changes: from seeking an accommodation of their demands within the Constitution, they proceed to delegitimize it, together with rule of law in Spain. In this clearly rupturist stage, disobedience to State institutions and, in particular, the Constitutional Court, is encouraged (Resolution 1/XI, of 9 November 2015). In the climax of the process, between September and October 2017, the Catalan Parliament passed the so-called disconnection laws on September 6th and 7th, the self-determination referendum prohibited by the Constitutional Court was held on October 1st, the Catalan Parliament passed the unilateral Declaration of Independence on October 27th and, in response to it,

[23] López Basaguren criticizes the biased reading of the Canadian case in the reports: "the Council's pretension to justify its position on the grounds of the Advisory opinion of the SC of Canada is unsustainable, as it not only simplifies the complexity of the arguments developed by that Court to the point of making a caricature of them, but it also takes as indisputable certain interpretations that contradict literal statements present in its doctrinal construction" (2016: 183–184).

[24] Resolution 479/X, of 16 January 2014, of the Parliament of Catalonia. Congress rejected this proposal.

the Senate passed on the same day the authorization for the State Government to adopt coercive measures against the *Generalitat.* Instead of a popular consultation, what is now discussed is a self-determination referendum; and instead of the right to decide, secession and the creation of the Catalan Republic. This was the moment when a manifesto of over two hundred Spanish Constitutional Law scholars was published, in which they declared their rejection of, among others, the Law on the referendum of self-determination of September 6th, which they contrasted with the situation of Quebec ("the Advisory opinion of the Supreme Court of Canada of 20 August 1998 is well known among scholars, which rejects the consistency with international law of a unilateral independence of Quebec"), while calling for respect for the rule of law and compliance with the rulings of the Constitutional Court by all public authorities (October 10th).[25]

The Invocation of the Reference of the SCC by the Constitutional Court in Judgement 42/2014

The above-mentioned resolution 5/X, passed by the Parliament of Catalonia in January 2013, was challenged before the Constitutional Court by the Government of the State. Judgement 42/2014 declared unconstitutional the section relative to the declaration of sovereignty but not that which referred to the right to decide, finding it consistent with the Constitution as long as it is interpreted as a "political aspiration." This decision includes an explicit citation to the Reference of the SCC of 1998: "within the framework of the Constitution an autonomous community may not unilaterally call a referendum of self-determination to decide on its integration in Spain. This conclusion is along the lines

[25] See https://elpais.com/elpais/2017/10/09/opinion/1507565032_310252.html (retrieved on 9 August 2018). On November 28th, Professors Albertí, Vintró (UB) and Barceló (UAB) responded with another manifesto in which they invoked Comparative Law as well: "the current crisis contrasts vividly with the way in which other countries in our vicinity have solved similar territorial conflicts, like Canada in relation to Quebec, and the United Kingdom in relation to Scotland. Although there are naturally some differences, basic similarities also exist which allow for a comparison. The main one, that the Constitutions of both countries (written in Canada, unwritten in Britain) allowed for a path towards a solution by means of a popular vote before they explicitly envisaged it. In any event, the great question that we all, as Constitutional Law scholars, have before us, is whether the current Spanish Constitution is able to provide a solution to this conflict."

of that reached by the Supreme Court of Canada in its opinion of 20 August 1998, in which it rejected the consistency of a project of unilateral secession by one of its provinces, not only with its Constitution, but also with the tenets of International Law" (FJ 3).

The Constitutional Court does not often use Comparative Law explicitly in its rulings. This quote is part of an attempt to approach the Canadian doctrine in the constitutional rejection of a unilateral secession, in the recognition of the "right to decide" as a legitimate political aspiration (although not as a right), and in the need of a constitutional reform in order to decide on the secession of a territory. The latter confirms that all the Spanish Constitution may be amended, and that the Spanish system is not that of a militant democracy (and, therefore, it is legitimate for a party to propose the secession of a territory). The decision draws a distinction between "preparatory acts" of the reform and the reform procedures themselves. Regarding the preparatory acts, the Court does not specify which ones may be carried out and which may not. Some scholars have accepted that they might include a previous referendum in order to prove the existence of a secessionist will among the Catalan population, before the reform itself begins, but it seems to us that this thesis cannot be supported in the light of a comprehensive interpretation of the legal basis of the decision and of the Spanish Constitutional order (Castellà Andreu 2016: 516 et seq.). By contrast, the Court seems to agree with the idea that a proposal for constitutional reform (proceeding form the Catalan Parliament) may not be rejected out of hand, without a debate in the *Cortes*, in the interest of fostering a constitutional debate.

But there are two other implicit references to the opinion of the SCC in judgement 42/2014. The first one is the mention of the principles that are to inspire the "right to decide." This aspiration can only be realized by means of "a process consistent with constitutional legality, respecting the principles of 'democratic legitimacy', 'pluralism', and 'legality'" (FJ 3). That is, the Court quotes the same principles that appear in the contested declaration of the Catalan Parliament, as the common space for a debate, which partly coincide with those of the 1998 Reference. The second implicit reference—which the Court reproduces in judgement 31/2015, FJ 6—is the defence and application of self-restraint when adjudicating such politically charged cases as those that derive from the will of a part of the State to alter its legal status[26]:

[26] See *Reference Re Secession of Quebec*, [1998] 2 S.C.R. 217, paragraphs 100, 101

"they may not be solved by this Court… for this reason, public authorities, very especially the territorial powers that form our Autonomic State, are those called to solve through dialogue and cooperation the problems that develop in this area… It is only incumbent upon this Court, at the petition of parties with legal standing to seek its intervention, to ensure that the procedures developed in the course of this dialogue are consistent with the requirements laid out by the Constitution" (FJ 4). It is a reminder to the petitioner (the Government of the State) of the limits of Constitutional justice when facing political problems like this one, and also a call to all public authorities and political actors involved to make efforts to find a solution. The Court recalls, however, its role as the supervisor of the consistency with the Constitution of the results of the dialogue, once it is invoked.

Fossas welcomed the mention of the Canadian Reference ("for it has become a worldwide reference, as it probably contains the most advanced constitutional doctrine on the right to secession"). At the same time, he criticizes the inaccuracy of the reference to the Opinion: in Canada, the unilateral secession of a province is rejected, but not so a unilateral referendum, which is consistent with its legal order (2014: 288). This is a basic difference between both systems, as in the Spanish one the constitutional provisions on the power to hold popular consultations require an authorization of the State so that an autonomic referendum may be held (Article 149.1.32 SC). Because of this, Bayona diminishes the relevance of the reference to the opinion in the decision of the Constitutional Court 42/2014: "the margin for action is [also] very limited from a legal viewpoint because the Constitutional Court… This particularly rigid doctrine is in contrast with the situation in Canada" (2017: 14–15).

Judgement 42/2014 represents the closest the Spanish Constitutional Court has ever been to the doctrine of the SCC of 1998. Neither before had it been thus (in its judgement 103/2008, on the vote in the Basque Country, it underscored that a decision of this kind corresponded to the legislator of a constitutional reform), nor would it be so again in the subsequent decisions on the Catalan secessionist process. In them, it takes a line in which it gives precedence to the defence of constitutional democracy in the face of the rupturist tendency of the process (especially in judgement 259/2015 and subsequent ones).

In Conclusion

In this work, we have reviewed (in a non-exhaustive way) the reception in Spain of the Reference of the SCC on the secession of Quebec by Constitutional Law scholars, as well as by political actors and even by the Constitutional Court. The existence of territorial tensions and, above all, the Catalan secessionist crisis that began in 2012, is the backdrop that explains the interest for the Reference and why it has been received with such intensity. This reception has been of a laudatory and uncritical tone, placing the Canadian doctrine as a "model" when facing specific internal situations of a secessionist nature. In some occasions, from "constitutionalist" positions, it sought to underscore the substantial parallels between the answers provided by both legal systems. In others, from the secessionist camp, it served to denounce the distance between the Spanish system and the Canadian one and, above all, to criticize the conduct and interpretation provided by national politicians and by the Constitutional Court. In most cases, the goal was to gain legitimacy for one's own position on the secessionist crisis by appealing to the Canadian case as an argument of authority. But, by doing so, the tendency is to "read" the Reference of the SCC in a selective fashion, highlighting those parts that offer a greater interest. Accordingly, it has been frequent among Spanish scholars to read the Reference from the perspective of its legislative concretion, particularly the Clarity Act of 2000, and, in other occasions, especially among the political and legal sovereignty movement, at least implicitly, in the light of the Quebec bill of 2001.[27]

The interest that the Canadian case has generated among promoters of the Catalan independence process deserves special attention. The selective and partial invocation of certain points of the Reference (especially the democratic principle and the obligation to negotiate) sought, first, to identify the Canadian (and British) model as the only fair and adequate one for a democracy of the twenty-first century (ignoring other approaches to the problem like those developed in Italy or Germany); second, to reproduce in Spain certain criteria they judged useful to their

[27] Especially along the same lines as the interpretation of Bill 99, consistent with the Constitution, recently provided by the Superior Court of Quebec (*Henderson c. Procureure générale du Québec*) in its decision of 18 April 2018.

cause, neglecting how it might fit in their own Constitutional system and casting aside other fundamental aspects of the Reference, such as clarity in the question and the required majority, as well as subjection to the principle of constitutionality, the rule of law, and respect for minorities (as the Venice Commission pointed out in the opinions regarding Montenegro, 2005 and Crimea, 2014); lastly, to delegitimize in the eyes of public opinion and the international community not only the way the constitutional order and the institutions of the State address the demands of secession, but also the democratic character of the State itself.

Acknowledgements This work is part of the project funded by MINECO DER2015-68160-C3-3-P, as well as of the activities developed by the Group of Studies on Democracy and Constitutionalism (GEDECO). I would like to thank Juan Tello for his assistance in the compilation of bibliography and Roger Boada for the translation.

References

Aja, Eliseo (2014), *Estado autonómico y reforma federal*, Alianza, Madrid.

Aláez Corral, Benito (2015), "Constitucionalizar la secesión para armonizar la legalidad constitucional y el principio democrático en estados territorialmente descentralizados como España", in *Revista d'Estudis Autonòmics i Federals* (22), 136–183.

Bayona Rocamora, Antoni (2017), "El futur politic de Catalunya: el paper del Parlament", in *Revista Catalana de Dret Públic* (54), 1–23.

Biglino Campos, Paloma (2016), "Cataluña, federalismo y pluralismo político", in *Teoría y Realidad Constitucional* (37), 449–460.

Calonge Velázquez, Antonio (2013), "El derecho de secesión en Canadá: una regulación jurídica completa y un problema político sin resolver", in *Revista de Derecho de la Unión Europea* (25), 107–124.

Caminal, Miquel (2002), *El federalismo pluralista: Del federalismo nacional al federalismo plurinacional*, Paidós, Barcelona.

Castellà Andreu, Josep Maria (2014), "Secesión y referéndum sobre el 'derecho a decidir' en Cataluña. Una aproximación desde el derecho constitucional", in Joan Oliver (ed.), *El futuro territorial del Estado español*, Tirant lo blanch, Valencia, 451–490.

Castellà Andreu, Josep Maria (2016), "Tribunal Constitucional y proceso secesionista catalán: respuestas jurídico-constitucionales a un conflicto político-constitucional", in *Teoría y Realidad Constitucional* (37), 561–592.

Chacón, Carmen and Ruiz Robledo, Agustín (1998), "El dictamen del Tribunal Supremo de Cañadá sobre el derecho a la secesión de Quebec", Translation, in *Cuadernos Constitucionales de la Cátedra Fadrique Furió Ceriol* (24), 129–180.

Consell Assessor per a la Transició Nacional (2013), *The Consultation on the Political Future of Catalonia*, First Report, Generalitat de Catalunya, Barcelona.

Consell Assessor per a la Transició Nacional (2014), *The Constituent process*, 10th Report, Generalitat de Catalunya, Barcelona.

Dion, Stéphane (2005), *La política de la claridad: Discursos y escritos sobre la unidad canadiense*, Alianza, Madrid.

Dion, Stéphane (2013), "Secesión y democracia: una perspectiva canadiense", Real Instituto Elcano, 11 de abril 2013, http://www.realinstitutoelcano.org/wps/portal/rielcano_es/contenido?WCM_GLOBAL_CONTEXT=/elcano/elcano_es/zonas_es/stephane-dion-secesion-democracia-secession-democracy-canada. Retrieved 9 August 2018.

Elkarri (2002), *Quebec: La obligación constitucional de negociar*, Ed. Elkarri, Donostia.

Fernández Manjón, Desiderio and Torrado Sancho, Julián (2009), "Autodeterminación en sistemas democráticos. El caso de la consulta en Euskadi", in *Revista Vasca de Administración Pública* (83), 281–314.

Ferreres Comella, Victor (2016), "Cataluña y el derecho a decidir", in *Teoría y Realidad Constitucional* (37), 461–476.

Fossas Espadaler, Enric (2014), "Interpretar la política. Comentario a la STC 42/2014, de 25 de marzo, sobre la Declaración de soberanía y el derecho a decidir del pueblo de Cataluña", in *Revista Española de Derecho Constitucional* (101), 273–300.

Gaudreault DesBiens, Jean François (2016), "Algunos de los desafíos legales y políticos que debe afrontar el movimiento de independencia de Quebec", in *Teoría y Realidad Constitucional* (37), 135–162 (see in this volume).

Guénette, Dave and Gagnon, Alain (2017), "Del referéndum a la secesión – El proceso quebequense de acceso a la soberanía y las lecciones aprendidas con respecto a la autodeterminación", in *Eunomía. Revista en Cultura de la Legalidad* (13), 9–30. Also published in French in la *RCDP* de l'Escola d'Administració Pública catalana (54), 2017.

Laforest, Guy (2013), "Trust and Mistrust Between Harper and Québec", in Alberto López Basaguren y Leire Escajedo (Eds.), *The Ways of Federalism in Western Countries and the Horizons of Territorial Autonomy in Spain*, Volume II, Springer, Heidelberg, 341–358.

López Aguilar, Juan Fernando (1998), "Reflexiones a propósito de la reciente Sentencia del Tribunal Supremo (TS) de Canadá acerca de la secesión de la provincia de Quebec", in *Repertorio Aranzadi del Tribunal Constitucional* (4), 519–526.

López Aguilar, Juan Fernando (1999), "Canadá y España: Una comparación desde el federalismo contractual", *Autonomies* (25), 7–36.

López Basaguren, Alberto (2013), "La secesión de territorios en la Constitución española", in *Revista de Derecho de la Unión Europea* (25), 87–106.

López Basaguren, Alberto (2016), "Demanda de secesión en Cataluña y sistema democrático. El *procés* a la luz de la experiencia comparada", *Teoría y Realidad Constitucional* (37), 163–185.

Pérez Tremps, Pablo (2004), *El marco (a)constitucional del debate sobre la secesión de Quebec*, Fundació Pi i Sunyer, Barcelona.

Requejo, Ferran (2003), *Federalisme plurinacional i estat de les autonomies. Aspectes teòrics i aplicats*, Proa, Barcelona.

Ruiz Rico, Gerardo (2016), "La reinvención constitucional del modelo territorial español y la propuesta soberanista en Cataluña", in *Teoría y Realidad Constitucional* (37), 309–346.

Ruiz Robledo, Agustín and Chacón, Carmen (1999), "Comentario del dictamen del Tribunal Supremo canadiense de 20 de agosto de 1998 sobre la secesión de Quebec", in *Teoría y Realidad Constitucional* (3), 275–284.

Sáiz Arnáiz, Alejandro (2007), "Constitución y secesión", in *Parlamento y Constitución. Anuario* (10), 33–56.

Tudela Aranda, José (2016), "El derecho a decidir y el principio democrático", in *Teoría y Realidad Constitucional* (37), 477–498.

Vintró Castells, Joan (2013), "La declaració de sobirania i el dret a decidir del poble de Catalunya. Un apunt jurídic", *Blog Revista Catalana de Dret Públic*, 7 February 2013.

Woehrling, José (1999), "El juicio del Tribunal Supremo de Canadá sobre la eventual secesión de Quebec", in *Revista Vasca de Administración Pública* (54), 405–436.

Woehrling, José (2006), "Una introducció al sistema federal canadenc", in *L'Abast de l'autonomia política del Quebec*, Parlament de Catalunya, Barcelona, 112–151.

The *Reference Re Secession of Quebec*, the Kosovo Advisory Opinion and the Questions They Leave Open: The Right to Decide, the Principle of Stability, and the Duty to Negotiate

Luigi Crema

Introduction

A reflection on the international law legacy of the Canadian Supreme Court's seminal decision on the secession of Québec,[1] particularly in the 2010 Advisory Opinion of the United Nations International Court of Justice (ICJ) on Kosovo,[2] is, unfortunately, not a satisfying task. Rather,

[1] Canadian Supreme Court, *Reference Re Secession of Quebec*, [1998] 2 S.C.R. 217.

[2] International Court of Justice, *Accordance with International Law of the Unilateral Declaration of Independence in Respect of Kosovo* (Advisory Opinion) (22 July 2010) ICJ Doc 2010 General List No. 141.

L. Crema (✉)
Università degli Studi di Milano, Milano, Italy
e-mail: luigi.crema@unimi.it

G. Delledonne and G. Martinico (eds.), *The Canadian Contribution to a Comparative Law of Secession*,
https://doi.org/10.1007/978-3-030-03469-6_5

for an international lawyer, it is an exercise in frustration, given the festival of missed opportunities put together by the ICJ. However, a close look at the positions of the intervening parties in the two proceedings reveals a fruitful loop between international lawyers, a domestic court, state positions on unilateral secession, and, eventually, an international jurisdiction (the ICJ—indeed, the most important of these bodies).

As the editors of this book correctly point out, in Re Secession of Quebec for the first time a Supreme Court had the bold (some people at The Hague would probably say, "inappropriate") courage to face the taboo of unilateral secession, and break it. In doing so, however, the Canadian judges did not embark alone, trusting only in their own forces like new Dantesque Ulysses. Instead, they were surrounded by several international lawyers—very expert ones—to help them navigate the powerful swells surrounding *Question 2*. This procession of ideas from international law to the Supreme Court of Canada was the first act of collaboration between Canada and international law (and it will be analysed in further detail in section "International Law and Re Secession of Quebec").

Then Canada returned the favour. Since 1998, the *Reference Re Secession of Quebec* has become a classic of international legal literature. The decision summarized the dominant positions in debates on this topic, touched upon the controversial ones, and had something to say (however briefly) about *each* (or, better, *many*, as section "International Law and Secession Today: The Right to Decide, the Principle of Stability, and the Duty to Negotiate—Drawing Inspiration to Address Contemporary Issues" below will explain) of the controversial issues related to self-determination of peoples. These topics included the relevance of the principle of territorial integrity; the question of what is a people; the role of recognition in a secessionist attempt; the possible existence of a right to self-determination in international law, beyond colonial and foreign occupation; and so on.

This multi-faceted analysis, together with the quality of the Court's reasoning, contributed to the fortune of the decision among international lawyers. Indeed, the decision appears not only in lengthy surveys on the topic, but even in university manuals intended to present the fundamental international law positions on the topic, where one would expect to see a case taken from an international tribunal (among many, see Treves [2005]; Brownlie and Crawford [2012]). Few domestic decisions are quoted so often by international lawyers—Re Secession of

Quebec probably shares the highest place on the figurative podium with the *Pinochet* cases. Notwithstanding the fact that Canadian Reference is just a domestic decision, its influence cannot be denied. Some of its most influential reasoning in current international law, and especially in the written briefs submitted by the states which intervened in the proceedings of the Kosovo Advisory Opinion, are highlighted below, in section "Re Secession of Quebec in International Law, and in Particular in the Proceedings of the Kosovo Advisory Opinion".

The Reference also had an unfortunate, indirect impact on the ICJ itself, which moved into the shadow of the Canadian decision, and eventually used it to avoid any direct engagement with the question of whether it exists a right to unilateral secession in international law (below, section "The 2010 Kosovo Advisory Opinion, Notwithstanding the 1998 *Reference Re Secession of Quebec*"). The different attitudes adopted by the two courts present a sad paradox (sad for an international lawyer): the most relevant issues regarding unilateral secession and international law were addressed by a domestic court, but left untouched by an international body.

Lastly, section "International Law and Secession Today: The Right to Decide, the Principle of Stability, and the Duty to Negotiate—Drawing Inspiration to Address Contemporary Issues" will sketch the relevance of Re Secession of Quebec in the light of the many contemporary requests for unilateral secession. These include elements that were not completely foreseen either in Ottawa or at The Hague: the so-called right to decide, the importance of the principles of effectiveness and stability, and the existence of a duty to negotiate between opposite parties.

International Law and Re Secession of Quebec

Before turning to the influence of the Canadian decision on the ICJ, it is important to consider the role played by international law and international lawyers in the decision Re Secession of Quebec. It is counterintuitive, but true, that international law played a much bigger role in the Canadian Reference than it did in the ICJ Advisory Opinion. There are two reasons for this.

First, it was the first time that a court was explicitly asked to deliver a judgement that specifically addressed self-determination. The ICJ had handled such questions in the past, but it had never been directly asked to clearly delineate the extent of the rights to unilateral secession and self-determination (e.g. in Western Sahara Advisory Opinion [16 October 1975], paragraph 70, and East Timor [Portugal v Australia] [30 June 1995], paragraphs 31, 37). These rights were generally considered in the form of incidental issues in advisory opinions concerning matters related to decolonization (Burri and Thürer 2008).

In Ottawa, one of the questions was clear and directly concerned *a right in international law*. The Canadian Supreme Court addressed three questions. While Question 1 concerned the Constitution of Canada,[3] Question 2 asked (*i*) if international law grants a right to unilateral secession to the public institutions which govern an administrative subdivision of a state, and (*ii*) if this process can be framed under the right to self-determination in international law:

> 2. Does international law give the National Assembly, legislature or government of Quebec the right to effect the secession of Quebec from Canada unilaterally? In this regard, is there a right to self-determination under international law that would give the National Assembly, legislature or government of Quebec the right to effect the secession of Quebec from Canada unilaterally?[4]

The other reason that international law played a highly relevant role in the Re Secession of Quebec Reference was due to the high quality of the interveners. The Canadian Supreme Court considered interventions from the most qualified international lawyers, creating an ideal forum to hear and adjudicate on international law. Prior to the proceedings in Re Secession of Quebec, in 1992, the Government of Quebec had requested an expert opinion from several professors of international law (Thomas Franck, Rosalyn Higgins, Alain Pellet, Malcom Shaw, and Christian Tomuschat) on "The Territorial Integrity of Québec in the Event of the Attainment of Sovereignty" (reproduced in Bayefsky 2000). Then, beginning in 1996, during the proceeding, the Supreme

[3]"1. Under the Constitution of Canada, can the National Assembly, legislature or government of Quebec effect the secession of Quebec from Canada unilaterally?", Questions posed by the Governor in Council, Order in Council P.C. 1996–1497, 30 September 1996, reproduced in *Reference Re Secession of Quebec*, paragraph 2.

[4]Ibidem. The third question concerned the relationship between that right and the domestic legal order: "3. In the event of a conflict between domestic and international law on the right of the National Assembly, legislature or government of Quebec to effect the secession of Quebec from Canada unilaterally, which would take precedence in Canada?"

Court of Canada considered expert opinions by some of the most prominent international lawyers. The Federal Government of Canada asked James Crawford, at the time Whewell Professor of International Law at the University of Cambridge (and whose earliest work was dedicated to the creation of states and the rights of peoples)[5] to deliver an opinion on the matter. The report, entitled "State Practice and International Law in Relation to Unilateral Secession", analysed state practice *since 1945* (the "UN Age", including, therefore, the end of colonialism, the Pakistan-Bangladesh issue, the dissolution of the Soviet Union, and of the Former Yugoslavia, etc., but *not* the nationalistic movements of the nineteenth century). It concluded that: (*i*) in international law, there is no unilateral right to secede based on a majority vote; (*ii*) in any case, it is a matter for the government of the relevant state to determine how to respond to such a call for independence; and (*iii*) the practice on self-determination during the decolonization phase, and the safeguard clause in UN General Assembly Resolution 2625 of 1970 (stating that a Government representing the whole people on the basis of equality complies with the principle of self-determination) confirm the first two points (Crawford 1997). Luzius Wildhaber, a Swiss judge, at the time President of the European Court of Human Rights, was asked to review and comment on James Crawford's opinion. He briefly agreed on his conclusions, stressing that, with the exception of a few scholars, legal literature almost unanimously denies a right of unilateral secession (Bayefsky 2000: 63 ff.).

In addition to these two expert opinions, other opinions by leading international lawyers were attached to an amicus curiae. As is well known, the Quebec Government refused to participate in the proceedings before the Canadian Supreme Court, and the Court itself asked a Québec City lawyer, Me André Jolie-Coeur, to present Quebec's point of view. The attached opinions were prepared by George Abi-Saab (HEI, Geneva), Thomas Franck (New York University), Malcom Shaw (University of Leicester), and Alain Pellet (Université de Paris-Nanterre), who were asked by the interveners to deliver an opinion on *Question 2*. Abi-Saab explained that states have no duty to grant self-determination to those unilaterally declaring independence, but that secession belongs

[5] Crawford, James (1979), *The Creation of States in International Law*, Oxford University Press, Oxford; Crawford, James (ed.) (1988), *The Rights of Peoples*, Oxford University Press, Oxford.

to the realm of facts rather than that of law, and that self-determination is part of a process of legitimization of a factual situation of effective self-governance. He added that one of its legal consequences would be that foreign interventions in favour of the new entity cannot be labelled as "illegitimate" (Abi-Saab 1997). Thomas Franck highlighted the limits of Crawford's position, explaining that, while there is no right to unilateral secession in international law, there is also no clear prohibition of it. He also directly contested Crawford's claim that "international law has always favoured the territorial integrity of states…" (Franck 1997: 83).

Alain Pellet and Malcom Shaw expressed similar criticisms to Crawford's, the former not excluding the possibility of an (eventually) legal, effective, unilateral secession, and the latter observing that international law neither authorizes nor precludes internal secessionist attempts, and that no prohibition exists in international law that would prevent secessionist attempts by persons or groups (Shaw 1997). An additional exchange of views followed between the same experts, throughout each retained their respective basic tenets on the issue.

Upon request by the Ad Hoc Committee of Canadian Women on the Constitution, Christine Chinkin was also asked to produce an opinion. Chinkin (the only female expert to intervene in the debate) contested a vision of self-determination based only on power, suggesting that the evolution of international law (and of its rules on self-determination) was incorporating human rights in its discourse, and that the equal participation of members of both sexes in the process of self-determination should be required (Chinkin 1998). This point, on the need to include human rights (equality of sexes, and beyond) into international law, is highly relevant to understanding some of the legal and political issues being raised by certain contemporary secessionist movements (see below, section "International Law and Secession Today: The Right to Decide, the Principle of Stability, and the Duty to Negotiate—Drawing Inspiration to Address Contemporary Issues").

As is clear from the findings of the Court, the voices of the international lawyers who participated in the proceedings found a significant place in the final decision of the Court. The Canadian decision reiterated the two cases recognized under existing international law practice as giving rise to a right to self-determination (*Reference Re Secession of Quebec*, paragraphs 132–134), but it also entertained the prospect of a third case, "remedial recession", and its scope (Cassese 1995; Palmisano 1997). In other words, the Canadian Court ventured onto the slippery terrain of defining nascent rules: "the right to self-determination may ground a right to unilateral secession [...] when a people is blocked from the meaningful exercise of its right to self-determination internally" (Canadian Reference, paragraph 134).

The major achievement of the Canadian judges was that they dared to summarize in judicial dicta what international lawyers up until that moment had only highlighted in their scholarly work, or in very political fora like the General Assembly:

> the international law right to self-determination only generates, at best, a right to external self-determination in situations of former colonies; where a people is oppressed, as for example under foreign military occupation; or where a definable group is denied meaningful access to government to pursue their political, economic, social and cultural development. In all three situations, the people in question are entitled to a right to external self-determination because they have been denied the ability to exert internally their right to self-determination. (Canadian Reference, paragraph 138)

Re Secession of Quebec in International Law, and in Particular in the Proceedings of the Kosovo Advisory Opinion

The Canadian Reference has had a tremendous impact on international law and legal scholarship in this area, even greater than that of the ICJ itself. As mentioned in the previous section, until 1998 the ICJ had addressed self-determination only incidentally, and even in the subsequent advisory opinions dealing with the topic, the ICJ has never framed a specific regulation of self-determination (Legal Consequences of the Construction of a Wall in the Occupied Palestinian Territory, Advisory Opinion [9 July 2004], paragraph 118, and the 2010 Kosovo Advisory Opinion, commented in the following section).

As a result, notwithstanding the fact that the Canadian Reference was handed down by a domestic court (and, therefore, amounts to a mere, individual act by a state organ in the neutral eyes of an international lawyer), the precision of the question, the quality of the participating interveners, and the quality of the answer coming from the Court have all contributed to its well-deserved success in providing the precision that is lacking from the ICJ.

Another factor in the far-reaching impact of the Canadian decision was the historical period in which it was handed down, which was particularly favourable to lending it a widespread audience. The decolonization process had been concluded, and the collapse of the Eastern block had led to the dissolution of the Soviet Union and of Yugoslavia. In a certain sense, one can say that it was the perfect moment to reflect on what had happened before and to crystalize the practice that had evolved up until that moment.

All these factors, taken together, contributed to granting the *Reference Re Secession of Quebec* a degree of relevance which goes far beyond other domestic decisions on rules of international law. As mentioned in the introduction, even in today's manuals of international law it is normal to find this 1998 judgement cited as a good summary of what international law has to say about self-determination.

Unsurprisingly, the Canadian Reference played a major role in the interventions of states before the ICJ for the advisory opinion on Kosovo, inspiring both those states which took positions more sensitive to the integrity of their state against possible secession (such as China, Romania, and Spain), and those states more sympathetic to the Kosovar cause (such as Albania). In their Written Statements and subsequent Comments, many states used the Canadian decision to explain various aspects of international law. For example, many sections of the Written Statements of Romania and Serbia were modelled on the Canadian reasoning.[6] Bolivia, in its Written Commentary, relied only on the Canadian Reference and past ICJ decisions to support its position.[7]

Written Statements and Comments used the Canadian Reference to comment on, in particular: (*i*) the role of recognition in the creation of a new state; (*ii*) the importance of the principle of integrity of a state; (*iii*) the limited, specific, extent of the right to self-determination in

[6]Written Statement of Romania, 14 April 2009, quoting in many parts paragraphs 112, 122, 126, and 134 of the Canadian Reference. The 370 pages Serbian brief, Written Statement of the Government of the Republic of Serbia, 17 April 2009, is full of references to the Canadian case, especially to limit external self-determination to the two only cases of former colonial occupation and foreign subjugation.

[7]Written Commentary by the Plurinational State of Bolivia, 17 July 2009, paragraphs 14–17, concluding at paragraph 17: "Applying the jurisprudence of the Court, and the conclusion of Canada's Supreme Court, Bolivia submits that international law does not grant Kosovo the legal right to secede unilaterally from Serbia".

international law and the possible existence and extent of remedial secession; (*iv*) the fact that international law ***neither prohibits nor authorizes*** unilateral secession; and (*v*) the definition of "people".

Albania, for example, quoted paragraph 138 of the Canadian Reference as a summary of the state of international law on self-determination, including remedial secession.[8] Many states used the immediately preceding paragraphs (134–135) both to deny the existence of remedial secession in international law, and to affirm its existence, but with a very well-defined scope.[9] Argentina relied extensively on the Canadian Reference, including for the purpose of underlining that international recognition is not a fundamental condition for a new entity to acquire statehood.[10] Serbia's position on recognition also contained very long quotes from the Canadian decision.[11] Austria and Ireland quoted

[8]Written Statement of the Republic of Albania, 14 April 2009, paragraph 83. Similar is the Written Statement of the Kingdom of Norway, 16 April 2009, paragraph 5, quoting paragraph 154 of the Canadian Reference.

[9]Written Statement of the Argentine Republic, 17 April 2009, paragraph 85, recalling paragraphs 134–135. Written Statement of the Republic of Estonia, 13 April 2009, paragraph 2.1.1, quoting paragraph 134 of the Canadian Reference and remedial secession. Statement of the Federal Republic of Germany, 15 April 2009, quoting in Section 2 paragraph 134 and the extreme situations under which a right to remedial secession arises; in general, Germany took in high consideration the expert opinions before the Canadian Supreme Court, cf. Section VI.1. Written Statement of the Kingdom of the Netherlands, 17 April 2009, paragraph 3.17. Written Statement of Romania, 14 April 2009, quoting paragraph 134 of the Canadian Reference. Written Statement of the Government of the Republic of Serbia, 17 April 2009, stressing that outside colonial subjugation and foreign occupation self-determination is fulfilled *internally* (referring to paragraphs 115, 126, 134–135 of the Canadian Reference). In the Written Comments of the Government of the Republic of Serbia, 15 July 2009, Serbia again drew on the clear statements of the Canadian Supreme Court in which the status of remedial secession is labelled as "unclear", paragraph 345, quoting paragraph 135 of the Canadian Reference. Written statement Addressed to the International Court of Justice by the Swiss Confederation, 25 May 2009, paragraphs 64, 65, recalling the distinction drew by the Canadian Supreme Court (paragraphs 126, 135) on internal and external self-determination, and the possible, exceptional, recourse to remedial secession. Written Statement of the UK, 17 April 2009, paragraph 5.32, quoting paragraphs 134–135 in which the Supreme Court of Canada opens to remedial secession.

[10]Written Statement of the Argentine Republic, 17 April 2009, paragraph 48, quoting paragraph 142 of the Canadian Reference; Argentina, see footnote above, referred also to the paragraphs dedicated to remedial secession.

[11]Written Statement of the Government of the Republic of Serbia, 17 April 2009 at paragraphs 1000–1005. See also Written Comments of the Government of the Republic of

the Canadian Reference to stress that international law neither prohibits, nor authorizes unilateral secession.[12] China and Ireland quoted the Canadian decision, in the part in which it says that international law recognizes the exercise of self-determination within the territorial integrity of states[13] Romania took a similar, but more detailed position.[14] Switzerland, among other quotes from the Canadian Reference, recalled paragraph 124, in which the Supreme Court affirmed that a people "may include only a portion of the population of an existing state".[15]

The oral phase of the ICJ proceedings naturally confirmed the centrality of the Canadian Reference in the way states regard unilateral secession. For example, many portions of the pleadings for the UK modelled their reasoning on the Canadian decision.[16] Even beyond specific issues, it is quite clear that states adopted the Canadian Reference as the best proxy on the state of the art concerning self-determination and secession in international law. Belarus, for example, simply affirmed that, "The Court's findings confirm the interpretation of the right of self-determination which was shaped within the United Nations framework during the second half of 20th century".[17]

Serbia, 15 July 2009, paragraphs 503–508, quoting paragraphs 142, 144, and 155 of the Canadian Reference.

[12]Statement by the Government of Austria, 16 April 2009, paragraphs 37–39, quoting the *Reference Re Secession of Québec*, paragraph 155. Statement of the Republic of Ireland, 17 April 2009, paragraph 21 (quoting paragraph 112 of the Canadian Reference): "international law contains neither a right of unilateral secession nor the explicit denial of such a right".

[13]Written Statement of the People's Republic of China to the International Court of Justice on the Issue of Kosovo, 16 April 2009, Section III.c, quoting paragraph 127 of the Canadian Reference. Statement of the Republic of Ireland, 17 April 2009, paragraph 28, quoting paragraph 122: "International law expects that the right to self-determination will be exercised by peoples within the framework of existing sovereign states and consistently with the maintenance of the territorial integrity of those states".

[14]Written Statement of Romania, 14 April 2009, quoting paragraph 122. The Romanian Statement constantly quotes the Canadian Reference, especially paragraphs 112, 122, 126, and 134—remedial secession as last resort.

[15]Written statement Addressed to the International Court of Justice by the Swiss Confederation, 25 May 2009, paragraph 76.

[16]Kosovo Opinion, Thursday 10 December 2009, at 10 a.m., verbatim record, doc. CR 2009/32.

[17]Elena Gritsenko (Belarus), Kosovo Opinion, Thursday 3 December 2009, at 10 a.m., verbatim record, doc. CR 2009/27, p. 29.

On 11 December 2009, Judge Koroma and Judge Cançado Trindade put two questions to the participants in the oral proceedings, showing that within the ICJ there was somebody trying to take a direct approach about self-determination, like in Ottawa. Judge Koroma asked:

> [I]t has been contended that international law does not prohibit the secession of a territory from a sovereign State. Could participants in these proceedings address the Court on the principles and rules of international law, if any, which, outside the colonial context, permit the secession of a territory from a sovereign State without the latter's consent?

Here, again, the States which replied relied on the Canadian Reference.[18] All of this, however, ended up being relegated to the background of the final opinion delivered by the ICJ.

The 2010 Kosovo Advisory Opinion, Notwithstanding the 1998 *Reference Re Secession of Quebec*

The ICJ, unfortunately, rather than addressing the legal place of unilateral secession head-on like the Supreme Court of Canada, decided to not take a position on many interesting arguments, and instead avoided pronouncing on them. The reasons for this were, first, the difference between the Canadian question and the ICJ one and, second, the reluctance of the ICJ judges.

[18] Albania, *Response by the Republic of Albania to the Questions Asked by the Judges*, 21 December 2009, paragraph 19, on the definition of people "According to the Court it is clear that a people may include only a portion of the population of an existing State". Argentina, *Reply of the Argentine Republic to questions posed by Judges Koroma and Cançado Trindade at the close of the oral proceedings*, paragraph 3, observes that the Canadian Supreme Court, in its reference concerning Quebec, correctly established the relationship between a power and a right: "A right is recognized in law: mere physical ability is not necessarily given status as a right. The fact that an individual or group can act in a certain way says nothing at all about the legal status or consequences of the act. A power may be exercised even in the absence of a right to do so, but if it is, then it is exercised without legal foundation." (Canadian Reference, paragraph 106) Finland, *Response Submitted by Finland to Questions of Judge Koroma and Judge Cançado Trindade*, 21 December 2009, p. 3, quotes the Canadian Reference, paragraph 138. Romania recalled the written statements (Romania Reply, paragraphs 4, 5). Pristina's authority, paragraph 6, recalled paragraph 138.

The question put to the ICJ by the UN General Assembly about Kosovo reads:

> Is the unilateral declaration of independence by the Provisional Institutions of Self-Government of Kosovo in accordance with international law?

This is, in part, similar, and, in part, very different from the Canadian question. Like the first part of Question 2 before the Canadian Supreme Court, this question insists on a unilateral power to secede. Where the two differ dramatically is that the Canadian question goes also straight to the point of the extent and limits of the right to self-determination under international law, while the question before the ICJ was less pointed. Serbia, which sought the advisory opinion, had to first obtain the approval of the UN General Assembly, and the question that went to the Court was, therefore, a political compromise, with the result that it stopped short of a request as direct as that brought before the Canadian Court and left the ICJ more flexibility in its answer.

In addition, the question was reformulated by the ICJ itself, rendering it even less direct. The Court reinterpreted the question to say: Is the unilateral declaration of independence by the Provisional Institutions of Self-Government of Kosovo prohibited by international law? Focusing only on the alleged prohibition of unilateral declarations in international law left the Judges room to avoid any specific description of the right to self-determination in international law (Tancredi 2010). On this finding, Judge Bruno Simma critically observed: "by unduly limiting the scope of its analysis, the Court has not answered the question put before it in a satisfactory manner" (Kosovo Advisory Opinion, Declaration of Judge Simma, paragraph 3; see also Christakis 2011: 73).

The ICJ, throughout the Advisory Opinion, often noted the importance of the question in structuring its answer.[19] In one of these instances, the ICJ explicitly addressed the difference between the question it had to answer and the Canadian ruling. Given that the Judges of The Hague stated this point in clear terms, it is best to let them speak for themselves, notwithstanding the long quote, rather than attempt to paraphrase:

[19] See especially Kosovo Advisory Opinion, paragraphs 49, 51–53, 56, 83.

> While many of those participating in the present proceedings made reference to the opinion of the Supreme Court of Canada in *Reference by the Governor in Council concerning Certain Questions relating to the Secession of Quebec from Canada* [...], the Court observes that the question in the present case is markedly different from that posed to the Supreme Court of Canada. [...] The question put to the Supreme Court of Canada inquired whether there was a right to 'effect secession', and whether there was a rule of international law which conferred a positive entitlement on any of the organs named. By contrast, the General Assembly has asked whether the declaration of independence was 'in accordance with' international law. The answer to that question turns on whether or not the applicable international law prohibited the declaration of independence. If the Court concludes that it did, then it must answer the question put by saying that the declaration of independence was not in accordance with international law. It follows that the task which the Court is called upon to perform is to determine whether or not the declaration of independence was adopted in violation of international law. The Court is not required by the question it has been asked to take a position on whether international law conferred a positive entitlement on Kosovo unilaterally to declare its independence or, a fortiori, on whether international law generally confers an entitlement on entities situated within a State unilaterally to break away from it. (Kosovo Advisory Opinion, paragraphs 55–56)

The ICJ concluded its reasoning on the Canadian case explaining the relevance of the different questions asked to the two courts:

> Indeed, it is entirely possible for a particular act – such as a unilateral declaration of independence – not to be in violation of international law without necessarily constituting the exercise of a right conferred by it. The Court has been asked for an opinion on the first point, not the second. (Kosovo Advisory Opinion, paragraph 56)

The ICJ used all the room that the reinterpreted question gave it to engage in "a tiring series of *dodges*" (Gradoni 2011), and avoided directly addressing the issue of the conditions necessary for legal unilateral secession. The Court very clearly distanced itself from every attempt to engage on the right to self-determination and its extent in international law, as well as the question of remedial secession:

> The General Assembly has requested the Court's opinion only on whether or not the declaration of independence is in accordance with international

> law. Debates regarding the extent of the right of self-determination and the existence of any right of 'remedial secession', however, concern the right to separate from a State. (Kosovo Advisory Opinion, paragraph 83)

This allowed the ICJ to sidestep what is probably the most original line of speculation coming from the Canadian Supreme Court decision: the possible existence of, and the conditions necessary for, remedial secession (criticism of the ICJ for failing *to stop* such speculation has been voiced by Pertile [2011: 91, 115–119]). The Court even deemed unnecessary the question of the relevance of international recognition in a process of unilateral secession (Kosovo Opinion, paragraph 51). This approach by the ICJ was harshly criticized by some of the Judges, namely Vice-President Tomka, Judge Bennouna, and, above all, Judge Koroma (Dissenting Opinion to the Kosovo Advisory Opinion, paragraph 3), who took a hard line against the majority (Bonafé 2011).

Ultimately, to answer to the question, the Court decided to focus on only two areas, which potentially contained a prohibition of unilateral secession: the principle of territorial integrity, and the relevant provisions of UN Security Council Resolutions (Wilde 2011).

Despite its cautions silence on many open questions, the ICJ *did* take some steps to define the status of unilateral secession under international law. It stated that the issue of recognition is *not necessary* to determine that an act is *in accordance with international law* (Kosovo Opinion, paragraph 51). It recalled that the principle of territorial integrity does not concern the relationship between the states and internal communities, but instead applies to relationships between states (paragraph 80). Lastly, it outlawed secessionist movements which violate *jus cogens* norms (paragraph 81). It also recalled the historical, controversial position of the international community on the topic: the ICJ grounded itself, once again, in the nineteenth century, and not just in the twentieth century (as certain arguments presented in the Canadian proceedings did, see above section "International Law and Re Secession of Quebec"). The narrative adopted by the ICJ was not one built on UN principles and post-war history, but invoked the nineteenth century and a time when sovereignty meant nation-building against the power of empires. This did not reflect a mere old-fashioned bent among the judges. What the ICJ did by basing its line of reasoning on the nineteenth century was to stress the difference between international law and the constitutionalized horizon of an existing state, by rejecting any attempt to frame contemporary, post-World War II international law as a system structured under the UN. Instead, the Court reminded all states of the roots of contemporary society: an anarchical society which amalgamated the nationalistic projects of communities rebelling against old empires and old colonial powers (Kosovo Opinion, paragraph 79). In other words, the ICJ was reminding states that, since they are the "owners" of international law, it would likely avoid any legal description of a process which runs counter to state interests (like internal, unilateral secession). For this reason, the Court did not endorse a right to secede. However, at the same time, the Court refused to entirely exclude the possibility, reminding the States that they, too, were young once, and that they themselves had often originated in acts of rebellion against cumbersome parents.

International Law and Secession Today: The Right to Decide, the Principle of Stability, and the Duty to Negotiate—Drawing Inspiration to Address Contemporary Issues

The legacy of the Supreme Court of Canada's *Reference Re Secession of Quebec* in international law is vast. It has become one of the most influential domestic decisions in the field. The reasons have been summarized above, and the extent of its influence can be seen in the analysis of the state briefs submitted to the ICJ during the proceedings on Kosovo's unilateral declaration of independence (section "Re Secession of Quebec in International Law, and in Particular in the Proceedings of the Kosovo Advisory Opinion"). Coming in 1998, after decolonization and the breakdowns of the Soviet Union and Yugoslavia, it presented an eager audience with a tribunal that, albeit from a domestic point of view, dared to take the tiger by its tail. For the Kosovo opinion States tapped into every level of the Canadian decision, from the paragraphs dedicated to the legal effect of recognition, to the importance of respecting the integrity of a state and its democratic and non-discriminatory order, until the part on remedial secession.

The Kosovo Opinion did not rule out any of these points, nor did it endorse them. It avoided them with the excuse of addressing a different question, but ultimately this choice validated the findings of the Canadian Supreme Court. So, in a certain way, we are still at the Canadian findings: secession justified by colonization, secession on the basis of oppression/occupation, and, maybe, remedial secession. The ICJ's real contribution was to provide a clear statement that unilateral secession is not prohibited by international law. If the Canadian Reference had the role of codifying certain rules on unilateral secession, the ICJ opinion did not contradict them and gave hope to many groups whishing to secede from their parent states.

In fact, even in the most recent attempts to unilaterally secede, one can find the imprint of that *status quo*. The Catalan activists for independence often attempt to couch their cause in the language of a remedial secession (they cite the 2010 decision by the Spanish constitutional court as unreasonably adverse, they point to the repression of their referendum and the criminal prosecution of Catalan leaders, and so on.). But Catalan and others (Venetians, for example, in Italy) have turned to new grounds as well. Today there are several independence claims being made that involve scenarios far removed from the three grounds for unilateral secession provided by the high court of Canada. In particular they invoke the "right to decide", a sort of ultimate expression of individual freedom, which claims the prerogative to deviate from anything, including from the structure which represents the state-level community of citizens and provides services in their name. The report drafted for the Catalan cause by Nicolas Levrat, Sandrina Antunes, Guillaume Tusseau, and Paul Williams, four professors of international law (respectively at the University of Geneva, Minho, Sciences Po in Paris and the American University, Washington, DC), revolves around this right (Levrat et al. 2017: 45–61). In a similar vein, two intellectuals involved in the referendum for the autonomy of the Veneto Region wrote a pamphlet claiming that *Io posso decidere*, "I can decide" (Favaro and Guadagnini 2015).

The claimed "right to decide" derails the trajectory that most other modern rights have followed and asks legal thinkers to reopen an old question: Is there a limit to individual rights? Contemporary rights tend to be structured as services which depend upon states to provide, subsidize, certify, enforce, or merely respect them (although this last category is diminishing). Indeed, in step with this, even the very image of the state has subtly shifted from that of the "sovereign" to that of the benevolent guarantor of rights and provider of the services to which its people are entitled. From the Canadian or American perspective, such rights are chiefly framed by the national constitution (in fact, the so-called right to decide can be perceived in the discussion under Question 1 of the

1998 *Reference Re Secession of Quebec*, where the principle of democracy is addressed). From the European point of view, on the other hand, these rights are also framed under the European Convention of Human Rights, and are, therefore, supranational. The rights expected by contemporary citizens at every stage of their lives, from assisted reproduction and abortion at the start of life to palliative care and assisted suicide at its end, with all the other rights and freedoms they enjoy in between (including the individual right to *secede*, in the form of divorce or separation, conditioned upon certain financial responsibilities, from one's partner, one's offspring, one's household), do not exist independent from a guarantor state which is called upon to provide or protect them.

The "right to decide" turns all of this on its head. It implies a right of rejection vis-a-vis the existing state, the entity ensuring all rights (Favaro and Guadagnini 2015). This takes the state's subtle shift from sovereign to service provider and makes it a crucial question. Indeed, if the state is nothing more than a neutral provider of services and guarantor of rights, why should people not be able to choose, just as they choose in all other areas (included the choice of other service providers)?

On the other hand, if the state is the basis of all freedoms, the rejection of it is problematic, because it would allow a small portion of the citizenry to refuse to participate and contribute to the whole, thus undermining the collective rights of all. This is an argument that the Canadian Reference addressed in general terms, talking about the responsibility of a federate community, and it is one that is often reduced to purely economic motives: "the wealthiest district wants to secede to avoid paying taxes that benefit everybody"; "that region wants independence because they have all the mines and oil"; etc. But isn't this just a classic appeal to sovereignty against individual freedoms, which are claiming (as they so often do) a "new right" (Cartabia 2010), in this case *the right to decide*? In contemporary legal theory, it would be difficult to try to answer this question relying on sovereignty alone. However, one might observe that the right to decide, by implying a rebellion against the state itself—the state that is, at least as conceived of under the traditional, positivistic approach, the origin of all rights—cannot be permitted.

Leaving these theoretical issues aside, international law takes a pragmatic approach. It gives priority to *stability*—and, therefore, to the unity of the preexisting state. What is striking about the Catalan situation, for example, is the silence of the European states and states in general. Catalonia is a wealthy and stable region in a stable state—other nations have not felt that the principle of non-intervention should be broken in order to deal with a crisis that Spain is able to handle on its own. With no effective secessionist power on the ground, there was no reason to break an already stable situation, and other states remained on the sidelines.

So, is *effectiveness* the determinative principle, the real principle at work, instead of stability? With an effective power on the ground, will states tend to intervene and recognize independence? Not necessarily, and here the reaction of the international community to a very effective power in Kurdistan is instructive. The Iraqi government in Baghdad does not have power in Kurdistan, and the Kurds have proven capable of administrating their own state without the help of Baghdad (Loqman 2014). But states do not recognize an independent Kurdistan because, among other reasons, the independence of Iraqi Kurdistan would trigger a series of claims in the surrounding Kurdish regions that would upend the already fragile balance in that region. Very clearly the Security Council felt legitimated in taking a position against the referendum in Iraqi Kurdistan in 2017, against secession and in favour of national unity:

> Calling on all political entities to intensify efforts to overcome divisions and work together in an inclusive and timely political process aimed at reaching consensus on a single vision for reconciliation and strengthening Iraq's national unity, sovereignty and independence and for Iraq's leaders to engage in dialogue that would contribute to finding a viable and sustainable solution to the country's current challenges… […] Underscoring the need for all segments of the Iraqi population to participate in the political process, in inclusive political dialogue, including through the equal participation of women, and in the economic and social life of Iraq, to refrain from statements and actions which could aggravate tensions, to reach a comprehensive solution on the fair distribution of resources, to promote stability, to develop a just and fair solution for the nation's disputed internal boundaries, and to work to strengthen national unity, including through cooperation between the Government of Iraq and the Kurdistan Regional Government in the spirit of genuine partnership… (UN SC Res. S/RES/2367 [2017], 14 July 2017).

Thus, the overall stability of the areas implicated by secessionists claims seems to be the pole star orienting international reactions to secessionist movements—and even effectiveness is valued according to its ability to lend stability.

In addition to its pragmatic preference for stability, international law should also base its reactions on human rights, something that Professor Chinkin, in part, brought up before the Supreme Court of Canada in her reference to gender equality (see above section "International Law and Re Secession of Quebec"). Let's envision a scenario in which a region strongly wants independence from a state. As seen above, at section "The 2010 Kosovo Advisory Opinion, Notwithstanding the 1998 *Reference Re Secession of Quebec*", international law does not recognize unilateral attempts to obtain independence through violations of "egregious violations of norms of general international law" (Kosovo Advisory Opinion, paragraph 81, referring to the examples of South Rhodesia, the northern Cyprus, and the Republika Srpska). By the same token, these same obligations bind states in their reactions against internal secessionist movements. If clashes between parent states and internal secessionist movements go unresolved, they can lead to extended situations of instability and escalating use of force resulting in human rights violations. Here the decision of the Supreme Court of Canada again extends a helping hand to international law, offering a potentially useful tool to avoid crises of this kind. In its reasoning, the Court discussed a principle which should be imported: a duty to negotiate with secessionists:

> Finally, we highlight that a functioning *democracy* [international community] requires a continuous process of discussion. [...] No one has a monopoly on truth, and our system is predicated on the faith that in the marketplace of ideas, the best solutions to public problems will rise to the top. Inevitably, there will be dissenting voices. A democratic system of government is committed to considering those dissenting voices, and seeking to acknowledge and address those voices in the laws by which all in the community must live.
>
> The Constitution Act, 1982, gives expression to this principle, by conferring a right [one can substitute, "International law does not prohibit"] to initiate constitutional change on each participant in Confederation. In our view, the existence of this right imposes a corresponding duty on the participants in Confederation to engage in constitutional discussions in order to acknowledge and address democratic expressions of a desire for change in other provinces. This duty is inherent in the democratic principle which is a fundamental predicate of our system of governance. [...]
>
> The federalism principle, in conjunction with the democratic principle, dictates that the clear repudiation of the existing constitutional order and the clear expression of the desire to pursue secession by the population

> of a province would give rise to a reciprocal obligation on all parties to Confederation to negotiate constitutional changes to respond to that desire.... (Canadian Reference, paragraphs 68–69, 88)

The international community is not linked by a federalist constitution, but when potentially "egregious violations of norms of general international law" (Kosovo Advisory Opinion, paragraph 81) are at stake, considering the international community in federalist terms can be useful. It would be difficult, indeed, to conclude that international law expresses nothing but complete indifference for opposing internal factions, until the relations between secessionists and the central government escalate enough to become a problem for the international community. The matter is particularly pressing where clear manifestations of independence arise from peaceable movements and referenda that do not recognize the old, unitarian political project as legitimate. What can the international community demand (if anything) from the two factions, before their divergent positions end up in open hostilities?

A duty to negotiate would take into account both the need to protect human lives and freedoms in the political struggle between parent states and secessionist movements and the international preference for stability. This could prevent what are today situations of avoidance and silent opposition from developing into full-fledged hostilities, since it is in no one's interest for Spain to become the new Balkans, or for Anglophone Cameroon to become a new Tamil region.

References

Abi-Saab, George (1997), "The Effectivity Required of an Entity That Declares Its Independence in Order for It to Be Considered a State in International Law", in Anne F. Bayefsky (ed.) (2000), *Self-Determination in International Law: Quebec and Lessons Learned*, Kluwer, The Hague, 69–74.

Bayefsky, Anne F. (ed.) (2000), *Self-Determination in International Law: Quebec and Lessons Learned*, Kluwer, The Hague.

Bonafé, Beatrice I. (2011), *Il potere della Corte internazionale di giustizia di riformulare la domanda di parere consultivo*, in Lorenzo Gradoni and Enrico Milano (a cura di), *Il parere della Corte internazionale di giustizia sulla dichiarazione di indipendenza del Kosovo. Un'analisi critica*, Cedam, Padova, 31–57.

Brownlie, Ian and Crawford, James (2012), *Brownlie's Principles of Public International Law*, Oxford University Press, Oxford.

Buchanan, Allen (2007), *Justice, Legitimacy, and Self-Determination: Moral Foundations for International Law*, Oxford University Press, Oxford.

Burri, Thomas and Thürer, Daniel (2008), "Self Determination", Max Planck Encyclopedia of Public International Law, Electronic Resource.

Cartabia, Marta (2010), *The Age of 'New Rights'*, Straus Working Paper 03/10, http://www.law.nyu.edu/sites/default/files/siwp/Cartabia.pdf.

Cassese, Antonio (1995), *Self-Determination of Peoples: A Legal Reappraisal*, Cambridge University Press, Cambridge.

Chinkin, Christine (1998), "Report for the Ad-Hoc Committee of Canadian Women on the Constitution", in Anne F. Bayefsky (ed.) (2000), *Self-Determination in International Law: Quebec and Lessons Learned*, Kluwer, The Hague, 231–240.

Christakis, Theodore (2011), "The ICJ Advisory Opinion on Kosovo: Has International Law Something to Say about Secession?", in *Leiden Journal of International Law* (24), 73–86.

Crawford, James (1997), "State Practice and International Law in Relation to Unilateral Secession", in Anne F. Bayefsky (ed.) (2000), *Self-Determination in International Law: Quebec and Lessons Learned*, Kluwer, The Hague, 31–61.

Crawford, James (2006), *The Creation of States in International Law*, 2nd ed., Cambridge University Press, Cambridge.

Favaro, Andrea and Guadagnini, Antonio (2015), *Io posso decidere*, Venezia.

Franck, Thomas M. (1997), "Opinion Directed at Question 2 of the Reference", in Anne F. Bayefsky (ed.) (2000), *Self-Determination in International Law: Quebec and Lessons Learned*, Kluwer, The Hague, 75–84.

Gradoni, Lorenzo (2011), "Conclusioni: questa non è una dichiarazione di indipendenza", in Lorenzo Gradoni and Enrico Milano (a cura di), *Il parere della Corte internazionale di giustizia sulla dichiarazione di indipendenza del Kosovo. Un'analisi critica*, Cedam, Padova, 227–255.

Hilpold, Peter (ed.) (2008), *Autonomy and Self-Determination: Between Legal Assertions and Utopian*, Edward Elgar, Cheltenham.

Levrat, Nicolas, Antunes, Sandrina, Tusseau, Guillaume and Williams, Paul (2017), "Catalonia's Legitimate Right to Decide Paths to Self-Determination", available at http://exteriors.gencat.cat/web/.content/00_ACTUALITAT/notes_context/FULL-REPORT-Catalonias-legitimate-right-to-decide.pdf.

Loqman, Radpey (2014), "The Legal Status of the Kurdistan Regional Government (KRG) in International Law", in *Journal of Social, Political and Economic Science*, (39), 397–435.

Palmisano, Giuseppe (1997), *Nazioni Unite e autodeterminazione interna*, Giuffré, Milano.

Pellet, Alain (1997), "Legal Opinion on Certain Questions of International Law Raised by the Reference", in Anne F. Bayefsky (ed.) (2000),

Self-Determination in International Law: Quebec and Lessons Learned, Kluwer, The Hague, 85–124.

Pertile, Marco (2011), "Il parere sul Kosovo e l'autodeterminazione assente: quando la parsimonia non è una virtù", in Lorenzo Gradoni and Enrico Milano (a cura di), *Il parere della Corte internazionale di giustizia sulla dichiarazione di indipendenza del Kosovo. Un'analisi critica*, Cedam, Padova, 89–129.

Shaw, Malcom N. (1997), "Re: Order in Council P.C. 1996–1497 of 30 September 1996", in Anne F. Bayefsky (ed.) (2000), *Self-Determination in International Law: Quebec and Lessons Learned*, Kluwer, The Hague, 125–148.

Tancredi, Antonello (2008), "Neither Authorized nor Prohibited? Secession and International Law after Kosovo, South Ossetia and Abkhazia", in *Italian Yearbook of International Law*, 18, 38.

Tancredi, Antonello (2010), "Il parere della Corte internazionale di giustizia sulla dichiarazione d'indipendenza del Kosovo", in *Rivista italiana di diritto internazionale*, 93 (4), 994–1052.

The International Court of Justice's Advisory Jurisdiction on Self-Determination.

Treves, Tullio (2005), *Diritto internazionale. Problemi fondamentali*, Giuffré, Milano.

Wilde, Ralph (2011), "Kosovo (Advisory Opinion)", Max Planck Encyclopedia of Public International Law, Electronic Resource.

Metaconstitutionalising Secession: The *Reference* and Scotland (In Europe)

Alastair MacIver

Introduction

This chapter considers the influence of the *Reference Re Secession of Quebec*[1] on the debate surrounding the Scottish independence referendum of 2014. Since the legal consequences of that vote on independence were clarified by the *Edinburgh Agreement*,[2] and given legal foundation by subsequent legislation of the Westminster and Scottish Parliaments,[3] the prospect of a unilateral secession of the kind considered in the

[1] *Reference Re Secession of Quebec*, [1998] 8 S.C.R. 217.

[2] *Agreement between the UK Government and the Scottish Government on a referendum on independence for Scotland* (2012).

[3] Scotland Act 1998 (Modification of Schedule 5) Order 2013 No. 242; the Scottish Independence Referendum (Franchise) Act 2013, 2013 asp 13; Scottish Independence Referendum Act 2013, 2013 asp 14.

This chapter presents the views of the author alone and not those of the Council or its Legal Service.

A. MacIver (✉)
Legal Service, Council of the European Union, Brussels, Belgium
e-mail: alastair.maciver@consilium.europa.eu

G. Delledonne and G. Martinico (eds.), *The Canadian Contribution to a Comparative Law of Secession*,
https://doi.org/10.1007/978-3-030-03469-6_6

Reference was, at least professedly, removed. Agreement on the legality of a Scottish independence referendum and its consequences *on that occasion* should not nonetheless be mistaken for a standing embrace by the British Constitution of *all* possible referendums on secession.[4] Indeed, the refusal of the UK Government to pre-commit to the legality of any prospective independence vote in the Scotland Act 2016 signals an ongoing fundamental duality on "the constitutionality, if not the legality, of future referendums in the half-twilight" between a textual analysis of the law and political acceptance of Scottish popular sovereignty (Tickell 2016: 344). Despite this interesting propensity to mould legal strictures to the *ad hoc* political constitution, in the concrete rather than in the abstract, this chapter does not propose to examine the influence of the *Reference* on the law of the UK. Instead, it offers an examination of its influence on EU law, especially as regards the possible accession of a Scottish successor state to the Union. The withdrawal of the UK from the EU will change some of the dynamics of any Scottish aspiration to independent member statehood, but the European dimension to the "Scottish Question" (Mitchell 2014: 285) looks certain to endure, and the influence of the *Reference* will therefore remain relevant as a point of orientation in the discussion.

European legal argument was a key feature and register of the campaign that preceded the 2014 vote. It is often remarked that Union law argument was frequently invoked in an instrumentalist manner by the official campaigns, and the UK and Scottish Governments (Bell 2016: 29). In unpolished terms, one could say that the foremost legal issue was not about whether the legislature or government of Scotland had the power to effect unilateral secession from the UK, but the question of the ease or automaticity of Scotland becoming a Member State of the EU. The assessment of the likelihood of seamless EU membership for a would-be independent Scotland ran in parallel lines with, or acted as a full proxy for, consideration of the merits of independence itself. The answer to this question, and whether Article 48 or 49 of the Treaty on European Union (TEU) was the correct procedure for accession, was subject to uncertainty that, on an institutional level, was refracted through laconic (or, one might even say, *ipse dixit*) statements by the European Commission (Barroso 2012), the UK Government's assessment of the *prima*

[4] See, in this connection: Scottish Parliament, Motion S5M-04710, 28 March 2017.

facie unlikelihood of expedited accession (Crawford and Boyle 2013: 100) and the agnosticism of the Scottish Government's *sui generis* approach (Scottish Government 2013: 221). In this chapter, I do not propose to concentrate on those institutional arguments, not least because they abstained from detailed Union law reasoning and were focused on the end destination of the putative new state. Instead, the chapter will seek out the influence of the *Reference* in scholarly analyses of what European law could contribute to evaluating, accommodating or deterring Scottish independence.

Transposing the holding and reasoning of the *Reference* from Canada to the EU is not a straightforward exercise. As already noted, the first-order problem is clearly different. But, more importantly, unlike the Constitution of Canada, the Treaties on which the EU is founded are emphatically not the expression of a singular people,[5] nor a statement of its will.[6] In other terms, the Union legal order is not host to any kind of foundational constitutionalism, in respect of which the *Reference* is most remarkable for lending it a radical responsiveness, by excavating underlying principles (Oklopcic 2018: 251). This facet of the Union, as harbouring a "constitution without constitutionalism" (Weiler 1995: 219), means that it lacks a historically grounded constitutional culture, or "historical lineage stretching back through the ages",[7] to produce confident categorical answers to problems like secessionism (Walker 2017: 42). Given those limitations, it is powerfully argued that the Union would have questionable legitimacy in repudiating diverse national "right answers" to secession and risk the EU becoming categorised as sort of federal state in the making that presumes to regulate these questions in the name of its Member States (Walker 2016: 18). The influence of the *Reference* on Union legal argument is therefore not to be found in any sort of crude attempt to assimilate the legal architecture of the EU to Canadian federalism.

In this chapter, I will argue that the influence of the *Reference* has manifested itself in arguments that, in fact, intrinsically base themselves on the absence of foundational constitutionalism in the EU. It will be shown that the *Reference* resonates in, what will be described as,

[5] *Reference Re Secession of Quebec*, paragraph 85.

[6] *Reference Re Manitoba Language Rights* [1985] 1 S.C.R. 721, 745.

[7] *Reference Re Secession of Quebec*, paragraph 49.

a normative influence and a methodological influence. A third influence on the conception of amending powers will also be suggested. These three influences all make use of the *Reference* not to identify underlying constitutional principles, but to derive the content of ***metaconstitutional*** ideas about the presuppositions of membership of the EU. Metaconstitutional is defined here as referring to principles that are external to positive EU law or the law of the Member States but which are recognised by those legal orders as constitutional in so far as they make up the building blocks of each order and make possible their coexistence (Walker 2000: 9). To be more concrete, such metaconstitutional ideas express different versions of plurality in the absence of a hierarchical relationship between Union and national law. These will be shown to be found in the *ethos* of membership, substantive normative commitments to democracy, and in the constitutional significance of admission to the Union. In different ways, like the *Reference*, the three influences I will point to here are sites that channel the "deep structure" (Haljan 2014: 269) of what sustains the normativity of Union law and its relationship with Member State constitutions.

This chapter will proceed as follows. Firstly, it will identify a normative influence of the *Reference*, especially in the argumentation of Joseph Weiler. Secondly, the chapter will demonstrate the methodological influence of the *Reference* on efforts to recast the division of power between the Union and the Member States, in the context of Scottish independence. Thirdly, a potentially fruitful influence of the *Reference*'s casting of amending powers on the procedural dilemma between Articles 48 and 49 TEU will be outlined. Fourthly, the chapter closes by reflecting on these transplantations of the *Reference* from the context of the foundational constitutional order of a state (Canada) to that of the EU.

Normative Influence

The *Reference* has had a normative influence on the European legal framing of a putative affirmance vote for Scottish independence by informing the content of a European *ethos* of tolerance (Weiler 2012: 594–595). In this respect, the Supreme Court's response to Question 2, on the right to self-determination under international law, has had most resonance. Most salient here was Weiler's argument that since Scotland, like Quebec, enjoyed extensive individual and collective freedom, not only is there no right to external self-determination under international law,[8] but there is no ethically sound justification for repudiating the "democratic discipline" (Weiler 2014: 14) of internal self-determination within the UK or Canada, which corresponds with a normative precondition for membership of the EU. In practical terms, Weiler argues that any people that rejects internal self-determination in a democratic state ethically disqualifies itself from any "safe harbour" (Weiler 2012) as a Member State of the EU.

To be clear, the *Reference* here does not contribute to the interpretation of public international law as received by the Union, but helps elaborate the substance of Weiler's normative "principle of constitutional tolerance" which he has affirmed a metaconstitutional minimum value to which all Member States subscribe (Weiler 2011). This distinct level of metaconstitutional argument is brought out clearly in the case of Scotland in particular because the need to have recourse to a right to external self-determination was obviated by the *Edinburgh Agreement*. In making his normative idea of tolerance a conduit for the *Reference*, Weiler seems to assimilate Canada and the UK to the EU; for him, the presupposition of discipline and self-abnegation that predicate being a component part of a democratic state equates to the metaconstitutional commitments needed to be a Member State of (and coexist with) the EU.

Weiler's use of the *Reference*, in the period preceding the 2014 vote, and the accompanying analogy with Canada nonetheless seems to understand the principle of constitutional tolerance in a way that defies the way he defined it in his original exposition, in which Canadian federal-provincial relations served as the ultimate counterexample to the sustaining *ethos* of Member State acceptance of Union norms. In its initial formulation, Weiler conceived of constitutional tolerance as predicated on *voluntary* submission distinguished from intra-state relations between central and federated levels of government characterised by *involuntary* submission. In the context of his normative criticism of secession, it is even more remarkable that constitutional tolerance fostered between the EU and its Member States was originally contrasted with the intra-state relationship between the province of Quebec (no stranger to secession crises) and the federal Canadian government. The distinction based on volition is so central to his understanding of constitutional tolerance that it is worth quoting the central passage in full:

[8] *Reference Re Secession of Quebec*, paragraph 136.

> The Quebecois are told: In the name of the People of Canada, you are obliged to obey. The French or the Italians or the Germans are told – In the name of the peoples of Europe, you are invited to obey. In both constitutional obedience is demanded. When acceptance and subordination is voluntary, and repeatedly so, it constitutes an act of true liberty and emancipation from collective self-arrogance and constitutional fetishism – a high expression of Constitutional Tolerance. (Weiler 2000)

Weiler seemed to be making clear that some form of voluntary self-abnegation—"when acceptance and subordination is voluntary" (Weiler 2011)—is essential to any demonstration of constitutional tolerance, and that the conditions for such "an act of true liberty and emancipation from collective self-arrogance and constitutional fetishism" (Weiler 2000) do not obtain in the intra-state relationship between Quebec and Canada, where the Quebecois are *obliged* to obey in the name of the people of Canada, and not *invited* to do so.

This comparison here between the intra-state relationship and that between the EU and its Member States is moreover not some incidental rhetorical flourish but entirely integral to Weiler's conception of constitutional tolerance. Specifically, he distinguishes the principle of constitutional tolerance from Neil MacCormick's constitutional pluralism (MacCormick 2003: 229) because voluntary submission to the constitutional discipline of the EU is not premised on the legal theoretical necessary incommensurability of constitutional authority but on the political fact of the absence of a European constitutional demos, attesting consent to be bound (Weiler 2011: 14). For Weiler the overlap of constitutional authority does not then pose any problems in the legal theoretical terms of the incommensurability of legal norms or the authority of legal orders (Weiler 1995). Rather, instead of there being a structural reason for the incommensurability of constitutional orders, as, for instance, between the Member States and the EU, where there is any such incommensurability it resides in the source of the authority of each constitution *as a political fact*, perceived in terms of political theory and not legal structure (Weiler 2011: 12–14). As Weiler has affirmed in a number of ways, the very specificity and nobility of the EU are precisely the absence of any single demos or any political fact establishing the constitutional authority of the EU which can unambiguously trump that of the Member States. There is only a political fact of incommensurability because of the absence of an EU demos. Whether or not one agrees with this characterisation of the EU, this understanding of nobility of the normative core of European constitutional project is, again and again, contrasted with the "relatively simple" (Weiler 2014: 14) case of a federal state in which the federal demos ("the people of Canada") trumps the demoi of the constituent units ("the people of Quebec, Alberta, etc."). The operation of the principle of constitutional tolerance is therefore marked out as being confined to a Europe in which there is incommensurability because of the lack of a super-demos. At the intra-state level (as between sub-state unit and central government), there is no such political (or, for that matter, legal) incommensurability because the state constitution is very explicitly grounded in a demos. Weiler's charge that the independence of a region of a Member State, which itself in political theoretical terms has a single demos, constitutes the rejection of the principle of constitutional tolerance in the EU, premised precisely on the absence of any demos, is hard to reconcile with the way he himself seems to have framed incommensurability. Weiler has, throughout his work, been very careful to distinguish the European constitutional construct from any banal form of nation-building within a state with a nation or people as its source of constitutional authority (Weiler 1999: 337). It follows from that that no act of self-abnegation, making constitutional tolerance a political fact, is possible on the part of a derivative sub-state entity since it is obliged to obey, and indeed exists because of, the constitution of the state as ordained by the demos. Crucially, there is no sense in which the accommodation of federal constitutional authority is *merely proposed*, rather it is required.

The normative influence of the *Reference* can therefore be seen in Weiler's reliance upon its characterisation of the right to self-determination under international law to supply the substance of a principle of constitutional tolerance. Nonetheless, the *Reference*'s rejection of an external right to self-determination for a people such as the Scots or the Quebecois cannot easily be likened with Weiler's metaconstitutional principle because that latter idea of tolerance has consistently and expressly been contrasted with the relatively banal case of "a people's pursuit of its political, economic, social and cultural development within the framework of an existing state".[9] Fundamentally, internal self-determination does not coherently equate to constitutional tolerance because it lacks the voluntary quality, as a purely political fact, that

[9] *Reference Re Secession of Quebec*, paragraph 126.

Weiler originally identified as arising from the absence of a European demos. While the *Reference* had an influence on the normative framing of the 2014 Scottish independence referendum in European legal thought, the ambiguous place of Canada *qua* EU in microcosm, and *qua* its Westphalian antithesis, stresses the complexities of translating public international law into metaconstitutional principle.

Methodological Influence

A second site which has elicited the influence of the *Reference* on the European legal imagination is the application of the principle of sincere cooperation in Article 4(3) TEU as regards a Scottish successor state. Douglas-Scott is notable here in drawing on the *Reference* to contend that an affirmative vote for Scottish independence would engage the Union law principle of democracy as a trigger for a duty to negotiate under sincere cooperation (Douglas-Scott 2016: 185). This influence proposes to make principles cognisable as more than mere "naked objectives" (Klamert 2014: 122). It defies the classic bounds of sincere cooperation which anchored duties to a power conferred on the Union (Neframi 2015: 70) or Union action that crystalises an objective of the Union (Klamert 2014: 122).

This projected way of making the European principle of democracy applicable as a free-standing norm, akin to its Canadian cousin in the *Reference*, imagines a new theory of sincere cooperation expressly premised on a "distinctive form of legal discourse that departs from the traditional law of integration" (Editorial Board 2014: 12). Douglas-Scott attaches this emancipation of the democracy principle in the project of building new federal philosophy of Union law that looks beyond competences (Azoulai 2014: 5). We can call this a "fact of membership" approach since it tries to give expression to values affirmed to be inherent in membership of the Union as a method of dividing power between the Union and the Member States. In Douglas-Scott's version attached to her invocation of the *Reference* (Douglas-Scott 2016: 188), "the fact of membership" approach sees principles, values, objectives and national identity as sufficient to trigger a legal duty of sincere cooperation. This search for a new kind of legal argument is also brought out in Armstrong's analysis of Edward's arguing for a duty to accommodate Scotland as a Member State (Edward 2013: 1163) on the basis *inter alia* of the principle of democracy, amounting to saying that if there is a "normative fit" with EU values, then Article 4(3) TEU is triggered (Armstrong 2017: 131). Douglas-Scott, however, is distinguished in joining the dots between the normative metaconstitutional convergence of the Member States on the principle of democracy, on the one hand, and the *Reference*'s application of the value in the secession context.

Some scepticism was expressed about this effort to build a new approach to the structure of Union law. For instance, the holding in the *Reference* case was distinguished from the Scottish accession to the Union on factual grounds (Closa 2016: 258). But this seems to ignore the *methodological* insight that the case presents from Douglas-Scott's point of view (Douglas-Scott 2016: 185). What is most salient about the *Reference* is that it is premised on the initial identification of four principles of federalism, democracy, constitutionalism and the rule of law, and respect for minority rights which "function in symbiosis".[10] It stood therefore more as a kind of template for how sincere cooperation would work in the "fact of membership" approach rather than working as a precedent for a particular outcome for a would-be successor state.

There was also some internal critique about what the principle of democracy would entail: becoming a third state was presented as a consequence of independence (Armstrong 2017: 129–130; Closa 2016: 255) and as a limiting feature of democracy. This risked reaffirming a premise as a conclusion (*petitio principii*) because the very purpose of the appeal to the principle of democracy was to identify *what the consequences are.*

The discussion of the *Reference* should therefore be read as a placeholder that speculates about the kind of new principles that could guide how powers are divided between the Union and the Member States in a "fact of membership" approach. This necessarily involves imagining a tentative theoretical model in terms of general principles, not strict adherence to the holding itself. The speculative nature of this "fact of membership" approach means it can be easily mistaken for an exhortation to political actors, through the proxy of legal argument, rather than any kind of legal theory about the scope of sincere cooperation. Indeed, Armstrong has contended that Edward's analysis of sincere cooperation, while using the language of legal obligation and duty to negotiate, asserts the primacy of the political decision. Armstrong reads Edward's presentation of the issue as conceding the difficulties as to legal basis and

[10] *Reference Re Secession of Quebec*, paragraph 49.

timescale that the law imposes on state succession but he nonetheless "seem[s] to suggest that whatever may be the legal difficulties, a political solution may be found" (Armstrong 2014: 185). Pursuant to this reading, Edward would not be understood to be making an argument about the constitutional structure of the Union but a claim about the ultimate recourse to politics when the law leads to arbitrary or inflexible solutions. Such a view seems to depict the Member States as the "Masters of the Treaties" bound only by a purely moral duty to accommodate a nascent state formed from the territory Member State, albeit that this duty is dressed up as a legal one.

In this connection, Armstrong offers a nuanced discussion of the relationship between law and politics that is apparent when questions such as withdrawal from the Union, secession are confronted (Armstrong 2014: 119). He concludes that certainty and legal order are elusive in such periods of political disruption, but the language of legal claims in which a number of plausible legal arguments are framed demonstrates the capacity of law to "manage political disorder" without definitively "rejurisdictionalising" by placing the relationships present in such disorder in a hard legal framework. If Armstrong's insight is correct, the sort of "fact of membership" approach, at which Douglas-Scott hints, needs to be read, not as positing a new legal division of power between the Union and the Member States, but as a sort of discussion of the totemic principles that underpin membership of the Union that need not be converted into legal norms. This, however, at least goes against Douglas-Scott's own framing of her approach, which roots itself in the broader project to elaborate a speculative new idea of the division of competences based on the normative convergence of membership, rather than understanding the invocations of sincere cooperation, based on values, as mere exhortations to politics informed by those principles. We should thus see those appeals to loyalty as speculation about a new way of casting Union law that does not view written law and politics as stark opposites.

In summary, the influence of the *Reference* has made itself known in the imagining of a whole new form of argumentation about the division of power between the Union and the Member States, in order to substantiate a duty to negotiate with a Scottish successor state. This "fact of membership" form of argumentation presents a site for the invocation of the equivalent of underlying principles as normative convergence that underpins the written text of the Treaties.

An Influence on Amending Powers

The *Reference* shows that constitutional amendments are the preeminent site for rendering the transformative event of secession into legal and constitutional terms. In this section, I argue that the *Reference* helps us to understand why the choice between the Union's amending procedures of Articles 48 and 49 TEU is not susceptible to a textual delineation. This argument has three elements to it. Firstly, I claim, against the predominant view, that the jurisprudence of the Court of Justice of the European Union (CJEU) rejects the resolution of the dilemma between Articles 48 and 49 TEU by reference to textual interpretation in the form of *lex specialis* legal basis formulae. Secondly, it is contended that the *Reference* helps us to understand why the appropriate procedure can only be identified in the light a prior characterisation of the transformative event of the secession of a constituent part of an EU Member State, like Scotland, in terms of "unwritten principles" (Haljan 2014: 275). Admittedly, this influence is merely suggested by the Supreme Court's translation of the secession of a province into the legal terms a constitutional amendment,[11] without specifying whether Section 38 (by majority provincial consent) or Section 41 (by unanimous provincial consent) of the Constitution Act 1982 is applicable.[12] The Supreme Court's decision to restrict itself to noting that the necessary amendments "could be radical and extensive"[13] while privileging "underlying principles" of the Constitution is nonetheless fleshed out by Haljan's emphasis on his "associative constitutionalism" above textual interpretation. Thirdly, it is argued that the Union law analogue of those "underlying principles" can be found either in a principle of solidarity or in a metaconstitutional standard, like Weiler's principle of constitutional tolerance.

Let us first consider the argument that a textual distinction between Articles 48 and 49 TEU is elusive. In Union law terms, the argument about Articles 48 and 49 TEU has tended to focus on legal basis, either in order to affirm one provision as more appropriate than the other. The typical starting point for this legal basis analysis of Articles 48 and 49 TEU is the long-established principle that the choice of legal basis for a Union legal measure must be based on objective factors which are

[11] *Reference Re Secession of Quebec*, paragraph 84.

[12] On this debate see Monahan (1995) and Webber (1997).

[13] *Reference Re Secession of Quebec*, paragraph 84.

amenable to judicial review[14] including the aim and content[15] of the measure. Applying that "aim and content" test, scholars propose Article 49 TEU as a *lex specialis* having regard to the projected aim and content of a hypothetical act admitting a successor state (Piris 2017: 86; Skoutaris 2016: 5). After all, legal basis is a question of "constitutional significance"[16] that is deeply embedded in the Union's identity as a polity of conferred powers.[17] Indeed, the need to point to a legal basis in the Treaties for any act of the institutions is expressive of the rule of law principle and more precisely what Von Bogdandy calls the principle of *positive legality*, the twin of the principle of *negative legality* (the requirement to respect hierarchically superior norms of Union law) (Von Bogdandy 2009: 51). But why the legal basis analysis fundamentally goes awry is because it looks past the insight that these rule of law principles of legality are premised on the "dichotomisation" (Von Bogdandy 2009: 53) of the EU Member States as both subject to Union law and excluded from the need to comply with it when, and provided that, they act as Treaty-makers creating the founding superior law. Concretely, the principle of positive legality demands that a legal act be anchored in a higher norm to give it legal authority; it would be contrary to the autonomy of Union law (Hartly 2010: 289) itself if a Treaty amendment was required to find a legal basis in an even higher norm to be validly adopted. In this connection, pursuant to Articles 1, first indent, 3(6), 4(1) and 5(1)-(2) TEU, the principle of conferral, on which the need for a legal basis is founded, refers to competences conferred *upon the Union by the Member States.* To treat Articles 48 and 49 TEU as legal bases would lead to the tautological conclusion that they are competences conferred on the Member States *by themselves*, running against the repeated framing of the conferral principle affirmed in the Treaties, not least Article 48(2) TEU itself which refers to the power "to increase or to reduce the competences conferred on the Union in the Treaties".

The "dichotomisation" of the Member States is equally reflected in the different treatment that Treaty amendments, on the one hand, and

[14] Case 45/86, *Commission v. Council* ('GSP'), ECLI:EU:C:1987:163, paragraph 11.

[15] Case C-300/89, *Commission v. Council* ('Titanium Dioxide'), ECLI:EU:C:1991:244, paragraph 10.

[16] *Opinion 2/00*, ECLI:EU:C:2001:664, paragraph 5.

[17] Opinion of Advocate General Kokott in Case C-13/07, *Commission v. Council* ('Vietnam WTO Accession'), ECLI:EU:C:2009:190, paragraph 105.

"Union legal measures", on the other, have received in the Court's understanding of acts that are apt for legality review. The requirement to point to a functional or sectoral basis, even in the terms of the case law[18] cited by proponents of a legal basis analysis, applies only to a "Community measure" or "act of the institutions". As such, amendments to the Treaties[19] and Accession Treaties are not Union legal measures or "acts of the institutions" for the purposes of Article 13(1) TEU,[20] Article 263 of the Treaty on the Functioning of the European Union (TFEU),[21] Article 267 TFEU,[22] Article 340 TFEU,[23] any other provision setting out the "general rules" the TFEU,[24] including a plea of illegality in the sense of Article 277 TFEU under Article 258 TFEU proceedings.[25] The review of the legality of the primary law including on the enumerated grounds of lack of competence or infringement of an essential procedural requirement is therefore precluded.[26] Likewise, the Court's jurisdiction to give rulings on the interpretation of the Treaties in Article 267(1)(a) TFEU, reasoning *a contrario* from subparagraph (b) jurisdiction regarding acts of institutions (Broberg and Fenger 2014: 107–108), is strictly delineated from jurisdiction to rule on the validity of primary law including as to its putative legal basis. In *Hoffmann-La Roche*, the CJEU has recently spelled

[18] Case C-338/01, *Commission v. Council* ('European Agricultural Guidance and Guarantee Fund'), ECLI:EU:C:2004:253, paragraph 54.

[19] Case T-584/93, *Olivier Roujansky v. Council*, ECLI:EU:T:1994:87, paragraph 15; Case C-253/94 P, *Olivier Roujansky v. Council*, ECLI:EU:C:1995:4, paragraph 11; Case T-113/96, *Edouard Dubois et Fils SA v. Council and Commission*, ECLI:EU:T:1998:11, paragraph 47; C-95/98 P, *Edouard Dubois et Fils SA v. Council and Commission*, ECLI:EU:C:1999:373, paragraph 21.

[20] The Member States are not one of the listed institutions in Article 13(1) TEU. See Case C-253/94 P, *Olivier Roujansky v. Council*, *ibid* for this analysis as regards ex Article 4 TEU (Maastricht).

[21] Joined Cases 31/86 and 35/86, *Levantina Agrícola Industrial SA (Laisa) and CPC España v. Council*, ECLI:EU:C:1988:211, paragraph 17; Case C-572/15, *F. Hoffmann-La Roche AG v. Accord Healthcare OÜ* ECLI:EU:C:2016:739, paragraph 30.

[22] Case C-204/01, *Tilmann Klett v. Bundesministerin für Bildung, Wissenschaft und Kultur*, ECLI:EU:C:2002:634, paragraphs 38 and 39.

[23] *Levantina Agrícola Industrial SA (Laisa)*, paragraphs 21 and 22.

[24] *F. Hoffmann-La Roche AG*, paragraph 31.

[25] Case C-313/89, *Commission v. Spain*, ECLI:EU:C:1991:415, paragraph 10.

[26] *Levantina Agrícola Industrial SA (Laisa)*, paragraph 17; *F. Hoffmann-La Roche AG*, paragraph 31.

out more detailed reasons for this comprehensive "difference in treatment" between acts of the institutions and Acts of Accession as "merely the consequence of the respective procedures chosen for the adoption of those provisions" which, therefore, the Court concludes, is "not arbitrary".[27]

Yet another reason to doubt a textual interpretation is that Articles 48 and 49 TEU may cover measures in the same substantive field. The Court suggests that acts adopted under Article 49 TEU, in so far as they amend primary law, *must* be later revised by Article 48 TEU.[28] This implicit reference to Article 48 TEU has appeared in every Act of Accession, with the most recent example being Article 7(1) of the 2011 Croatian Act of Accession. The amendment of Acts of Accession has also been carried out in practice by ordinary Treaty revisions under Article 48 TEU or its antecedents. Article 3(2) of the Greenland Treaty, adopted under Article 236 EEC, the predecessor of Article 48 TEU, amends the 1972 Act of Accession. More emphatically, Article IV-437(2) of the Constitutional Treaty, also a putative ordinary Treaty revision (under Article 48 TEU [Nice]), repealed *all* the past Acts of Accession, notwithstanding their partial simultaneous insertion in appended protocols.

But the most important reason to doubt a purely textual interpretation here is that Articles 48 and 49 TEU mark out, what Schütze calls, "external limits" on the exercise of Union competences. Keeping general for the moment, and to put this in other words, Articles 48 and 49 TEU act as a barrier on recourse to a legal basis, even when within the "internal limits" of a given competence, if the act would achieve a "qualitative leap" (Schütze 2009: 139) such that would change the constitutional identity of the Union "by the back door" (Schütze 2009: 139). Before we turn to the case law that substantiates this proposition, the consequence of this internal and external distinction should be laid out. It is submitted that the function of both procedures as external limits suggests that rather than being distinguished by aim and content (i.e. the internal limits of legal bases), they are distinguished by the nature of the constitutional change.

[27] *F. Hoffmann-La Roche AG*, paragraph 31; See likewise on the "alleged arbitrary difference of regime": *Levantina Agrícola Industrial SA (Laisa)*.

[28] *Levantina Agrícola Industrial SA (Laisa)*, paragraph 12; Opinion of Advocate General Lenz in *Levantina Agrícola Industrial SA (Laisa)*, ibid., paragraph 20; Case C-445/00, *Austria v. Council*, ECLI:EU:C:2003:445, paragraph 62.

It is submitted that the jurisprudence indicating when an Article 48 TEU amendment is the appropriate procedure to bring about a fundamental constitutional change aligns with case law that tacitly compels recourse to Article 49 TEU. In *Opinion 2/94*,[29] the CJEU affirmed that the Article 48 TEU amendment procedure is required because of the systematic constitutional significance of a change contemplating "fundamental institutional implications". In *Opinion 2/94*, the change under examination was accession by the then Community to the European Convention on Human Rights through use of the flexibility clause in Article 235 EC (now, as amended, Article 352 TFEU). Rather than suggesting that the terms of Article 235 EC were exceeded (Alston and Weiler 1999: 24–25), the Court relied instead on the constitutional significance of the change. The "external limits" of constitutional identity determined recourse to Article 48 TEU rather than the "internal limits" of a legal basis test as applied to Article 235. There is less jurisprudence on the need for an accession procedure, simply because few acts of the Union institutions conceivably amount to the admission of a Member State "by the back door". Nonetheless, the reasoning in *Région wallonne*,[30] pursuant to which the Union cannot "comprise a greater number of Member States than the number of States between which they were established" without undermining the "institutional balance provided for in the Treaties", reflects the same rationale as that in *Opinion 2/94*. Although Article 49 TEU is not mentioned in *Région wallonne*, the Court obliquely refers to accession by defining Member States as "States party to the Treaties establishing the Communities and the Accession Treaties".

Having established that a textual interpretation of Articles 48 and 49 TEU in terms of legal basis sits awkwardly with the jurisprudence of the CJEU, let us now consider the second claim in the argument: the *Reference* could help us understand deeper reasons why the amending powers effecting a transformation like secession or accommodating a successor state cannot be understood in a narrowly textual way. On one level, the Von Bogdandy's "dichotomisation" of the Member States and the pronouncements of the CJEU are just the formal inference to be drawn from the conferral principle. But on another level understanding the choice between Articles 48 and 49 TEU as markers of "external

[29] *Opinion 2/94*, ECLI:EU:C:1996:140, paragraph 35; Case 43/75, *Gabrielle Defrenne v. Société anonyme belge de navigation aérienne Sabena*, ECLI:EU:C:1976:56, paragraph 58.

[30] Case C-95/97, *Région wallonne v. Commission*, ECLI:EU:C:1997:184, paragraph 6.

limits" forces us to confront basic questions about what underpins the Union in normative terms and what the Member States have in common. More pointedly, it also forces us to reckon with change in those terms. In this way, the written text of the Treaties comes to be seen as either giving rise to horizontal principles about the commitments of membership or the product of the Member States, whether guided or not by the objectives that caused them to associate. This is particularly driven home by *Opinion 2/94*, which, like in the *Reference*, holds an amendment that is necessary because some change to the basic structure of the polity is in view. Like the *Reference*, *Opinion 2/94* and *Région wallonne* identify a challenge to the written law and channel it through an amendment, not because of the subject matter of the amendment but because of foundational principles[31] that oblige it to be effected in that way.

In terms of reception by scholars, the *Reference*'s identification of "underlining principles" which "inform and sustain the written text"[32] and act as the "lifeblood"[33] of the Constitution readily correlates with Haljan's notion of "associative constitutionalism" which sees the formal constitution as "the articulation of the foundational associative commitments gluing us together as a polity" (Haljan 2014: 70). This notion of associative constitutionalism seems to be transposable to the EU, since the kind of "association" it articulates may be subject to a "pluralist conception of multiple centres of controlling power and influence" (Haljan 2014: 55). Haljan's framework clearly entails a very sophisticated reconstruction of the concept of law, but the practical implication of seeing written legal law as only the expression of "associative commitments" has a clear implication for Canada's dilemma between Section 38 and 41 of the Constitution Act 1982: the procedure is collateral to determining what the implications of the transformation of secession mean in the light of "associative commitments" and whether the will to secede by the given group is constitutionally recognisable (Haljan 2014: 274). In like terms, the nature of Articles 48 and 49 TEU seems to place the procedure downstream to understanding why the admission of a successor state would be constitutionally significant in terms of what membership of the Union requires and how far a would-be Scotland's desire to be

[31] *Reference Re Secession of Quebec*, paragraph 88.

[32] *Reference Re Secession of Quebec*, paragraph 49.

[33] *Reference Re Secession of Quebec*, paragraph 51.

both independent and a Member State of the EU converges with those "associative commitments" of membership.

Let us now look at this in more detail. If we are to reject the straight-jacket of textual interpretation in favour of "associative commitments", in what terms are the equivalents of "underlying principles" articulated in Union law? In Schütze's terms, it remains unclear what the "external limits" of the Union are in detail. In fact, from *Opinion 2/94*, it seems that discerning what the "external limits" actually entail is a circular process: it affirms in essence that recourse to Articles 48 and 49 TEU will be required where the use of Union competence is "unconstitutional [because] it goes beyond the constitution" (Schütze 2009: 142). The reason given for this circularity is that it is a demonstration of the "dialectical nature of all constitutional interpretation" (Schütze 2009: 142) as the task of reconciling a single provision with the sum of all the provisions and *vice versa* does help to distinguish more clearly what those limits might be. The consequence of this "paradox as old as the interpretation of foundational texts" is that the answer to where the "Europe's legal universe" ends is bifurcated (Schütze 2009: 142). On the one hand, the *Opinion 2/94* formula seems to leave the ultimate associative commitments of the Union up to the Member States in the specific changes they render to the text. But, on the other hand, the general scheme of the principles of the Treaty as interpreted by the Court point to where recourse to the Member States is needed in the first place. This dialectic of the general and the specific leads us into something of an interpretative dead end but it also points to two ways out of the impasse: one vests the say on the constitutional identity of the Union in the CJEU and the other in the collective of the Member States. These two views also might correspond with different ideas of the associative commitments or presuppositions of Union membership: one based on adherence to metaconstitutional principles determined by the *cercle* of Member States (which allow *ad hoc* specific changes or refusals to change) and the other on adherence to the classic Copenhagen Criteria as "conditions of eligibility" in the text of Article 49 TEU (based on a reading of Treaties as a whole). Let us now turn those two versions of "underlying principles" in detail.

We begin by examining the idea that the external limits of the Union, to which both *Opinion 2/94* and *Région wallonne* point us, are to be found in metaconstitutional values. In the context of the Scottish debate, this viewpoint has been most notably expressed by Joseph Weiler. It holds that what matters when deciding whether a successor state should be granted admission to the Union is not whether it fulfils the substantive and procedural requirements of Article 49 TEU (Weiler 2014: 4), but whether that state adheres to the normative core of European integration. This core is, in Weiler's analysis, to be found in a "principle of constitutional tolerance" examined above (Weiler 2014: 4). What is of importance here is not the content of the metaconstitutional values, but that metaconstitutional values (whatever their form) themselves constitute the external limits or associative commitments of Union membership. This primacy of metaconstitutional values has the consequence that practical time constraints of the classical application of Article 49 TEU, and the possibility of a temporal gap between independence and accession, are to be dismissed as artificial legal chicanery (Weiler 2014: 4). Indeed, in Weiler's analysis, from the perspective of positive law alone, *ceteris paribus* a successor state could be accommodated within the Union instantaneously on its achievement of independence (Weiler 2014: 9). He thereby asserts hypothetical legal flexibility in the hands of the collective of the Member States. This flexibility is, however, eclipsed by the innate failure of an independent Scotland, which by its very creation repudiates the tenets of constitutional tolerance (Weiler 2014: 4), from adhering to the metaconstitutional substance of what it is to be a Member State. It is therefore a metaconstitutional idea—Weiler's constitutional tolerance—that acts as signpost towards the associative commitments of the Union.

Against this purely metaconstitutional view is a formalised conception of associative commitments that inheres in the new textual reference in Article 49 TEU to the "conditions of eligibility agreed upon by the European Council", added by the Lisbon Treaty. Hillion believes that that latter change is confirmation that the Copenhagen Criteria have become a fully constitutionalised part of EU law (Hillion 2017: 69). There is a familiar story of the progressive incorporation of the Copenhagen Criteria into the text and practice of the accession process but this nonetheless tells us nothing explicit about the constitutional significance of the change that admission of a new Member State entails. In Schütze's terms, we still need to ask: do the Copenhagen Criteria constitute an external limit of the Union's constitutional identity? In practical terms, does the admission of a new Member State require the conditions of eligibility and admission to be applied because they have a systemic role in defining the associative commitments of the Union? Such questions are crucial because they indicate the constitutional change upon which Member States are compelled to decide by *Opinion 2/94* and *Région wallonne* as the element that stands still while a textual change is happening. Cremona's excavation of the deeper foundations of accession conditionality within the Article 49 TEU process shows that the formal membership criteria give procedural expression to solidarity and mutual trust between the Union and a potential candidate, acceding state or eventual Member State (Cremona 2005). But this notion that the Copenhagen Criteria stand for an "in principle" premise of the Union's relations with candidates for membership (and Europe *as a continent*) might also point us towards the status of such formal criteria as kinds of external limits on the Union's constitutional identity. Let us first look at the role of solidarity in accession before considering the latter possibility that they represent external limits.

Solidarity is a value that emerges from a horizontal and purposive reading of the Treaties and the application of constitutionality during accession negotiations (Cremona 2005: 7). In Cremona's analysis, the solidarity which underpins the Criteria is based first on "an unconditional welcome" (Cremona 2005: 9) from the Union to all European states; membership should be an option for them all on the basis of a common European identity. But, secondly, solidarity is also based on "compliance with specified conditions or meeting targets", like the Copenhagen Criteria, as well as burden-sharing by both parties (Cremona 2005: 15). The accession criteria should therefore be understood not only as constitutionalised but as a *process*-based expression of the horizontal Treaty value of solidarity and even of "constitutional tolerance" (Cremona 2005: 7) itself. The crescendo of this solidarity is in the period between signature and accession itself. That is, when adaption to the Copenhagen Criteria has been achieved and solidarity and mutual trust thereby demonstrated. As such, the state changes from being a *candidate* to an *acceding state*, an effective synonym for future Member State. At that advanced stage, each side is bound, in the words of the Court, by "principles of equality, good faith and solidarity among current and future Member States".[34]

But we can go even further and understand the Copenhagen Criteria and the solidarity they represent as marking out external limits that require the Member States to decide on amendments to the Treaties so as to ensure that formalised criteria, as kinds of associative commitments, are respected by any new state. Two arguments can militate in favour of this idea of the Criteria as external limits and as commitments

[34] Joined Cases C-413/04 and C-414/04, *Parliament v. Council*, ECLI:EU:C:2006:742, paragraph 68.

that underpin membership. Firstly, the limited amendment procedure of Article 49 TEU that narrows the nature of changes to "adjustments" and secondly, the CJEU's idea of membership as a status that primarily supports mutual trust because of Article 49 TEU. Indeed, *Opinion 2/13*[35] offers some guidance on what external limits could be. Most germane to the Article 48 or 49 TEU debate is what the Court says about membership and the role of values in Article 2 TEU, which are explicitly affirmed in Article 49 TEU. The Court affirms a "fundamental premise that each Member State shares with all the other Member States, and recognises that they share with it, a set of common values on which the EU is founded, as stated in Article 2 TEU".[36] What emerges then from *Opinion 2/13* is that presumed Member State compliance with certain values, which are given in explicit form in Article 2 TEU, is part of the special characteristics of the Union and Union law—akin to Schütze's external limits—which cannot be amended without express warrant by the Treaty-maker. Given that Article 49 TEU establishes a process-driven system to ensure compliance with Article 2 TEU and, as such, makes accession the foundation of a presumption of adherence to values, *Opinion 2/13* seems to compel the use of the Article 49 TEU procedure to ensure that the associative commitments of membership are respected.

To tie these two ideas of external limits back to a potential influence of the *Reference* on amending powers, in short they demonstrate that the choice between amending procedures is driven by characterising the basic commitments of membership of the polity and not the written text. In this argument, the EU's corollary to the "underlying principles" of federalism, democracy, constitutionalism and rule of law, and respect for minority rights turns out to be the process-driven establishment of solidarity in the Copenhagen Criteria or recourse to a purely metaconstitutional idea like Weiler's principle of constitutional tolerance. These may seem like rather esoteric counterparts to Canada's fourfold principles and indeed to be so removed from those of the *Reference* so as to strain the analogy. But the divergence between the nature of the Canadian and European principles tallies with the differences in the nature of the two polities. This argument for amending powers as a potential site eliciting the influence of the *Reference* on the Union law framing of an

[35] *Opinion 2/13*, ECLI:EU:C:2014:2454.

[36] *Opinion 2/13*, paragraph 168.

independent Scotland built itself on the marginalisation of textual arguments by CJEU, the place of legal text in associative constitutionalism and the excavation of principles that bind the European association together.

Conclusion: Metaconstitutionalising Secession

What arises from this exploration of the influence of the *Reference Re Secession of Quebec* on the debate surrounding the Scottish independence referendum of 2014 is that the European imagination has somewhat played "fast and loose" with the holding and reasoning of the Supreme Court's seminal contribution. This is not to be pejorative but to acknowledge that the *Reference*'s interpretations of Canadian and public international law have migrated not only across jurisdictions but also across registers and into ethical principles and interpretive philosophies that orient the EU. We saw here that the Court's response to Question 2 of the *Reference* informed the content of a normative concept of the "principle of constitutional tolerance" which Weiler identified as generating an imperative to preclude a Scottish successor state from membership of the Union. Despite its inconsistencies, Weiler's objections were argued to reach beyond a mere form of political morality; both the *Reference* and the federal–provincial relationship between Quebec and Canada supplied normative building blocks for the metaconstitutional substance of membership of the EU which Weiler proposed as the key to the Scottish question. Secondly, the Supreme Court's answer to Question 1 of the *Reference* had a methodological influence on those, like Douglas-Scott, who sought to formulate a European legal response to a would-be Scottish "yes" vote in the light of a novel "fact of membership" approach to the structure of Union law. Drawing on the *Reference*, such an approach aspired to make the unstated premises of the European project legally cognisable by privileging the importance of the principle of democracy on which the Union is premised. Thirdly, it was argued that the *Reference* could present a way of resolving the well-rehearsed procedural dilemma between Articles 48 and 49 TEU, by suggesting a turn to the associative commitments in which those two amending powers are each nested. The chapter has shown that the *Reference* has had a widely dispersed influence on attempts to apprehend secession in terms of principles that underpin the association of the Member States and the Union.

References

Alston, Philip and Weiler, Joseph (1999), "An 'Ever Closer Union' in Need of a Human Rights Policy: The EU and Human Rights", in Philip Alston, et al. (eds.), *The EU and Human Rights*, Oxford University Press, Oxford.

Armstrong, Kenneth (2014), "After 'Ever Closer Union': Negotiating Withdrawal, Secession, and Accession", in *Fordham International Law Journal*, 37, 119.

Armstrong, Kenneth (2017), "The Reach and Resources of European Law in the Scottish Independence Referendum", in Carlos Closa (ed.), *Secession and Withdrawal from the EU: Troubled Membership*, Cambridge University Press, Cambridge.

Azoulai, Loïc (2014), "Introduction: The Question of Competence", in *The Question of Competence in the European Union*, Oxford University Press, Oxford.

Barroso, Jose Manuel, Letter to Lord Tugendhat, 10th of December 2012, *BARROSO (2012) 1300171.*

Bell, Christine (2016), "International Law, the Independence Debate, and Political Settlement in the UK", in Aileen McHarg, et al. (eds.), *The Scottish Independence Referendum: Constitutional and Political Implications*, Oxford University Press, Oxford.

Broberg, Morten and Fenger, Niels (2014), *Preliminary References to the European Court of Justice*, Oxford University Press, Oxford.

Closa, Carlos (2016), "Secession from a Member State and EU Membership: The View from the Union", in *European Constitutional Law Review*, 12, 240.

Crawford, James and Boyle, Alan (2013), *Annex A Opinion: Referendum on the Independence of Scotland—International Law Aspects*, Crown Copyright, Edinburgh.

Cremona, Marise (2005), "EU Enlargement: Solidarity and Conditionality", in *European Law Review*, 30 (1), 3.

Douglas-Scott, Sionaidh (2016), "Scotland, Secession, and the EU", in Aileen McHarg, et al. (eds.), *The Scottish Independence Referendum: Constitutional and Political Implications*, Oxford University Press, Oxford.

Editorial Board (2014), "Union Membership in Times of Crisis", in *Common Market Law Review*, 51, 1.

Edward, David (2013), "EU Law and the Separation of Member States", in *Fordham International Law Journal*, 36, 1151.

Haljan, David (2014), *Constitutionalising Secession*, Hart Publishing, Oxford.

Hartley, Thomas (2010), *The Foundations of EU Law*, Oxford University Press, Oxford.

Hillion, Christophe (2017), "Overseeing the Rule of Law in the EU: Legal Mandate and Means", in Carlos Closa and Dimitri Kochenov (eds.), *Reinforcing the Rule of Law Oversight in the EU*, Cambridge University Press, Cambridge.

Klamert, Marcus (2014), *The Principle of Loyalty in EU Law*, Oxford University Press, Oxford.

MacCormick, Neil (2003), *Legal Theory and Legal Reasoning*, Oxford University Press, Oxford.

Mitchell, James (2014), *The Scottish Question*, Oxford University Press, Oxford.

Monahan, Patrick (1995), "The Law and Politics of Secession", in *Osgoode Hall Law Journal*, 33, 1.

Neframi, Eleftheria (2015), "'Within the Scope of EU Law' Beyond the Principle of Conferral?", in Jeffrey Ellsworth and Johan van der Walt (eds.), *Constitutional Sovereignty and Social Solidarity in Europe*, Nomos Publishing, Baden-Baden.

Oklopcic, Zoran (2018), *Beyond the People*, Oxford University Press, Oxford.

Piris, Jean-Claude (2017), "Political and Legal Aspects of Recent Regional Secessionist Trends in some EU Member States (I)", in Carlos Closa (ed.), *Secession and Withdrawal from the EU: Troubled Membership*, Cambridge University Press, Cambridge.

Schütze, Robert (2009), *From Dual to Cooperative Federalism: The Changing Structure of European Law*, Oxford University Press, Oxford.

Scottish Government (2013), *Scotland's Future: Your Guide to an Independent Scotland*, Crown Copyright, Edinburgh.

Skoutaris, Nikos (2016), *From Britain and Ireland to Cyprus: Accommodating 'Divided Islands' in the EU Political and Legal Order*, EUI Working Papers, Academy of European Law AEL 2016/02.

Tickell, Andew (2016), "The Technical Jekyll and the Political Hyde", in Aileen McHarg, et al. (eds.), *The Scottish Independence Referendum: Constitutional and Political Implications*, Oxford University Press, Oxford.

Von Bogdandy, Armin (2009), "Founding Principles", in Armin Von Bogdandy and Jurgen Bäst (eds.), *Principles of European Constitutional Law*, Hart Publishing, Oxford.

Walker, Neil (2000), "Flexibility Within a Metaconstitutional Frame: Reflections on the Future of Legal Authority in Europe", in Grainne de Burca, et al. (eds.), *Constitutional Change in the EU: Between Uniformity and Flexibility*, Hart Publishing, Oxford.

Walker, Neil (2016), "Federalism in 3D: The Reimagination of Political Community in the EU", in *Católica Law Review*, 1 (1), 67.

Walker, Neil (2017), "Internal Enlargement in the EU: Beyond Legalism and Political Expediency", in Carlos Closa (ed.), *Secession and Withdrawal from the EU: Troubled Membership*, Cambridge University Press, Cambridge.

Webber, Jeremy (1997), "The Legality of a Unilateral Declaration of Independence under Canadian Law", in *McGill Law Journal*, 42, 281.

Weiler, Joseph (1995), *The State Über Alles: Demos, Telos and the German Maastricht Decision*, EUI RSC 1995/19.

Weiler, Joesph (1999), "To Be a European Citizen: Eros and Civilisation", in J.H.H. Weiler (ed.), *The Constitution of Europe*, Cambridge University Press, Cambridge, 337.

Weiler, Joseph (2000), *Federalism and Constitutionalism: Europe's Sonderweg*, Harvard Jean Monnet Working Paper 10/00.

Weiler, Joseph (2011), "Prologue: Global and Pluralist Constitutionalism—Some Doubts", in G. de Búrca and J.H.H. Weiler (eds.), *The Worlds of European Constitutionalism*, Cambridge University Press, Cambridge, 12–14.

Weiler, Joseph (2012), "Editorial: Catalonian Independence and the EU", in *European Journal of International Law*, 23, 909–913.

Weiler, Joseph (2014), "Introductory Remarks", in Carlos Closa (ed.), *Troubled Membership: Dealing with Secession from a Member State and Withdrawal from the EU*, EUI Working Paper RSCAS 2014/91.

Constitutional Migrations in the Commonwealth: The *Quebec Secession Reference* and Sri Lankan Constitutional Discourse

Asanga Welikala

Introduction

The legal issues concerning sub-state nationalism, the self-determination of peoples and secession that were dealt with by the Canadian Supreme Court in the *Reference Re Secession of Quebec* (1998) have been of central relevance to Sri Lankan constitutional debates for decades. Sri Lanka has struggled to find a viable constitutional settlement for the politico-territorial claims of its main minority Tamil people since before independence. While the thirty-year armed conflict between the Sinhala-Buddhist dominated Sri Lankan state and Tamil secessionist militants ended in 2009 with the military defeat of the latter, no further attempt at constitutional accommodation has been made aside from the existing framework of limited devolution. It is in the context of this need for a

A. Welikala (✉)
School of Law, University of Edinburgh, Edinburgh, Scotland, UK
e-mail: Asanga.Welikala@ed.ac.uk

G. Delledonne and G. Martinico (eds.), *The Canadian Contribution to a Comparative Law of Secession*,
https://doi.org/10.1007/978-3-030-03469-6_7

resolution of protracted ethnic conflict that the *Reference* has been of interest in Sri Lanka.

The intricate balance that the Canadian Supreme Court struck between competing norms of international and constitutional law has, perhaps unsurprisingly, inspired Sri Lankan liberal federalists about the possibilities of a principled approach to a resolution of their own conflict. For them, the judgement not only clarified the key principles applicable to accommodating Tamil autonomy within a united Sri Lanka, but it also added normative depth, through the transferable discussion of the 'unwritten principles' of the Canadian constitution, to the design of the federal-type institutional architecture that is needed for a Sri Lankan settlement.

The judgement has been less well received among nationalists on either side of the ethnic divide. For Sinhala-nationalist defenders of the unitary state, the concessions to sub-state nationalism as were held to arise from the normative dictates of democracy, and in particular the notion of internal self-determination, were too much to stomach. For secessionist Tamil nationalists, the presumption against a unilateral right to secede and the high threshold for, and the reciprocal duties attached to, the triggering of such a right were unpalatable. With mutual antagonism inflamed by decades of violent conflict, the implied duty to engage in principled negotiations with each other in effecting a separation consistent with the rule of law was anathema to both.

In concrete terms, the *Reference* has made an appearance in Sri Lankan constitutional discourse at two key moments, and in both instances, what has been of most relevance to the Sri Lankan context has been the concept of 'internal self-determination'. In the first instance, its influence was clearly visible in the Oslo Communique of 2003, issued during the peace process (2001–2006) facilitated by Norway between the government of Sri Lanka and the Liberation Tigers of Tamil Eelam (LTTE). This was a joint statement of intent that outlined the core of a future constitutional settlement to be negotiated between the two sides. It stated:

> Responding to a proposal by the leadership of the LTTE, the parties agreed to explore a solution founded on the principle of internal self-determination in areas of historical habitation of the Tamil-speaking people, based on a federal structure within a united Sri Lanka. The parties acknowledged that the solution had to be acceptable to all communities. (Welikala 2008: 206)

This was the first time the Sri Lankan government had agreed to a formulation that included federalism and the first time the LTTE agreed to one that acknowledged the unity of the Sri Lankan state. During the third round of talks that led to this agreement in December 2003 at Oslo, the parties were assisted by a technical team of the Canadian non-governmental organization, the Forum of Federations, the members of which actively subscribed to the principles enunciated in the *Reference*. Although the Oslo Communique articulates the substantive parameters of one possible constitutional model for Sri Lanka that remains relevant, both the government and the LTTE soon retreated from their commitments, and the peace process collapsed.[1]

The second occasion on which the *Reference* made a somewhat more explicit appearance was in 2017, when the Sri Lankan Supreme Court relied on its authority in apparently coming to the conclusion that the Tamils were a people within Sri Lanka entitled to a right to internal self-determination in the case of *Chandrasoma v. Senathiraja*.[2] This seemingly radical but simultaneously ambiguous decision will be the focus of this chapter below. But a preliminary comment on the context of this attempted migration of constitutional ideas seems apposite, because this is relevant to an assessment later whether *Chandrasoma* is regarded as a turning point in Sri Lankan constitutionalism, or a mere flash in the pan.

The Comparative Context

It is perhaps unremarkable that there should be some cross-fertilization in the thinking of legal and political actors within two common law jurisdictions faced with the similar constitutional challenge of having to deal with the fundamental claims to autonomy, recognition and representation of sub-state national minorities divided from the majority by linguistic, territorial and cultural cleavages. Canada and Sri Lanka also enjoy the historical and cultural bonds of the Commonwealth, and an older tradition of legal transplantation and especially judicial borrowing that characterizes the legal technique of this community of nations.

[1] I discuss these issues and the failed peace process of 2001–2006 in greater detail in Welikala (forthcoming).

[2] *Chandrasoma v. Senathiraja and Others* (2017), SC SPL 03/2014, SC Minutes, August 4, 2017, http://www.supremecourt.lk/images/documents/sc_spl_03_2014.pdf.

But these similarities are rendered quite superficial when the differences between the two are weighed into the comparative scale. Canada and Sri Lanka have met their shared constitutional challenge in profoundly different ways. In dealing with Quebec, Canada has led the world in accommodationist techniques of managing multinational politics, both through developing the normative content of liberal democracy and through institutional variations of federalism (Choudhry 2008a).[3] The post-colonial Sri Lankan state has evolved into a Sinhala-Buddhist ethnocracy that has preferred hegemonic control over accommodation or even integration (Uyangoda 2011: 52–58). Under the decisive influence of the majority nationalism, it has constitutionally entrenched a highly centralized unitary state that constantly claws back what is offered by way of devolution to the periphery (Anketell 2017; Welikala 2016).

While too much must not be made of the theoretical dichotomy between civic versus ethnic nationalisms, it is undeniable that the character of nationalisms in the two cases is also a salient factor in comparing the two. For all their differences, Anglophone Canada and Quebec share basic liberal democratic ideals and a cultural heritage stemming from the European Enlightenment which equip them with a common language of constitutional negotiation, whereas the more ethno-culturally defined Sinhala and Tamil communities have struggled to find common ground based on a shared past or shared values in ways that permit multinational coexistence within the island.

Moreover, the Sri Lankan Supreme Court cannot be compared to its Canadian counterpart as a player in constitutional politics. Setting aside differences in qualitative attributes such as intellectual rigour or doctrinal sophistication, the Sri Lankan court operates in a politico-legal system in which the 'legal constitution' of which it is the interpreter is distinctly subordinate to the 'political constitution' defined by the ethnocratic values and structures of the ethnic majority, of which political players are the enforcers, in matters of constitutional politics such as ethnic pluralism (Welikala 2017). The Sri Lankan court's pronouncements, while important, are not decisive in these matters, especially if they go against the grain of the ethnocratic postulates of the political constitution, as the decision in *Chandrasoma* purports to do. The court, and the legal

[3]For excellent introductions to the accommodation v. integration debate in comparative politics and constitutional law, see Choudhry (2008b) and McGarry et al. (2008).

constitution it upholds and interprets, can be and often is ignored by the more dominant political actors in these situations.

Seen in these stark terms, the contextual differences between Canada and Sri Lanka appear to describe two cases that are so fundamentally divergent that any attempt at transplanting the Canadian model in whole or even in part in Sri Lanka would prove futile. If this is true, then it is very unlikely that the Sri Lankan Supreme Court's laudable attempt at establishing a juristic position based on liberal principles in relation to the question of the Tamils' collective identity and rights would gain any traction whatsoever in constitutional politics. Perhaps the deafening silence with which the judgement was greeted in political debates is the best portent of this likely eventuality.

The Unresolved Tamil Nationality Claim

Debates about the constitutional form of the Sri Lankan state have been ongoing since the late colonial period with no settled consensus, in a polity characterized by rich ethnic and religious pluralism, albeit with an overwhelming Sinhala-Buddhist majority that regards itself as the dominant historic national community of the island. According to the latest 2012 census, the total population of Sri Lanka is 20,359,439, of which Sinhalese are 15,250,081 (74.9%), the Sri Lankan Tamils 2,269,266 (11.15%), Sri Lankan Moors (Muslims) 1,892,638 (9.3%) and the Indian Tamils 839,504 (4.12%).[4] While all aspects of this societal pluralism have cultural and political salience for constitutional debates, it is the schism between the Sinhalese and the Tamils that has defined the deep divide at the heart of Sri Lanka's constitutional unsettlement.

In the Sinhala-Buddhist nationalist worldview, the island is the only homeland of the Sinhalese people, who are, moreover, the inheritors of a sacred duty to preserve and protect Theravada Buddhism. This is the heritage of race and religion that the Sinhala-Buddhists have defended with much sacrifice and resilience from time immemorial. These central elements of Sinhala-Buddhist nationalism are elaborated and reproduced in a powerful tradition of historiography, which continues to inform contemporary political and cultural discourse, in particular in relation

[4] Department of Census and Statistics, "Census of Population and Housing of Sri Lanka 2012", Table A3, http://www.statistics.gov.lk/PopHouSat/CPH2011/Pages/Activities/Reports/FinalReport/Population/FinalPopulation.pdf.

to a specific view of the form and foundations of the Sri Lankan state (Tambiah 1991: 93–102). The three major elements of post-colonial Sinhala-Buddhist nationalism's constitutional agenda—the recognition of a special place for Buddhism and the Sinhala language, and a centralized unitary state—were constitutionally entrenched when the country became a republic in 1972 (Welikala 2012). In this view, there is no distinction between the collective identity of the ethnic majority and the Sri Lankan nation state (Roberts 1978).

The Sri Lankan Tamils, distinct from the Indian Tamils and the largely Tamil-speaking Muslims, see themselves as the other historic national community within the island (Tambiah 1991: 102–113), whose claims to constitutional accommodation are based on three cardinal principles: that they are a distinct nation, with a traditional homeland in the north-east of the island, and entitled on these grounds to the right to self-determination (Edrisinha et al. 2008: Ch. 15). On this basis, they have asserted an entitlement to self-government in the preferred form of autonomy within a federal Sri Lankan state.[5] The main vehicle of these claims has been the *Ilankai Thamil Arasu Katchi* (ITAK) or better known in English as the Federal Party, formed a year after independence in 1949.

It is thus the persistence, even after the military defeat of armed secessionism, of the Tamil claim to distinctive nationhood, and the demand for constitutional accommodation on that specific basis, that renders Sri Lanka empirically a multinational polity (Wilson 2000). And it is in this context that the concept of internal self-determination, of which the Canadian *Reference* case is an important comparative articulation, assumes continuing relevance for Sri Lankan debates on constitutional reform.

The Current Constitutional Framework

It necessary to have an understanding of the framework of the 1978 Constitution and the key doctrines that underpin it as they relate to questions arising from sub-state nationalism, before we attempt an

[5] Tamil nationalism's attempts to encompass the Muslims of the north and east within the Tamil nation under the rubric of 'Tamil-speaking people' have been resisted by the Muslims, who insist on their separate religion-based identity. The Indian Tamils, the descendants of indentured labour in the British colonial plantation economy, do not make territorial claims.

analysis of the implications of the *Chandrasoma* case. The unitary state principle in both its formal and substantive aspects, the constitution's concept of sovereignty and peoplehood, the Sixth Amendment which comprehensively prohibits even the peaceful advocacy of secession and the Thirteenth Amendment which establishes a framework of devolution within the unitary state are the key elements germane to this discussion.

Sri Lanka has been governed by three constitutions since independence, all of which have been unitary in nature to the extent that none have contemplated nor permitted federal-type diffusion of power, institutional pluralism, and the division and sharing of sovereignty (Edrisinha 2008). The independence constitution of 1948 was silent on its self-classification, and it was only with the establishment of the republican state in 1972 that Sri Lankan constitutions have contained the express self-description of 'unitary state' (Jayawickrama 2012). In the period between the grant of independence and the establishment of the republic, the increasingly hostile relationship between the majority Sinhala-Buddhist and minority Tamil nationalisms came to be characterized by the latter's demand for federal autonomy and the former's resistance to it. At the level of legal contestation, therefore, this political relationship between the two nationalisms maps on to the conventional either/or dichotomy of formal classification as between federal and unitary constitutions.

When the Constituent Assembly was established in 1970 to draft, enact and operate a republican constitution, the Tamil Federal Party presented proposals for the establishment of a federal state (Edrisinha et al. 2008: Ch. 11). These proposals were resoundingly and indeed predictably rejected in the Constituent Assembly, whereupon the Federal Party terminated its participation in its deliberations (Wickramaratne 2010). Instead, what became the 1972 Constitution reflected a radical centralization of all political power and legal authority in the legislature, the National State Assembly, which would necessarily have implied a structurally unitary state order (1972 Constitution: §§. 5, 44 and 45). The incorporation of this undiluted form of parliamentary sovereignty, however, was further reinforced by Section 2, which stated that, 'The Republic of Sri Lanka is a Unitary State'. The same provision was replicated in the successor 1978 Constitution as its Article 2, with the additional protection of entrenchment by referendum (Article 83), which is the current constitution of Sri Lanka.

Given that the theme of centralization characterizes Sri Lanka's constitutional evolution from the consolidation of the British colonial state by the Colebrooke-Cameron reforms of 1833 (Mendis 1956; Wilson 1988), the express inclusion of the term 'unitary state' in Section 2/ Article 2 of the republican constitutions may not seem a revolutionary change or innovation. But in registering the wholesale repudiation by the Sinhalese majority represented in the Constituent Assembly of Tamil aspirations to autonomy within a united and republican but federal state, it had the momentous consequence of driving the political transformation of Tamil nationalism from parliamentary agitation to armed secessionism (Loganathan 1996; Wilson 2000; Edrisinha et al. 2008: Chs. 12, 13). Nevertheless, the unitary state clause remained largely a descriptive, if symbolically divisive, feature of the republican constitutional order, until political circumstances forced the government to introduce devolution in 1987 through the Thirteenth Amendment to the 1978 Constitution, which was when it assumed major significance as a source of normative guidance for constitutional adjudication.

By 1987, the Sri Lankan state and Tamil militants were in a state of active and escalating armed conflict. The Thirteenth Amendment was the result of the Indo-Lanka Accord of 1987, by which the neighbouring government of India, by then an active participant in the Sri Lankan conflict, undertook to disarm the Tamil rebels in return for the commitment of the government of Sri Lanka to devolve power to newly created Provincial Councils, including a Tamil-majority Council in the Northern and Eastern Provinces (Loganathan 1996). At this time, devolution was actively opposed by the Sinhala majority in the south and it was even less popular than ever because of the perception of India's strong-arm tactics on the Sri Lankan government. At the other end of the ethnic divide, the devolution settlement agreed between the Indian and Sri Lankan governments was far short of the federal constitution that even parliamentary Tamil nationalists demanded, although many of them returned to Parliament following the Thirteenth Amendment under pressure from India. More extreme Tamil groups like the LTTE rejected the deal and went to war with the Indian Peace Keeping Force sent under the terms of the Indo-Lanka Accord, and subsequently with the Sri Lankan military, until they were finally defeated on the battlefield in 2009.

The legal scheme of devolution, in the form of a lengthy constitutional amendment and consequential ordinary legislation, was challenged at Bill-stage before the Supreme Court by a large number of petitioners for inconsistency with a number of provisions of the 1978 Constitution, including the provision declaring Sri Lanka to be a unitary state. This provision is entrenched against amendment by the procedural requirements of a two-thirds parliamentary majority and a referendum. While the government in 1987 did enjoy the necessary majority in Parliament, it was reluctant in the extreme to put the proposal to referendum, where it more than likely would have been defeated. Thus, the Supreme Court's determination that the Thirteenth Amendment Bill was *intra vires* the constitution assumed crucial political significance.

Among the provisions entrenched in Article 83 of the 1978 Constitution are Articles 2 and 3, which some petitioners in the *Thirteenth Amendment Case* argued were affected by the provisions of the proposed Thirteenth Amendment and Provincial Councils Bills (Peiris 1989).[6] As already noted, Article 2 provides that 'The Republic of Sri Lanka is a Unitary State'. Article 3 states that 'In the Republic of Sri Lanka, sovereignty is in the People and is inalienable. Sovereignty includes the powers of government, fundamental rights and the franchise'. Thus, two of the main questions put to the Supreme Court in this case were whether devolution in the form set out in the two impugned Bills was inconsistent with the republic being a unitary state, and whether the devolution of legislative and executive powers to Provincial Councils was an unconstitutional alienation of the sovereignty of the people. If the Supreme Court determined that devolution in terms of the two Bills affected the unitary state and the sovereignty of the people in a material way, then a referendum would become necessary in addition to a two-thirds majority in Parliament to validly enact them.

In view of the political and constitutional significance of the matter, the Chief Justice nominated a full bench of all nine judges of the Supreme Court to hear the case. Chief Justice Sharvananda and three other judges, Justices Colin-Thomé, Atukorale and Tambiah, held that the Thirteenth Amendment Bill did not require a referendum, and once the Thirteenth Amendment was enacted by Parliament, the Provincial Councils Bill would also be constitutional. One judge, Justice Ranasinghe, agreed with this view, but held that two clauses of the Thirteenth Amendment Bill would require a referendum. Four other judges, Justices Wanasundera, de Alwis, Seneviratne and de Silva, held that the two Bills required a

[6] *In Re the Thirteenth Amendment to the Constitution and the Provincial Councils Bill* (1987) 2 SLR 312.

referendum. The government deleted the two clauses which Justice Ranasinghe held to require a referendum, thereby securing a narrow majority for the view that neither Bill required a referendum, and proceeded to enact both Bills, which were both certified as validly enacted on 14 November 1987 (as the Thirteenth Amendment to the Constitution, and the Provincial Councils Act, No. 42 of 1987).

In coming to their conclusion that the system of devolution sought to be introduced by the Thirteenth Amendment was consistent with the constitution, the majority of judges had to interpret Articles 2 and 3—and define the concept of the unitary state and the location of sovereignty—in view of the argument that the proposed structure was federal or quasi-federal in nature. The judgement of the majority provided the following definition:

> The term 'unitary' in Article 2 is used in contradistinction to the term 'Federal' which means an association of semi-autonomous units with a distribution of sovereign powers between the units and the centre. In a Unitary State the national government is legally supreme over all other levels. The essence of a Unitary State is that the sovereignty is undivided, in other words, that the powers of the central government are unrestricted. The two essential qualities of a Unitary State are (1) the supremacy of the central Parliament and (2) the absence of subsidiary sovereign bodies. It does not mean the absence of subsidiary law-making bodies, but it does mean that, they may exist and can be abolished at the discretion of the central authority. (*In Re the Thirteenth Amendment to the Constitution and the Provincial Councils Bill* [1987] 2 SLR 312 at 319)

Considering the structure of devolution set out in the two Bills against this conceptual definition, the majority judgement concluded that,

> The question that arises is whether the 13th Amendment Bill under consideration creates institutions of government which are supreme, independent and not subordinate within their defined spheres. Application of this test demonstrates that both in respect of the exercise of its legislative powers and in respect of exercise of executive powers no exclusive or independent power [is] invested in the Provincial Councils. The Parliament and President have ultimate control over them and remain supreme. (ibid.: 320)

The other major argument put to the Supreme Court by the petitioners was that devolution was inconsistent with Article 3 read with Article 4, which provides that legislative power shall be exercised by Parliament, executive power by the President and judicial power through the courts. Relying on the 'basic structure' doctrine then being developed by the Indian Supreme Court, it was argued that these two provisions established the basic institutional structure of the state for the exercise of the sovereignty of the people (Edrisinha et al. 2008: Ch. 26). It was contended that devolving legislative and executive powers to the proposed Provincial Councils would be an unconstitutional alienation of sovereignty contrary to Article 3, and a contravention of the basic structure of the constitution, since Article 4 did not contemplate any institutions (such as Provincial Councils) other than Parliament, the President and the courts as being entitled to exercise sovereign power (the Thirteenth Amendment Bill did not seek to add Provincial Councils as a separate category of (devolved) institution to those already mentioned in Article 4). It should be noted that Article 4 is not one of the provisions entrenched by Article 83, and therefore, the petitioners were asking the court to regard Article 4 as an inseparable part of Article 3 (which is entrenched).

The majority rejected this argument, while the minority embraced it.[7] It referred to the drafting history of Article 83 to conclude that the framers of the constitution intended to exclude Article 4 from entrenchment, and therefore, it was not open to the court to interpret Article 4 itself as an entrenched provision, or as a part of the entrenched Article 3, when the framers had expressly excluded it. The majority of judges also argued that it was possible to introduce new institutions for the exercise of legislative and executive power, other than those mentioned in Article 4, so long as this did not impinge on the sovereignty of the people as provided in Article 3. In the view of the majority, the Provincial Councils system proposed in the Bills, which exercised only powers delegated by Parliament and the President, did not involve an alienation of the sovereignty of the people.

[7]There is now considerable confusion on this point. Contrary to the majority in the *Thirteenth Amendment Case*, the Supreme Court in *In Re the Nineteenth Amendment to the Constitution* (2002) 3 SLR 85 held that Articles 3 and 4 must be read together, whereas the court in its determination of constitutionality of the latest Nineteenth Amendment Bill (see *Parliamentary Debates* 234(3), 9 April 2015: Cols. 261–284) held that since Article 4 is not entrenched, not all violations of Article 4 would result in a violation of Article 3. There is thus no coherent general account of the relationship between these two provisions in the constitutional case law.

The judges in the minority, especially the main dissenting opinion of Justice Wanasundera (*In Re the Thirteenth Amendment to the Constitution and the Provincial Councils Bill* [1987] 2 SLR 312 at 333–383), offered a powerful critique of these findings of the majority. In their view, the framework of devolution proposed by the two Bills would establish a federal or quasi-federal form of government that was contrary to the unitary state and the basic structure of the 1978 Constitution. Justice Wanasundera noted that the Provincial Councils would have the power to make statutes 'which enjoy at least parity with laws made by Parliament', enact statutes 'that can suspend or render inoperative laws made by Parliament', that they would enjoy 'plenary power' to legislate in respect of competences set out in the Provincial Council List, and enjoy 'terms of equality' with Parliament in respect of the competencies in the Concurrent List. He further noted that the institutional structure and the devolved distribution of legislative and executive competences in the Thirteenth Amendment would be entrenched by virtue of the special procedures in Article 154G, and that 'Parliament has disabled itself by placing fetters upon itself in the exercise of legislative power' in matters in which it hitherto had enjoyed unlimited power (ibid.: 351–352). This being a quasi-federal system that would alter the basic unitary structure of the constitution, the minority concluded that the approval of the people at a referendum was necessary to validly enact the two Bills. However, as noted above, the government made changes to the Thirteenth Amendment Bill so as to address Justice Ranasinghe's concerns and thereby secured a majority in the Supreme Court for the view that a referendum would not be necessary.

In reconciling the devolution of power with the existing structure of a centralized unitary state as envisaged by the 1978 Constitution, the interpretational choices available to the majority in the Supreme Court were perhaps limited, in the presence of Articles 2 and 3 in the constitutional text and the arguments put to court with regard to them. The majority were impelled to stress that ultimate power and supremacy continued to be vested with the central Parliament and the President. Notwithstanding the views of the minority (subsequently endorsed by some commentators as being the better view in law: Egalahewa 2010), this meant that Provincial Councils came to be regarded from the outset as subordinate bodies to central institutions. This had implications for the way in which devolution was implemented, with administrative practices and subsequently enacted central legislation clearly being based on a notion of central supremacy and superiority (Welikala 2010).

The introduction of devolution therefore was the occasion on which the normative force of the unitary principle and its pervasive reach within the constitutional architecture of the Sri Lankan state became most visible. While it did not prevent devolution—as it would have had the minority view in the Supreme Court prevailed—the express unitary state provision certainly ensured the subordination of any form of devolved institution to a hierarchical relationship with central institutions, in addition to its implied limitation on any further spatial devolution.

Furthermore, the textual/interpretational link between Articles 2 and 3 emphasized the conceptual nexus between the unitary state and a unitary sovereignty, reposed in a unitary 'People'. The unitary state as the emblem of a unitary sovereignty has been one of the principal arguments of those opposed to the accommodation of Tamil claims through power-sharing and especially territorial autonomy (de Silva 2008: Ch. 5). Implicit in this unitary view of sovereignty is not only the notion that it is illimitable and indivisible, but also that it can only be reposed and exercised by a people (or political community or nation), defined in monistic terms, resident within a single territory. Moreover, in this view, the nation is synonymous with the state. Thus, the unitary view with regard not only to constitutional form, but also sovereignty, territory and the nation, has presented major ideological and theoretical impediments to the recognition of plural national identities in Sri Lanka, as indeed it has elsewhere (Tierney 2006; Norman 2006). The explicit association of the majority ethno-religious nationalism with the power and indeed the very identity of the state as a whole (Roberts 1978, 2013) exacerbates the effect of this problem for constitutional approaches to the accommodation of pluralism in general, and the Tamil claim to distinctive nationhood in particular.

Ethnic relations in post-colonial Sri Lanka reached its nadir with the anti-Tamil pogrom of July 1983, which also marked the onset of civil war. In the wake of the riots, Parliament enacted the Sixth Amendment to the 1978 Constitution, which introduced a comprehensive prohibition on even the peaceful advocacy of secession and banned any political party or association from having as its aims and objectives the establishment of a separate state within the territory of the island. This was made a criminal offence triable directly by the Court of Appeal, and upon conviction, a person could be deprived of civic rights for seven years and to forfeiture of property. A new oath of office including a specific undertaking to desist from advocating secession was also introduced, and all elected officers including MPs and local councillors expected to take it, with failure to do so leading to loss of office. The Sixth Amendment also set down a procedure whereby any person could move the Supreme Court for a declaration that a party or association had secession as one of their aims or objectives, and if the court made such a declaration, the party would be proscribed and its members exposed to the criminal and civic liabilities just mentioned. This was the procedure that was triggered by a petitioner leading to the judgement in *Chandrasoma v. Senathiraja*, and this was the first occasion it was set in motion.

The Judgement in *Chandrasoma v. Senathiraja*

The present case was triggered by a petitioner in March 2014 by applying to the Supreme Court for a declaration that the Federal Party had secession as one of its aims, and for the consequent application of a proscription on it as required by the Sixth Amendment. In terms of the Sixth Amendment, the Secretary to the Federal Party was cited as the principal respondent in the application. The judgement was delivered by Chief Justice Dep, with Justices Abeyrathne and Goonerathne agreeing.

The court quickly found that some averments of the petition were misdirected in that they were based on a misunderstanding of the Tamil language formulations of clauses of the Federal Party constitution, in particular whether certain substitutions of Sanskrit-origin words with Pure Tamil words in 2008, served to shift the party's substantive aims from federalism to confederation. These were disposed of by clarifications sought and provided by the Official Languages Department, and conceded by the petitioner (*Chandrasoma v. Senathiraja* 2017: 3–10).

Another matter that was disposed of without too much trouble was the petitioner's contention that the Federal Party had at one time subscribed to the controversial Vaddukoddai Resolution (1976), which brought together nearly all Tamil nationalists both parliamentary and militant, in demanding a separate and independent Tamil state (Edrisinha et al. 2008: Ch. 12). It was conceded by the respondent that there was a period in which the Federal Party and its members had subscribed to the principle of a separate state, and had accordingly forfeited their seats in Parliament, but that this had not been the case since 1987 (or before 1976). In 1983, when the Sixth Amendment was passed, all Federal Party MPs including the then Leader of the Opposition refused to take the oath and thus lost their seats. They returned to Parliament (and took the Sixth Amendment oath) following the enactment of the Thirteenth Amendment in 1987. It was moreover established that it was an umbrella political organization known as the Tamil United Liberation Front (TULF) rather than the Federal Party itself that had subscribed to the Vaddukoddai Resolution, and the TULF was not a party to the present proceedings (*Chandrasoma v. Senathiraja* 2017: 10–11).

In assessing the arguments of the petitioner and respondent, the court recounted a compact history of the evolution of Tamil constitutional claims since independence and in doing so relied *inter alia* upon the *Quebec Secession Reference* and the views of Judge Cançado Trindade of the International Court of Justice in the *Kosovo Advisory Opinion* (2010) in elucidating a number of critical constitutional concepts, including sovereignty, federalism and most prominently, the principle of self-determination of peoples. Chief Justice Dep was persuaded that the Federal Party's claims to shared sovereignty and federal autonomy within the framework of a united and undivided Sri Lanka, as repeatedly reaffirmed in public statements including election manifestoes, were legitimate political claims which did not amount to an advocacy of secession in breach of the Sixth Amendment (ibid.: 17). The application was accordingly dismissed without costs.

Discerning the court's own views on key substantive points, however, is made somewhat difficult by the way the judgement is written and structured. In large part, the judgement is a presentation of the petitioner's arguments followed by the respondent's responses. In the light of its final conclusions being based on the court's acceptance of the respondent's arguments almost entirely, it is reasonable to assume that the recitation of the respondent's arguments must be construed as being endorsement rather than mere narration. If this is true, then the court appears to accept the following contentions.

The first point of significance is the court's acknowledgement that the old constitutional classification as between unitary states and federations is now increasingly blurred and unstable (even though it premises this observation on a distinction between 'federation' and 'confederation', the presumed clarity of which is, arguably, equally unstable). According to Chief Justice Dep,

> It is established that there is a clear distinction between [the] words 'federation' and 'confederation'. The main issue in this case is whether advocating the establishment of a federal state [is] tantamount to establishment of a separate state … The labelling of states as unitary and federal sometimes may be misleading. There could be unitary states with features or attributes of a federal state and vice versa. In a unitary state if more powers are given to the units it could be considered as a federal state. Similarly in a federal state if the centre is powerful and the power is concentrated in the centre it could be considered as a unitary state. Therefore sharing of sovereignty, devolution of power and decentralization will pave the way for a federal form of government within a unitary state. The Thirteen Amendment to the Constitution devolved powers on the provinces. The ITAK is advocating for a federalist form of government by devolving more powers to the provinces within the framework of a unitary state. Advocating for a federal form of government within the existing state could not be considered as advocating separatism. (ibid.: 17)

While these observations might seem irredeemably confused and confusing for those who prefer neat positivist categories of constitutional classification, it can be argued that the court is describing complex state-formation phenomena in plural polities that are now widely accepted in comparative politics and constitutional law (Keating 2001: Ch. 4). More specifically in relation to Sri Lanka, it is important to note that the court is not sanctioning federalization through some sort of potential 'holding together' process (Stepan 1999), because it only contemplates the possibility of 'a federalist form of government by devolving more powers to the provinces *within the framework of a unitary state*'. It is questionable whether this is actually the position of the Federal Party, which, as readily apparent from the policy documents cited by the court itself, has consistently demanded federalism within a 'united state', not a 'unitary state'. Whether this is a mistake, or the result of a sleight of hand, is open to conjecture, although the court's observation in the last paragraph of the judgement that 'It is established that the ITAK support or advocate the establishment of a federal State within [a] *united Sri Lanka*' suggests error and a lack of care—common in Sri Lankan discourse—as to the significance of the difference (*Chandrasoma v. Senathiraja* 2017: 18, emphasis added).

However, in recognizing that forms of federalism can, in fact, exist within formally unitary states through processes of devolution and multilevel governance, the court is implicitly acknowledging a well-known distinction between 'federalism' and 'federation' that has been made in comparative politics and constitutionalism for quite a while (King 1982; Burgess 2006: 2). But this is a completely novel proposition to make in Sri Lankan constitutional discourse, which as the discussion in the preceding section demonstrated has remained stubbornly wedded to the older formalist categories. Any inconsistency of this substantively fluid attitude to multilevel governance with the rigidly formalist definition of unitary and federal states in the key precedent of the *Thirteenth Amendment Case* does not seem to trouble Chief Justice Dep, who cited the argument of the respondent with seeming approval on this point:

> ...advocacy for sharing sovereignty along federal lines does not tantamount [sic] to demanding a separate State. Instead, as per the interpretation of federalism in the judgment given by Chief Justice Sharvananda, in the Thirteenth Amendment Determination, it is merely a "distribution of sovereign powers between the units and the centre" unlike in a unitary State where sovereignty is undivided. (*Chandrasoma v. Senathiraja* 2017: 10)

Some may find this casual treatment of potentially incommensurable approaches an imprecise use of language that obfuscates a genuine conceptual separation between federal and unitary states, while others may criticize it for its inadequacy of reasoning. However, to the extent that the court was simply concerned with the question of whether or not the advocacy of federalism also amounted to an advocacy of potential secession—as seems to have been the underlying thrust of the petitioner's argument—then it was surely right in concluding that they are in no sense the same thing.

More broadly, this judicial endorsement of an approach to the vertical internal structuring of the state that is less concerned with classificatory formalism and more with what is required substantively and normatively by the demands of societal pluralism is a refreshing contribution to Sri Lankan constitutional discourse. It could help future constitution makers transcend the otiose and reductionist unitary v. federal debate on which so many constitutional debates have foundered in Sri Lanka, and focus attention on the more constructive path of conceiving of devolution and power-sharing based on practical needs and realities rather than abstract and artificial classifications.

The petitioner's argument with regard to the Federal Party's claim of a Tamil right to self-determination was that this necessarily includes an implicit assertion of a right to secession at will, even if that option is not for the time being exercised, because if a people are to fully control their political status, self-determination must necessarily include the right to form an independent state (ibid.: 14–15). In response, the respondent asserted that the Tamils were a people for the purposes of the international law principle of self-determination, including the right in the form expressed in the two Covenants. However, they qualified this by reference to the internal/external distinction in the exercise of the right recognized by the International Court of Justice in the *Kosovo Advisory Opinion* and by the framework established by the Canadian Supreme Court in the *Quebec Secession Reference* by which there would be no unilateral right to external self-determination unless conditions were such that the internal exercise of the right was systematically prevented or violated (ibid.: 15–17). The court also adduced the academic views of the Canadian scholar of federalism, Ronald Watts, in support of the accommodationist view that internal autonomy for group claims to self-determination abates if not precludes secessionist movements and sentiments (ibid.: 16).

This is a more contemporary view of self-determination, taking into account new developments in international law and practice as well as comparative constitutional law (Cassese 1998: Ch. 5; Barten 2015; Welikala 2008). The old principle of self-determination which was almost always regarded as applying only to decolonizing contexts is now of course understood to be much broader (to include sub-state national claims within existing states), deeper (to include general democratic entitlements within existing states) and more focussed (by refining the objective circumstances of secession as a remedy of last resort, through the development of the internal aspect of self-determination for sub-state peoples).

In all these respects, the Supreme Court agreed with the Federal Party's contentions in holding that '…it is clear that the right to self-determination has an internal dimension, in that it could be exercised within the country to the benefit of a "people" inside the country. Thus, the invocation of self-determination does not amount to a demand for a separate State, as the right is sometimes to be used internally within the territory of an existing State' (ibid.: 17).

While of course the principle of self-determination so implemented bars a unilateral right to secession, as the Canadian court held, the necessary implication of this conclusion is that Sri Lanka seems now to have been judicially recognized as a multi-*demoi* polity, with the Tamils having an entitlement to some form of constitutional accommodation of their claim to internal self-government. It follows, further, from this pluralistic understanding of the societal foundations of the Sri Lankan state that the monistic concept of sovereignty underpinning the current constitutional order would have to be reconsidered.

In the Indo-Lanka Accord preceding the Thirteenth Amendment in 1987, the Sri Lankan government had acknowledged that Sri Lanka is a 'multi-ethnic, multilingual and multi-religious plural society' (Loganathan 1996). Such a conception of societal pluralism is entirely consistent with a monistic view of Sri Lankan nationality and sovereignty. The implications of the present judgement, however, are much more fundamental. Because of the normative charge added, through the notion of internal self-determination, to the Tamil federalism demand, the logic of the judgement opens up major questions of re-territorialization and pluralization of peoples and sovereignties. Only a plurinational and asymmetric—and not an orthodox, mono-national—form of federalism (or other non-federal devolved constitutional structure or autonomy arrangement) can accommodate a sub-state exercise of collective internal self-determination. In short, it appears the Supreme Court has indirectly—or unwittingly—endorsed the principles encapsulated in the Oslo Communique of 2003.

The Constitutional Implications of *Chandrasoma v. Senathiraja*

In assessing the deeper constitutional implications of the judgement, it must be clearly acknowledged in fairness to the court that all it was doing was to draw conclusions, on the facts and arguments put before it, about whether the policy stances of the Federal Party in relation to federalism, Tamil peoplehood and self-determination amounted to the advocacy of secession as prohibited by the Sixth Amendment. It was not, for example, pronouncing upon a concrete constitutional amendment proposal. In concluding that the Federal Party had not violated the Sixth Amendment, the court was not seeking to alter settled law or reinterpret doctrines established in prior cases such as the *Thirteenth Amendment Case*. This may explain why it made no effort to engage with its precedents on these matters in any great depth. However, it cannot also be doubted that in accepting propositions like the Tamil claim to peoplehood for the purposes of the international law of self-determination, or that a right to internal self-determination is available to Tamils within Sri Lanka so understood, the court was giving judicial approval to normative perspectives on these principles that are fundamentally at odds with the tenor of its previous approaches to such questions. This is why the sparsity of its reasoning in this case constantly raises questions in the reader as to the extent to which the court has fully contemplated the conceptual ramifications of its conclusions.

If we take what the court has said at face value, however, there are number of serious questions of constitutional theory that arise, of which two are especially important. The first concerns the necessary disaggregation of 'nation' and 'state' that must follow if it is accepted that there are more than one 'people' (or nation) within the state, which then requires a fundamental reappraisal of the notion that the republic of Sri Lanka is a 'nation state'. The second implication, which flows from the first, is that the unitary conception of sovereignty that has so far informed Sri Lankan constitutional self-understandings likewise requires a major re-evaluation. Let us briefly consider these issues in turn.

The equation of nation and state in the orthodox modernist conception of the nation state that underpins the Sri Lankan constitution becomes epistemologically untenable once it is conceded that the Tamils are a people for the purposes of the international law of self-determination. This communally pluralistic understanding of the empirical character of the Sri Lankan polity goes beyond the recognition of mere ethnic, cultural or linguistic diversity to a full-blown acknowledgement that the polity is, in fact if not in law, composed of multiple nations. The idea that there is, or can be, only one 'People' within Sri Lanka, as the constitution repeatedly affirms, has been fatally undermined by the Supreme Court. The only type of constitutional design that is appropriate for an adequate reflection of these plural societal foundations of Sri Lanka, it follows, is not only one that is federalist rather than unitary in form, but one that is normatively informed by the principles of plurinational constitutionalism grounded on the rejection of the 'monistic *demos* thesis' of traditional accounts of the nation state (Tierney 2007: 230).

Second, the *Chandrasoma* decision sends reverberations down the highly formalistic and positivist conception of sovereignty that dominates

Sri Lankan constitutional discourse. In this respect, Sri Lankan legal discourse is a classic example of its kind as a former British colony that has inherited the doctrines, concepts and modes of thinking of nineteenth-century English public law and remains fossilized in the colonial age. Unlike in the Canadian experience in which the challenge of sub-state nationalism gave birth to an efflorescence in post-imperial constitutional thought, Sri Lankan legal elites have only retreated into the comfort of orthodoxy in the face of the challenge. Hence the repetitive invocations in Sri Lankan legal discourse of the monistic conception of the nation (or 'the People'), the unitary and static conception of sovereignty (and hence of the necessary constitutional form of the state), and the positivist legalism that clothes an ideologically particularistic view of the state in an apparently politically impartial language of legal legitimacy, objectivity and universalism.[8]

But this orthodox version of unitary sovereignty and constitutional form no longer holds if it is accepted, as the Supreme Court has done, that there are multiple sub-state peoples exercising self-determination, which if even only internally within the existing territory of the state must surely entail entitlements to self-government that demand major changes to the unitary state. In other words, the logic of the argument accepted by the Supreme Court in this case is that there are multiple sovereignties within the Sri Lankan polity attaching to the plural peoples within its territory, the exercise of which is constrained only by the presumption of consistency with the territorial integrity of the state, and that too subject to the exemptions identified in the Canadian *Reference* (and by the International Court of Justice in the *Kosovo Advisory Opinion* of 2010). This analysis lays bare the profound inadequacies and structural injustices of the current constitutional framework of Sri Lanka, and points to a radical reopening of major normative and institutional questions about how the Sri Lankan state is internally restructured in appreciation of its multinational character.

[8]For an illustration of this viewpoint, see, e.g., de Silva (2008: 74). For the judicial expression of a broadly similar perspective, see the dissenting opinion of Justice Wanasundera *In Re the Thirteenth Amendment to the Constitution and the Provincial Councils Bill* (1987) 2 SLR 312 at 333–383, which is critically discussed in Coomaraswamy (1997: Ch. 7).

Conclusion

There is some satisfaction to be gained from the fact that the petitioner's excess of zeal in trying to trigger the draconian Sixth Amendment—for the first time in over thirty years since its enactment—to get the moderate Federal Party proscribed, or at the least, subjected to major embarrassment, boomeranged when the Supreme Court instead agreed with the respondent's contentions in a wholly unexpected way. But whether or not this decision reflects a liberal turn in Sri Lankan constitutional law and judicial attitudes remains to be seen. It is not at all clear if the court itself appreciated the deeper consequences of its conclusions, and it may well resile from them if and when it does. In any case, the doctrine of precedent in Sri Lanka does not operate as strongly as it does in other common law jurisdictions, and it is not unlikely that a future court may distinguish it as cursorily as this bench did with the *Thirteenth Amendment Case*, or indeed, simply ignore the decision.[9] Perhaps more importantly, the liberal potential of the deeper implications of the judgement is likely to prove far too radical for Sri Lanka's conservative and majoritarian political culture. Any attempt to use it as a cue for a rejuvenation of constitutional reform in a pluralistic direction is thus likely to meet with a stiff ethnocratic backlash from Sinhala-Buddhist nationalists. It would seem, therefore, that a quiet burial in the dusty annals of the Supreme Court's case law is the most likely fate of this otherwise praiseworthy judgement.

References

Anketell, Niran (2017, December), "The Unitary State, Parliamentary Sovereignty, and the Sovereignty of the People: A Reappraisal", in *Bar Association Law Journal*, Colombo, 2.

Barten, Ulrike (2015), *Minorities, Minority Rights and Internal Self-Determination*, Springer, Dordrecht.

Burgess, Michael (2006), *Comparative Federalism: Theory and Practice*, Routledge, London.

Cassese, Antonio (1998), *The Self-Determination of Peoples: A Legal Appraisal*, Cambridge University Press, Cambridge.

Choudhry, Sujit (2008a), "Does the World Need More Canada? The Politics of the Canadian Model in Constitutional Politics and Political Theory", in Sujit

[9] See, e.g., note 7, *supra*.

Choudhry (ed.), *Constitutional Design for Divided Societies: Integration or Accommodation?* Oxford University Press, Oxford, Ch. 5.

Choudhry, Sujit (2008b), "Bridging Comparative Politics and Comparative Constitutional Law: Constitutional Design in Divided Societies", in Sujit Choudhry (ed.), *Constitutional Design for Divided Societies: Integration or Accommodation?* Oxford University Press, Oxford, Ch. 1.

Coomaraswamy, Radhika (1997), *Ideology and the Constitution: Essays on Constitutional Jurisprudence*, Konark, New Delhi.

Department of Census and Statistics, Government of Sri Lanka (2012), "Census of Population and Housing of Sri Lanka", Table A3, http://www.statistics.gov.lk/PopHouSat/CPH2011/Pages/Activities/Reports/FinalReport/Population/FinalPopulation.pdf.

de Silva, Herman Leonard (2008), *Sri Lanka a Nation in Conflict: Threats to Sovereignty, Territorial Integrity, Democratic Governance and Peace*, Visidunu Prakasakayo, Colombo.

Edrisinha, Rohan (2008), "Sri Lanka: Constitutions Without Constitutionalism, A Tale of Three and a Half Constitutions", in Rohan Edrisinha and Asanga Welikala (eds.), *Essays on Federalism in Sri Lanka*, Centre for Policy Alternatives, Colombo, Ch. I.

Edrisinha, Rohan, Gomez, Mario, Thamilmaran, V.T. and Welikala, Asanga eds. (2008), *Power-Sharing in Sri Lanka: Constitutional and Political Documents, 1926–2008*, Centre for Policy Alternatives, Colombo.

Egalahewa, Uditha (2010), "The Judicial Approach to the Devolution of Power: The Interpretation of the Thirteenth Amendment to the Constitution", in Lakshman Marasinghe and Jayampathy Wickramaratne (eds.), *13th Amendment: Essays on Practice*, Stamford Lake, Colombo, Ch. 5.

Jayawickrama, Nihal (2012), "Reflections on the Making and Content of the 1972 Constitution: An Insider's Perspective", in Asanga Welikala (ed.), *The Sri Lankan Republic at 40: Reflections on Constitutional History, Theory and Practice*, Centre for Policy Alternatives, Colombo, Ch. 1, http://republicat40.org/wp-content/uploads/2013/01/Reflections-on-the-Making-and-Content-of-the-1972-Constitution1.pdf.

Keating, Michael (2001), *Plurinational Democracy: Stateless Nations in a Post-Sovereign Era*, Oxford University Press, Oxford.

King, Preston (1982), *Federalism and Federation*, Croom Helm, London.

Loganathan, Ketheshwaran (1996), *Sri Lanka: Lost Opportunities—Past Attempts at Resolving Ethnic Conflict*, Centre for Policy Research and Analysis, Colombo.

McGarry, John, O'Leary, Brendan and Simeon, Richard (2008), "Integration or Accommodation? The Enduring Debate in Conflict Regulation", in Sujit Choudhry (ed.), *Constitutional Design for Divided Societies: Integration or Accommodation?* Oxford University Press, Oxford, Ch. 2.

Mendis, Garrett C. ed. (1956), *The Colebrooke-Cameron Papers: Documents on British Colonial Policy in Ceylon, 1796–1833*, Oxford University Press, Oxford.

Norman, Wayne (2006), *Negotiating Nationalism: Nation-Building, Federalism and Secession in the Multinational State*, Oxford University Press, Oxford.

Peiris, Gamini Lakshman (1989), "Provincial Autonomy Within a Unitary Constitutional Framework: The Sri Lankan Crisis", in *Comparative and International Law Journal of Southern Africa*, XXII, 166.

Roberts, Michael (1978), "Ethnic Conflict in Sri Lanka and Sinhalese Perspectives: Barriers to Accommodation", in *Modern Asian Studies*, 12 (3), 353–376.

Roberts, Michael (2013), "Mixed Messages and Bland Oversimplification in President Rajapaksa's Independence Day Speech", *Groundviews*, February 11, 2013, http://groundviews.org/2013/02/11/mixed-messages-and-bland-over-simplification-in-president-rajapaksas-independence-day-speech/.

Stepan, Alfred C. (1999), "Federalism and Democracy: Beyond the US Model", in *Journal of Democracy*, 10 (4), 19–34.

Supreme Court of Sri Lanka, *In Re the Nineteenth Amendment to the Constitution* (2002) 3 SLR 85.

Supreme Court of Sri Lanka, In the Matter of Applications Under Article 121(1) of the Constitution, A Bill entitled 'Nineteenth Amendment to the Constitution', *Parliamentary Debates*, 234 (3), April 9, 2015, Cols. 261–284.

Supreme Court of Sri Lanka, *Chandrasoma v. Senathiraja and Others* (2017), SC SPL 03/2014, SC Minutes, August 4, 2017, http://www.supremecourt.lk/images/documents/sc_spl_03_2014.pdf.

Tambiah, Stanley Jeyarajah (1991), *Sri Lanka: Ethnic Fratricide and the Dismantling of Democracy*, University of Chicago Press, Chicago.

Tierney, Stephen (2006), *Constitutional Law and National Pluralism*, Oxford University Press, Oxford.

Tierney, Stephen (2007), "We the Peoples': Constituent Power and Constitutionalism in Plurinational States", in Martin Loughlin and Neil Walker (eds.), *The Paradox of Constitutionalism: Constituent Power and Constitutional Form*, Oxford University Press, Oxford, Ch. 12.

Uyangoda, Jayadeva (2011), "Travails of State Reform in the Context of Protracted Civil War in Sri Lanka", in Kristian Stokke and Jayadeva Uyangoda (eds.), *Liberal Peace in Question: Politics of State and Market Reform in Sri Lanka*, Anthem Press, London, Ch. 2.

Welikala, Asanga (2008), "The Right to Internal Self-Determination in International Law", in Rohan Edrisinha and Asanga Welikala (eds.), *Essays on Federalism in Sri Lanka*, Centre for Policy Alternatives, Colombo, Ch. VII.

Welikala, Asanga (2010), "Devolution Within the Unitary State: A Constitutional Assessment of the Thirteenth Amendment with Reference to the Experience in the Eastern Province", in *Devolution in the Eastern*

Province: Implementation of the Thirteenth Amendment and Public Perceptions, 2008–2010, Centre for Policy Alternatives, Colombo.

Welikala, Asanga ed. (2012), *The Sri Lankan Republic at 40: Reflections on Constitutional History, Theory and Practice*, Centre for Policy Alternatives, Colombo, http://republicat40.org.

Welikala, Asanga (2016), *The Sri Lankan Conception of the Unitary State: Theory, Practice and History*, CPA Papers on Constitutional Reform No. 3, July 2016, http://constitutionalreforms.org/wp-content/uploads/2016/06/CPA-Working-Paper-1.pdf.

Welikala, Asanga (2017), *The Idea of Constitutional Incrementalism*, CPA Working Papers on Constitutional Reform No. 14, January 2017, http://constitutional-reforms.org/wp-content/uploads/2016/06/Working-Paper-14.pdf.

Welikala, Asanga (Forthcoming), "The Limits of Elite-Led Constitutional Transitions: Sri Lanka's Failed Peace Process and the Continuing Challenge of Ethno-Territorial Cleavages", in George Anderson and Sujit Choudhry (eds.), *Territory and Power in Constitutional Transitions*, Oxford University Press, New York.

Wickramaratne, Jayampathy (2010), "1972 in Retrospect", in Tissa Jayatilaka (ed.), *Sirimavo: Honouring the World's First Woman Prime Minister*, The Bandaranaike Museum Committee, Colombo, 63–77.

Wilson, Alfred Jeyaratnam (1988), *The Break-Up of Sri Lanka: The Sinhalese-Tamil Conflict*, Hurst & Co., London.

Wilson, Alfred Jeyaratnam (2000), *Sri Lankan Tamil Nationalism: Its Origins and Development in the 19th and 20th Centuries*, Penguin, New Delhi.

The *Reference* and Ethiopian Constitutionalism

Erika Arban

> Every Nation, Nationality and People in Ethiopia has an unconditional right to self-determination, including the right to secession.
>
> [Article 39(1) of the Constitution of the Federal Democratic Republic of Ethiopia]

Introduction

At first blush, it might appear that an imaginary thread links together the *Secession Reference* (hereinafter, the "*Reference*") to the current Ethiopian Constitution: in fact, although the latter predates the

Erika Arban is a Postdoctoral research fellow at the Centre for Comparative Constitutional Studies, Melbourne Law School; lecturer at the Faculty of Law, University of Antwerp. This research was fully funded by the Australian Government through the Australian Research Council (ARC) Laureate Program "Balancing Diversity and Social Cohesion in Democratic Constitutions."

E. Arban (✉)
University of Melbourne, Melbourne, VIC, Australia
e-mail: erika.arban@unimelb.edu.au

G. Delledonne and G. Martinico (eds.), *The Canadian Contribution to a Comparative Law of Secession*,
https://doi.org/10.1007/978-3-030-03469-6_8

Reference by a few years, it seems to explicitly address some of the major points raised in it by the Supreme Court of Canada (hereinafter, "SCC"), first and foremost the entrenchment of a secession clause in Article 39(1) Const. However, at a closer scrutiny, this link between the two becomes less obvious, due to the unique genesis and evolution of the Ethiopian federal and constitutional architecture.

The important legacy of the *Reference*, however, goes well beyond the discussion on the legitimacy and viability of secession under Canadian law. In fact, this decision is rich with insightful reflections on fundamental constitutional principles such as federalism, democracy, constitutionalism and the rule of law, and respect for minorities: all these principles have been embraced—to a more or less extent—by many democratic systems around the world, including Ethiopia. The *Reference* has thus bequeathed to posterity an invaluable testament to constitutional law, and this volume offers a unique opportunity to rediscover this precious legacy and explore it comparatively.

After a brief historical introduction in Part I, this chapter proposes to broadly revisit the principles discussed in the *Reference* to assess their role and impact in the Ethiopian Constitution. More specifically, Part II offers an overview of the principle of federalism in Ethiopia, while Part III discusses respect for minorities and ethnicity as central tenets of the current Ethiopian federal architecture. Part IV is devoted to constitutionalism and the rule of law, and Part V thoroughly analyses the secession clause as combined with the democratic principle. The conclusion will assess lessons and legacy of the *Reference* in the Ethiopian context.

From a methodological standpoint, the approach used for this contribution is mainly doctrinal, in the sense that I look at the text of the Constitution and assess how it resonates with the *Reference*. I am, however, aware that gaps exist between the text and the actual practice, particularly in complex scenarios such as Ethiopia.

Historical Background

Although it shares many features (e.g. ethnicity) with most African countries, a unique characteristic that distinguishes Ethiopia from the rest of the continent is that, in addition to enjoying a long history of statehood, it has never succumbed to European colonialism, except for a very short period of Italian occupation[1] (Abdullahi 1998; Henrard and Smis 2000). In the late 1880s, emperor Menelik reunified the various small kingdoms scattered on the Ethiopian territory with the intention of modernizing the country by building infrastructures such as schools or hospitals (Medlock Wigger 1998). These transformative policies were continued by Haile Selassie, whose main merit was to grant Ethiopia its first written Constitution in 1931, thus establishing a constitutional monarchy with absolute imperial authority (Medlock Wigger 1998). In 1935, Italy did invade Ethiopia, but this occupation was brief, as Haile Selassie defeated the Italians in 1941 with the help of the UK (Medlock Wigger 1998). Haile Selassie revised the Constitution in 1955 to include the protection of certain civil rights and liberties such as freedom of religion and freedom of speech, as well as provisions intending to transform Ethiopia into an attractive foreign investment country (Medlock Wigger 1998). He also pursued centralization and assimilation policies through the imposition of the Amharic language, culture and religion to the other ethnic groups (Van der Beken 2015). Haile Selassie's ruling time came to an end in 1974 after proving himself unable and unwilling to control a horrific famine that devastated parts of the country. Haile Selassie was deposed by the DERG, a military coalition whose chairman Mengistu Haile Mariam became the Head of State (Medlock Wigger 1998). The DERG established what was supposed to be a temporary military regime and secured the support of numerous Ethiopians who were ready to cut ties with the imperial legacy (Medlock Wigger 1998). However, this temporary military government quickly turned into a 17-year rule, during which the DERG not only suspended the existing Constitution, but also implemented social policies inspired by Marxism-Leninism, accepting the financial support of the Soviet Union to militarize Ethiopia (Medlock Wigger 1998; Van der Beken 2015; Henrard and Smis 2000). The influence of Leninist theory profoundly shaped Ethiopian federalism, as will be further explained *infra*. The DERG regime escalated into a dictatorship led by Mengistu and aggravated by another devastating famine in the mid-1980s (Medlock Wigger 1998).

[1] Italy occupied Ethiopia at the end of the XIX century but was defeated by Menelik's army in the battle of Adowa in 1896. A treaty signed in the aftermath left Italy in control only of its colony in Eritrea (Medlock Wigger 1998).

Eventually, this regime collapsed in 1991, when the EPRDF (Ethiopian People's Revolutionary Democratic Front) took over and a transitional government was established, supported by other liberation movements (Medlock Wigger 1998). In this scenario, the TPLF (Tigray People's Liberation Front) became a major player in transforming Ethiopia into a decentralized system of government in 1991, thus paving the road to federalism (Mengie 2015), introduced as part of a major reform project which also included democratization and economic liberalization (Vaughan 2013). The early 1990s were marked also by the secession of Eritrea from Ethiopia, formalized in 1993 (Bihonegn 2015a; Henrard and Smis 2000). The current Constitution—drafted in 1994 and entered into force in 1995—is characterized by the entrenchment of a federal system of government featuring ethnic pluralism and the acknowledgement of extensive rights to the various ethnic groups.

In comparative terms, the Ethiopian legal system is interesting as it blends a number of different legal traditions: in fact, most of the substantive legal codes derive from the civil law tradition, whereas procedural laws are moulded according to the common law, with *shari'a* courts deciding on matters of family and succession law disputes for individuals following Islamic law (Hessebon and Idris 2017).

Ethiopia and the Federalism Principle

In listing it as one of the "four fundamental and organizing principles" of Canadian constitutionalism, the SCC clarifies in the *Reference* that federalism was the "legal response to the underlying political and cultural realities" that have historically existed in Canada, and the "political mechanism by which diversity could be reconciled with unity" (*Reference*, at 43). Furthermore, the SCC indicates that the federal-provincial division of powers, enshrined in the *Constitution Act, 1867*, "was a legal recognition of the diversity that existed among the initial members of Confederation" (*Reference*, at 43).

The choice to opt for federalism in Ethiopia was intended to address similar concerns of reconciliation of (ethnic) diversity and social cohesion: in a country profoundly divided along ethnic, linguistic and cultural-religious lines, federalism seemed to be the only tool that could help compromising among centripetal and centrifugal forces and thus "accommodate that diversity within a single nation" (*Reference*, at 43). In fact, with a population of over 96 million people, Ethiopia is one of the most populated countries in Africa, with a considerable ethnic and religious diversity: out of about 80 different ethnic groups sharing its territory, only 10 have a population of more than one million people (Hessebon and Idris 2017).

The federal nature of Ethiopia is explicitly stated in Article 1 of the 1994 Constitution in the following terms:

> This Constitution establishes a <u>Federal</u> and Democratic State structure. Accordingly, the Ethiopian state shall be known as The <u>Federal</u> Democratic Republic of Ethiopia. (emphasis added)

The Constitution further provides that Ethiopia is composed by federal and state governments (Article 50(1)(2)), the nine states in which it is divided being Tigray, Afar, Amhara, Oromia, Somalia, Benshangul/Gumuz, Southern Nations, Nationalities and Peoples, Gambela Peoples, and Harari Peoples (Article 47(1)).[2] None of these states is ethnically *pure* (in the sense that their population does not belong to one ethnic group only, although in some states one ethnic group may constitute the numeric majority), and internal minorities are often blended with regional majorities (Fessha and Van der Beken 2013; Van der Beker 2013).[3] However, more than 85% of the population live in five states, which are named after the dominant ethnic group in each of them (Tigray, Amhara, Oromia, Somalia, and Afar). Although they all enjoy the same powers, the various regional states are de facto asymmetrical when it comes to population, socio-economic development, composition, etc. (Bihonegn 2015a).

Legislative, executive and judicial powers are divided between federal and state governments (Article 50(2) Const.). In this regard, the Constitution enumerates the legislative powers belonging exclusively to

[2] Although the Constitution refers to them as "states," they are also called "regional states" or "regions" (a legacy of the terminology adopted in the pre-federation period (1991–1995)) (Regassa 2004). In Amharic language, these constituent units are called *kilils*: the *kilil* of Southern Nations, Nationalities and Peoples is the most heterogeneous, being the home of more than 56 different ethnic groups (Bihonegn 2015a, citing Vaughan and Tronvoll).

[3] A further classification is commonly made between *indigenous* and *non-indigenous* minorities, depending on whether these minorities inhabit their region or not. Indigenous internal minorities can claim more extensive rights protection based on federal and regional constitutions than the non-indigenous counterparts (Fessha and Van der Beken 2013).

the federal government (Article 51) as well as the (more limited) powers exclusively vested in the states (Article 52(2)), which also enjoy residual powers (Article 52(1)). When necessary, the federal government may delegate to the states its exclusive powers (Article 50(9)). Some powers—mainly in the ambit of taxation—are shared between the federal and states governments (e.g. Article 98 Const.), although the fiscal powers of the states are extremely limited, a choice that was justified by the need to address regional inequalities and socio-economic development (Hessebon and Idris 2017; Bihonegn 2015a). The capital city of Addis Ababa and the city of Dire Dawa are chartered federal cities. Finally, the Constitution also contains some sort of *federal loyalty* clause when it expressly mandates that both federal and state governments shall respect each other's powers (Article 50(8)). While federalism represented an ideal mechanism to reconcile diversity and social cohesion, the federal architecture engineered by the 1994 Constitution (and particularly the long list of federal powers as opposed to the more limited number of state powers) has been criticized by many scholars for being too centralized, to the point that Ethiopia works in practice as a unitary state (Hessebon and Idris 2017).

Although the Constitution provides for only two levels of government—federal and state—and is silent about the local level, states are free to determine their own subregional administrative structures so long as they grant adequate power "to the lowest units of government to enable the People to participate directly in the administration of such units" (Article 50(4) Const.) (Hessebon and Idris 2017). Pursuant to this provision, most state constitutions guarantee both a two-tiered system of local self-government and special local governments that accommodate minority ethnic groups (Hessebon and Idris 2017).[4] This duty clearly reminds of some sort of *subsidiarity* principle funnelling powers to the bottom to empower individuals and local communities to be in charge of their local affairs. In this sense, one first step that Ethiopia could take in its path to economic, social and political growth is to follow the recommendation of

[4] Regional state constitutions provide for *zonal, wereda* and *kebele* local administrations (Hessebon and Idris 2017). *Zones* and *wereda* are "ethnic-based territorial administrations" whose goal is to allow ethnic groups to exercise their constitutionally protected right to self-determination through the establishment of their own territorial administration, although not all ethnic groups have their own *zone* or *wereda*. Normally, regional constitutions treat *zones* and *wereda* as having identical status powers and functions, although *wereda* are established for "smaller and territorially strongly concentrated ethnic groups" (Van der Beken 2013).

the SCC when it argues in the *Reference* that "[t]he federal structure ... facilitates democratic participation by distributing power to the government thought to be most suited to achieving the particular societal objective having regard to this diversity" (*Reference*, at 58). Although the SCC does not say it openly, this can be seen as an invitation to embrace the principle of subsidiarity: therefore, a concrete adoption of subsidiarity may be the road to travel for Ethiopia in the future.

The Unique Role of the House of Federations

Besides the secession clause, which will be discussed in Part V, there is one other unique feature that singles out the Ethiopian federal arrangement in comparative terms: the role and functions of the House of Federations. In federalism scholarship, federations are usually characterized by the presence of a *federal* Senate or Upper Chamber whose main role is to represent—at federal level—the interests of the constituent units of a federation and to participate in (federal) lawmaking: in this way, constituent units may have a say in the federal legislation that directly affects their interests. Ethiopia, however, is exceptional in this regard. While the Parliament is composed of two branches, the House of Peoples' Representatives (the highest authority at federal level, as indicated by Article 50(3) Const.) and the House of Federations (hereinafter, "HoF") as a second chamber, the latter is basically a non-legislative house vested with other important federal powers (Hessebon and Idris 2017; Abbink 1997). Listed in Article 62 Const., they include (but are not limited to) the power to interpret the Constitution; to decide on issues relating to the rights of self-determination and secession of the various *nations, nationalities* and *peoples* (hereinafter, "NNPs") (see Part III); to determine the formula to distribute federal transfers to regional states; to solve disputes between states; to determine civil matters on which federal legislation is needed; and to authorize federal interventions within the states. Most importantly, it is the role of the HoF to settle conflicts of competences between federal and states governments, thus transforming it into an "adjudicative chamber" (rather than a legislative one), which is unusual considering that in federal states this power is normally vested in Supreme or Constitutional Courts. In light of the above, it emerges that the HoF is tasked with safeguarding the interests of the Ethiopian federation as a whole, while promoting equality and unity among the NNPs and preserving the constitutional order, as scholars have pointed out (Bihonegn 2015b).

In the HoF, each NNP is represented by at least one representative, with one additional representative for every one million of each group's population (Article 61(2) Const.). HoF members are elected by state councils, either directly appointing them or through democratic elections (Article 61(3) Const.). This is also quite exceptional in comparative perspective: in fact, rather than representing the constituent units (or states) of the federation—as is the case with most federal upper chambers—the HoF represents the individual ethnic groups, even if it is normally called to decide on matters that interest the states more than the NNPs (Bihonegn 2015b).[5]

While the HoF is entrusted with the interpretation of the Constitution and act as umpire in case of conflicts between federal and state governments, it is assisted by the Council of Constitutional Inquiry ("CCI"), an organ mainly composed of legal experts (Hessebon and Idris 2017). This is also quite unique: in fact, although it establishes a Federal Supreme Court entrusted with "supreme federal judicial authority" (Article 78(2) Const.), the Ethiopian Constitution does not expressly provide for the power of judicial review (Hessebon and Idris 2017), as it is the HoF with the assistance of the CCI that serves as the Constitution's ultimate interpreter (Hessebon and Idris 2017). This means that the Ethiopian judiciary—and in particular the Federal Supreme Court—does not play any major role in devising doctrines, principles and rules because it is precluded the power of judicial review and constitutional interpretation (Hessebon and Idris 2017; Vibhute 2014).

In spite of being exceptional, these features of the HoF do have their own rationale. For instance, the choice to represent the various ethnic groups rather than the states in the HoF is justified by the fact that, in Ethiopia, federalism is considered not a compact among the federal government and the states but among NNPs which are, in fact, the repository of (internal) sovereignty (see Part III *infra*) (Bihonegn 2015b; Fiseha 2007). This point resonates well with the idea of federalism as a legal mechanism to bring together the very diverse ethno-cultural, linguistic and political communities and reconcile unity and diversity. Likewise, constitutional interpretation was regarded as the power to amend the Constitution by giving specific meaning to the constitutional

[5] Addis Ababa and Dire Dawa—the two autonomous cities—have no representation in the HoF, since they are non-ethnic administrations, although some of the tasks of the HoF might be relevant to them (Bihonegn 2015b).

text itself: because the NNPs enjoy sovereign powers, it was seen as undemocratic to grant the power to indirectly modify the Constitution to unelected judges (Hessebon and Idris 2017; Fiseha 2007). Also, the Constitution is considered a political—rather than a merely legal—document, so its interpretation should not be regarded as a "technical exercise" for professionals but a political act in which the various NNPs should have a say: in other words, there was a fear that judicial interpretation would undermine the constitutional order by fostering judicial activism (Hessebon and Idris 2017; Fiseha 2007). This is why it is a political organ such as the HoF—and not a court—that enjoys the power to interpret the Constitution and settle the disputes on allocation of powers between the states and the federal governments (Hessebon and Idris 2017). All this notwithstanding, very little constitutional jurisprudence on federalism has been developed by the HoF so far (Hessebon and Idris 2017). This rather unique situation is rooted in the peculiar connotation of Ethiopian federalism: in fact, federal-state disputes are unlikely to be debated in courts or before the HoF because the EPRDF (the controlling party) controls directly or indirectly all state governments, the HoF and the federal government (Hessebon and Idris 2017). The EPRDF is a very hierarchical and centralized party—a tradition that is somehow rooted in its genesis as an armed group—and it is therefore unlikely that its members will engage in legal battles before the HoF: differences in opinions will thus be addressed inside the party (Hessebon and Idris 2017).

In conclusion, it might be worth underlining how the absence of constitutional jurisprudence on federalism may—in the long run—constitute an obstacle in the development of the federal arrangement. As noted above, Ethiopian federalism is criticized for being too centralized and, in this sense, it faces similar challenges than Canadian federalism at the beginning: in fact, the SCC recalls that, at the time of Confederation "the federal government retained sweeping powers which threatened to undermine the autonomy of the provinces" (*Reference*, at 55). It was only over time, and with the substantial contribution of the Privy Council first, and the SCC case law later, that Canadian federalism reached full maturity and a more balanced equilibrium between federal and provincial powers. Because in Ethiopia courts have not substantially engaged in federalism disputes so far, this inertia may prevent bridging the gap between the constitutional text and the actual federalism practice, thus thwarting to adapt the Constitution to real life.

Ethnicity and Protection of Minorities: The Reconciliation Between Unity and Diversity

The accommodation of internal minorities is one of the major struggles that multinational federations deal with. This is why the SCC in the *Reference* identifies the protection of minorities as one of the unwritten constitutional principles underlying the Canadian constitutional scaffolding. Over time, this principle—which originally mainly served to find a point of reconciliation between the anglophone majority and the francophone minority—has been extended to the respect for all minorities in the country, including Aboriginal people, and has been translated into a number of provisions to protect minority languages, religion and education rights (*Reference*, at 79). Although the SCC in the *Reference* does not speak in terms of *ethnicity*—preferring to use the expression "protection of minorities"—ethnicity has played a major role in Canada: in fact, as Gaudreault-DesBiens explains in this volume, the Quebec nationalism that led to the referendum on secession—with its bundle of linguistic and religious diversity—was in fact ethnic.

In this regard, Ethiopia is not different. As a country of minorities, the reconciliation between unity and diversity is pivotal: for this reason, it would be incomplete and at the same time impossible to discuss Ethiopian federalism without referring to ethnicity. In fact, Ethiopia is a notorious example of *ethno*-federalism, as federalism and ethnicity are two intimately intertwined concepts that profoundly forge each other and that need to be read and understood together.

Differently than other African countries, the significant ethnic variety and richness of Ethiopia is not the result of Western colonization; rather, it is the direct consequence of the attempts made in the late 1800s by Menelik to expand the Abyssinian empire from its heartland territories (located in the north of present-day Ethiopia and mainly composed of Orthodox Christians speaking Amharic and Tigrigna) to the south, east and west, with the result that peoples of very diverse languages, religion, cultural and socio-economic fabric joined the empire (Van der Beken 2015). Of all the various ethnic groups, the *Oromo* presently represents the largest group, followed by the *Amhara* and the *Somali* (Fessha and Van der Beken 2013). However, none of these ethnic groups accounts for the majority of the population and, for this reason, Ethiopia is commonly defined as a country of minorities (Fessha and Van der Beken 2013). In terms of religious diversity, the Ethiopian Orthodox

Christianity and Islam are the dominant faiths, whose roots in the country go back to time immemorial (Hessebon and Idris 2017; Henrard and Smis 2000).

The close connection between federalism and ethnicity (or respect for minorities) can be perceived also in the promises of federalism when it was first discussed in the early 1990s. In fact, the belief was that it would foster

> respect for local languages and cultures, training and staffing of local authorities with local people who spoke the relevant languages and were sensitive to the culture, and more access to regional and state institutions by members of smaller ethnic minorities or disadvantaged groups. (Abbink 2006)

Although the problem of ethnicity is not unique to Ethiopia but is common to the rest of Africa (Bihonegn 2015b), what is exceptional about the Ethiopian system is that ethnic identity "has been declared the ideological basis of political organization and administration" (Abbink 1997) and has become "the foundation of its constitutional order" rather than insisting on territorial integrity as other African states and federations have done (Bihonegn 2015b). In fact, as Turton has aptly observed, "Ethiopia has gone further than any other African state … in using ethnicity as its fundamental organizing principle" (Turton 2006). It could thus be argued that ethnicity is part and parcel of Ethiopia's federalism and constitutional identity.

Similarly to Canada, the Ethiopian Constitution does not use the term *ethnicity* (or derivates thereof), but prefers to employ the expression *nations, nationalities* and *peoples* to refer to the various ethnic groups (Bihonegn 2015b). As already noted, these numerous NNPs occupy a prominent place in the constitutional scheme. First, Article 39(5) Const. defines each NNP as

> a group of people who have or share a large measure of a common culture or similar customs, mutual intelligibility of language, belief in a common or related identities, a common psychological make-up, and who inhabit an identifiable, predominantly contiguous territory.

The criteria used by this constitutional provision to define NNPs include common culture or customs, mutual language, common heritage and territorial sharing. In this regard, scholars have observed that the constitutional text does not make any reference to common religion as an identifying feature, probably because the vast majority of Ethiopians belong either to Christianity or Islam (Abdullahi 1998). The role of the various NNPs is further strengthened by the fact that they (and not Ethiopian peoples as a whole) are the repositories of sovereign constituent powers and are the main actors that have come together to join the federal compact (Hessebon and Idris 2017; Mengie 2015). This is expressly declared in Article 8(1) Const. mandating that "[a]ll sovereign power resides in the Nations, Nationalities and Peoples of Ethiopia" whereas Article 8(2) Const. posits that "[t]his Constitution is an expression of their sovereignty." Likewise, Article 8(3) Const. indicates that "[t]heir sovereignty shall be expressed through their representatives elected in accordance with this Constitution and through their democratic participation" this last paragraph suggesting that ethnicity is also strictly connected to the democratic principle discussed in Part V. But also the constitutional preamble starts off with the words "We, the Nations, Nationalities and Peoples of Ethiopia" (reminiscent of the more celebrated *We the People* opening the preamble of the 1787 US Constitution) as a clear statement of the prominent place occupied by ethnic groups in the Ethiopian constitutional architecture as repositories of sovereignty. The common opinion among scholars is that the eminent place granted to the NNPs means that the Ethiopian population as a whole "is no longer perceived or presented as one homogeneous community – as was the case during most of the twentieth century" but rather "as a body composed of various ethnic limbs" (Fessha and Van der Beken 2013).

The Ethiopian Constitution enshrines several provisions aiming at protecting both individual and group-specific minority rights of the various NNPs (Fessha and Van der Beken 2013). For example, among the individual rights protecting internal minorities, there is the right to equality and non-discrimination (Article 25 Const.), freedom of movement and choice of residence (Article 32 Const.), as well as the right to vote and be elected without discrimination based on ethnicity (Article 38 Const.) (Van der Beken 2013). Likewise, in awarding a right to self-determination (including secession) in its first paragraph, Article 39 Const. grants important "group-specific" rights. For example, it grants language and cultural rights to ethnic groups (Article 39(2) Const.) (Fessha and Van der Beken 2013), but also the right to self-government which includes both a right to establish governmental institutions and to an equal representation in federal and state governments which, in practice, means a right to "territorial self-rule" (Article 39(3) Const.) (Fessha and Van der Beken 2013). This provision should be read in conjunction with Article 47(2) Const. vesting the various NNPs within a state with the right to establish their own state at any time (Fessha and Van der Beken 2013; Van der Beken 2013). As already noted, the right to self-determination includes the right to secede from the federation (Article 39(1) Const.). Finally, the Constitution expressly allows the various states that compose the federation to enact their own constitutions, which thus become the ideal places where states can not only decide their internal administrative and institutional structure, but also accommodate internal ethnic cleavages and protect individual and group-specific rights (Articles 50(5) and 52(2)(b) Const.) (Van der Beken 2013).

Ethnicity is a major criterion also in dividing political positions both at federal and regional levels, as well as in the organization of the federal cabinet (Mengie 2015). In particular, the Constitution requires "equitable representation" of the various ethnic groups in both levels of government, in a commitment "to accommodate intra-regional diversity" (Article 39(3) Const.) and to ensure that these institutions reflect the ethnic plurality of the Ethiopian society, although the actual realization of this ultimately depends on regional constitutions (Fessha and Van der Beken 2013). Most regional governments also offer representation to indigenous internal minorities at executive level, even if state constitutions do not enshrine any guarantee in this regard (Fessha and Van der Beken 2013).

On the one hand, scholars contend that, while the ethno-federal system in place in Ethiopia has supported ethnic groups in promoting and protecting their identity, this was done at the expenses of a common Ethiopian identity and of what should be shared values such as common history, humanity and culture (Mengie 2015), to the point that it is not a helpful tool in preserving unity and diversity (Mengie 2016). Likewise, it has been contended that the various NNPs are in reality rival groups, a situation that has exacerbated after the institutionalization of ethnicity in the 1990s (Mengie 2015).

In general terms, ethnic tensions in Africa—not only in Ethiopia—are a major cause of state disintegration, mainly because the *tribe* still plays a very important role (Abdullahi 1998). These struggles are caused mainly by factors such as inequalities among the various groups, discrimination and other forms of rights abuses, partly resulting from the absence of any constitutional provision mediating among ethnic groups (Abdullahi 1998). Furthermore, in Ethiopia, many conflicts that occur are about land and boundaries between the various ethnic groups, even when these conflicts are flagged as "ethnic": in fact, because land remains the most important resource in the country, access to land plays a pivotal role in local and domestic conflicts among groups (Abbink 2006).[6]

In light of the above, the principles of federalism and ethnicity—which are not unwritten but are clearly spelled out in the Ethiopian Constitution—are closely connected and need to be read and understood together, as the former represents the framework where the latter finds its actualization.

Constitutionalism and the Rule of Law

In including constitutionalism and the rule of law among the four fundamental and unwritten constitutional principles in Canada, the SCC defines the rule of law as providing a "shield for individuals from arbitrary state action" (*Reference*, at 70). Furthermore, drawing on previous decisions, it argues that it includes "a sense of orderliness, of subjection to known legal rules and of executive accountability to legal authority" (*Reference*, at 70). Although conceptually not identical, it bears a close connection with constitutionalism, a principle requiring compliance with the Constitution (*Reference*, at 72). More precisely, constitutionalism requires compliance by federal and provincial governments with the Constitution, while the rule of law demands all government action to be in compliance with the law, including the Constitution (*Reference*, at 72). Furthermore, constitutionalism and rule of law are essential to democracy, as they create "an orderly framework within which people may make political decisions" (*Reference*, at 78).

At least on paper, the Ethiopian legal system is anchored on the rule of law by an express provision enshrined in the constitutional preamble saying that

> We, the Nations, Nationalities and Peoples of Ethiopia:

[6] In this sense, scholars point out that land has been the source of power for nobility, both ecclesiastical and secular. And since Ethiopia is an agrarian society, control over land means control over people (Abbay 2009).

> Strongly committed ... to building a political community founded on the rule of law and capable of ... guaranteeing a democratic order .... (emphasis added)

This principle is reaffirmed in Article 52(2)(a) Const. in regard to state powers, which shall include the establishment of a democratic order based on the rule of law.

In addition to implying a supreme Constitution and the rule of law, which represent its major pillars, constitutionalism is often understood also as characterized by other elements such as an independent judiciary enjoying the power of judicial review, separation of powers, checks and balances, protection of fundamental rights, etc. (Regassa 2010). Formally, the Ethiopian Constitution reflects a strong commitment to constitutionalism. For example, constitutional supremacy is expressly entrenched in Article 9(1) Const., so that any decision made by public officials in contravention of the Constitution is void. Furthermore, it is a duty of all citizens, state organs and political associations and organizations to observe and obey the Constitution (Article 9(2) Const.), and state power cannot be assumed in contrast to the Constitution (Article 9(3) Const.). Furthermore, the Constitution provides for democratic government and the protection of a large array of rights in the bill of rights (Article 10 and 13 to 44 Const.), in addition to providing for an independent judiciary (Regassa 2010). However, some scholars have pointed to the fact that, despite the constitutional text, constitutionalism remains weak in Ethiopia, mainly because of three elements: poor performance in the protection of human rights; absence of a true form of judicial review because of the unique role of the HoF as described *supra;* and concerns on whether elections are actually free (Regassa 2010).

The Right to Self-Determination and the Secession Clause: Reflections upon the Democratic Principle

As one of the four fundamental unwritten principles of Canadian constitutionalism, in the *Reference* the SCC defines democracy as a political system of "majority rule" (*Reference*, at 63) expressing "the sovereign will of the people" (*Reference*, at 66). However, democracy is also construed as a principle connected to the promotion of self-government and to the accommodation of cultural and group identities (*Reference*, at 64), thus tracing it back to the principles of federalism and respect for minorities.

Furthermore, the SCC reads the democratic principle as "the process of representative and responsible government and the right of citizens to participate in the political process as voters … and as candidates" thus suggesting that democracy implies that provincial and federal legislatures are "elected by popular franchise" (*Reference*, at 65). At the same time, the SCC argues, democracy shall be considered not in isolation, but along with the other three constitutional values of federalism, respect for minorities and constitutionalism and the rule of law (*Reference*, at 66).

With regard to secession, which is neither expressly authorized nor prohibited by the Canadian Constitution (*Reference*, at 84), the SCC argues that it would radically change the current constitutional architecture (*Reference*, at 84): consequently, the joint operation of the federal and democratic principles requires that any repudiation of the existing constitutional scaffolding, expressed by a clear desire to secede by one province, "would give rise to a reciprocal obligation on all parties to Confederation to negotiate constitutional changes to respond to that desire" (*Reference*, at 88). As a result, all parties involved (the seceding province, the other provinces and the federal government) would be obliged to enter into negotiations in compliance with the aforementioned constitutional principles (*Reference*, at 88). On the one hand, secession cannot be seen as an "absolute legal entitlement" whereby one province dictates the terms of secession to the others in contrast to the principles of democracy, federalism and the rule of law (*Reference*, at 91). On the other hand, the rights of the other provinces and of the federal government cannot deny the right of one province to pursue secession, should there being a "clear majority" of people willing to proceed in this sense (*Reference*, at 92). In other words, the decision of a "clear majority" of people in one province on a "clear question to pursue secession" should be reconciled to the rights and obligations of all the other parties involved (*Reference*, at 93).

How can all this be integrated in the narrative of Ethiopian federalism? In this part, the democratic principle and the rights to self-determination and secession embedded in the Ethiopian Constitution will be discussed in relation to the *Reference*.

The Principle of Democracy

Article 1 Const. defines Ethiopia not only as a *federal* but also as a *democratic* country: the democratic principle is thus expressly spelled out in the constitutional text. However, Ethiopia has moved to democracy after experiencing a period of "feudal autocracy until 1974 and socialist totalitarianism until 1991," and this transition requires people to be introduced and familiarize to the democratic culture (Abbay 2009). In other words, democracy has been introduced into a paternalistic society deeply accustomed to authoritarianism, with a state not at the service of people but to which people owed loyalty and obedience (Abbay 2009).

As noted, democracy is a principle that goes past the simple "majority rule" to encompass, among other things, other values such as free and fair elections, freedom of expression and organization, and real power to govern granted to those who win elections, in addition to their full accountability (Abbay 2009). However, scholars lament that, in spite of the many rights and freedoms entrenched in the constitutional text, including freedom of speech and press, democracy in Ethiopia "remains uncertain" mainly because of the presence of a peasant culture and society which has a smaller urban population, is divided along ethnic lines and, consequently, is not yet fully prepared to embrace democratic values (Abbay 2009). This means that, although the principle of democracy is explicitly spelled out and pervades the Constitution, there is still a "poor democratic culture" in Ethiopia (Mengie 2016).

The Rights to Self-Determination and Secession

As noted *supra,* Article 39(1) Const. enshrined what is perhaps the most intriguing and contested feature of the Ethiopian ethno-federal arrangement—the right to secession—in the following terms:

> Every Nation, Nationality and People in Ethiopia has an unconditional right to self-determination, including the right to secession. (emphasis added)

It was observed above how the secession clause is part of a broader constitutional provision embedding other rights belonging to the NNPs. However, the right to self-determination prominently displays not only in the text of this constitutional provision but is also captured in the opening sentence of the 1994 constitutional preamble as follows:

> We, the Nations, Nationalities and Peoples of Ethiopia: strongly committed, in full and free exercise of our right to self-determination, to building

> a political community founded on the rule of law and capable of ensuring a lasting peace, guaranteeing a democratic order, and advancing our economic and social development … (emphasis added)

The rights embedded in Article 39 Const. originate in the *interim* charter adopted during the transition period (Abdullahi 1998). In particular, Article 2 of that document mandated that

> The right of nations, nationalities and peoples to self-determination is affirmed. To this end, each nation, nationality and people is guaranteed the right to: a) Preserve its identity and have it respected, promote its culture and history and use and develop its language; b) Administer its own affairs within its own defined territory and effectively participate in the central government on the basis of freedom, and fair and proper representation; c) Exercise its right to self-determination of independence, when the concerned nation/nationality and people is convinced that the above rights are denied, abridged or abrogated. (as quoted in Abdullahi 1998) (emphasis added)

There is thus a *continuum* between the transitional charter and the 1994 federal Constitution in guaranteeing secession, although no explicit reference is made to secession as such in the older document (but only to independence) (Bihonegn 2015a): yet, the seed of what will become Article 39 was planted.

This right to self-determination, granted to all NNPs, is so important that it has been considered the "cornerstone" of Ethiopia's federalism (Hessebon and Idris 2017). The inclusion of a right to self-determination (and secession) was justified mainly on historical grounds, being a legacy of the "socialist-communist thinking" that has influenced Ethiopia, as indicated *supra* (Abbink 1997). Turton argues that

> [t]he theory of federalism developed by Lenin, during the communist revolution in Russia, was designed, from the start, to provide a degree of autonomy and self-determination for minority groups in the former Russian Empire. It was this model of federalism which most clearly influenced the framers of the constitution … (Turton 2006)

In fact, the formation of modern Ethiopia was widely seen as an "imperial project" that had led to the "subjugation and assimilation of various ethnic groups": self-determination, secession and the overall identity-based federalism were thus seen as the ideal solution to address these past injustices (Hessebon and Idris 2017). Consequently, although the secession clause seems to virtually respond to some of the issues and concerns raised in the *Reference*, its genesis rests in fact on very different grounds.

A closer scrutiny of Article 39(1) Const. reveals that the twin rights to self-determination and secession are granted to every NNP—the repository of sovereign powers—and not to the nine constituent units (states) that compose the federation (Abbink 1997). Technically speaking, only the various NNPs enjoy a right to secede, not only from the federation pursuant to Article 39 but also from the state to which they belong, as expressly mandated by Article 47(2) Const. (Abbink 1997). In other words, the Constitution allows NNPs to pursue both internal and external independence, by granting them the right to establish their own state in Ethiopia or to seek secession from Ethiopia altogether (Mengie 2015): because of this right, both the states and the union are "destructible" as Mengie posits (Mengie 2016). In entrenching the right to self-determination in the Constitution, the drafters were inspired also by the International Covenant on Civil and Political Rights, as well as the African Charter on Human and Peoples' Rights (Henrard and Smis 2000).

Article 39 Const. sets forth an elaborate mechanism to pursue secession, entrusting the Ethiopian government—and in particular the HoF—with a facilitating role (Abdullahi 1998). More specifically, Article 62(3) Const. mandates that the HoF shall "decide on issues related to the rights of Nations, Nationalities and Peoples to self-determination, including the right to secession" in accordance with the Constitution. However, in spite of this central role of the HoF, scholars have argued that decisions on self-determination and secession do not necessarily involve constitutional issues but political ones: in other words, the right to secession is regarded as a *political*—rather than *constitutional*—question (Vibhute 2014).

Demands for secession shall be approved by two-thirds majority of the members of the legislative council of the specific NNP seeking to secede (Article 39(4)(a) Const.). The rationale for this demand is twofold: first, it addresses the need to provide some form of control against "any thoughtless or purely jingoistic agitation for secession" (Abdullahi 1998). Second, secession can be first triggered only by the initiative of the local legislative assembly, thus ensuring that the will of the people is sanctioned by their democratically elected representatives (Abdullahi 1998).

The subsequent step involves the federal government, called to organize a referendum within three years after the reception of the vote of the local legislative council (Article 39(4)(b) Const.). Again, the rationale is to ensure that there is enough democratic support for secession within the state, especially in light of the requirement of a majority vote in support of the referendum (Article 39(4)(c) Const.) (Abdullahi 1998). Once these steps have been completed, the federal government will transfer its powers to the people seeking secession (Article 39(4)(d) Const.), in a virtual "handover" from the federal government to the newly formed state (Abdullahi 1998). Finally, Article 39(4)(e) Const. requires that all assets be divided between the federal government and the new state pursuant to the law.

Despite its exceptional character, the introduction of the secession clause has not been welcomed with unanimous enthusiasm. Some scholars acknowledge that the right to secession has become "the most cherished provision in the federal constitution" to the point that it is "non-derogative even during state of emergency" (Bihonegn 2015a).[7] Likewise, it has been argued that this provision not only gives constitutional recognition to the various NNPs, but it also "creates equality, checks and balances and assures that unlike most Africa, the institutions of the state is not dominated by just one tribe" (Abdullahi 1998). Furthermore, by empowering the various NNPs with the power to self-determination, the Ethiopian Constitution also limits the power of the central government, historically seen as "organ of oppression" (Abdullahi 1998). The right to secession has also been labelled as "a radical experiment in democracy" that should be followed by other African states, especially those torn along ethnic lines (Abdullahi 1998). Also, considering that secession in Africa (and elsewhere) has often been pursued or achieved through violence or civil wars, the constitutional entrenchment of secession might lead to a more peaceful way to solve ethnic conflicts (Abdullahi 1998). In fact, according to this idea, the

[7] Article 93 Const. deals with the declaration of state of emergency, and Article 93(4)(c) protects the right of secession and self-determination from limitation or suspension in such extreme circumstances: "[i]n the exercise of its emergency powers the Council of Ministers cannot, however, suspend or limit the rights provided for in Articles 1, 18, 25, and sub-Articles 1 and 2 of Article 39 of this Constitution."

inclusion of a secession clause does not necessarily mean that it would lead to an easy dismemberment of the state: on the contrary, it would make it "more responsive and caring to the wishes and aspiration of all of its constituencies" (Abdullahi 1998), thus deterring—rather than encouraging—secessionist threats (Bihonegn 2015a).

Other scholars have dismissed the secession clause as a negative, useless and dangerous addition to Ethiopian federalism: one common fear is that its entrenchment would "stimulate a surge of nationalism" in addition to being a "recipe for disaster" although the hope is still that the clause would "defuse ethnic discontent" with a consequent enhancement of peace and stability (Brietzke 1995). Another major concern is that most ethnic groups in the country would not be able to become viable sovereign states (Van der Beken 2013). Other scholars have pointed to the fact that the right to secession (construed as an "extreme interpretation of 'national self-determination'") is a unique feature in democratic constitutions, but while Ethiopia might be exceptional in many ways, it is not so special to require the entrenchment of a secession clause (Abbink 1997). Another paradox has been identified in the fact that, while the Ethiopian Constitution grants the right to secede, at the same time it withholds from the constituent units some basic federal powers, being it a very centralized federation (Bihonegn 2015a): for this reason, experts have suggested that granting some "real federal autonomy" to the constituent units would serve their interests better than a secession clause (Abbink 1997). More generally, classic federalism scholarship has traditionally resisted the introduction of secession clauses in federal constitutions as against the federalism principle (Wheare 1963). In the Ethiopian case, the secession clause has also been read as contrary to the principles of democracy and constitutionalism (Bihonegn 2015a).

In line with the *Reference*, the articulate procedure to achieve secession under Article 39 Const. virtually responds to some of the concerns raised by the SCC: the involvement of the federal government through the HoF implies that obligations arise both for the seceding party and national institutions. However, the democratic principle does not provide for actual negotiations among the various parties involved—as suggested by the *Reference*—so secession is seen not only as "unconditional" but also as a unilateral privilege in Article 39 Const. (Mengie 2016). Yet, democracy is triggered when the approval of the members of the local legislative council of the seceding NNP by a super-majority vote of two-thirds is required; it is also triggered in the subsequent steps, e.g. in the referendum that the federal government shall organize in the seceding territory after a three-year time lapse before eventually handing over all powers. In other words, scholars have pointed to the fact that

> what is constitutionally incorporated in Ethiopia and what is decided by the Supreme Court of Canada regarding secession are substantially different. While the Ethiopia's Constitution grants unconditional and unilateral right to secede, the Supreme Court of Canada rejected such unilateral and unconditional right to secede. (Mengie 2016)

To this date, however, the secession clause has not been invoked yet, so it is difficult to assess whether the procedure set forth in Article 39 Const. is functional or not.[8]

Conclusion

This chapter explored federalism, respect for minorities, constitutionalism and the rule of law, and democracy—all discussed by the SCC in the *Reference* as fundamental organizing principles of Canadian constitutionalism—to assess their role and place in the unique context of Ethiopia. Differently than Canada, however—where these principles are not explicitly entrenched in the constitutional text and are therefore "underlying"—the Ethiopian Constitution expressly makes them all part of the written document, in addition to entrenching secession as a recognized right for all NNPs.

Comparing Canada and Ethiopia might seem inappropriate, especially if one considers that the 1994 Ethiopian Constitution predates the *Reference* by a few years, and the secession clause originates in the Marxist-Leninist

[8]While secession has not yet been invoked to secede from Ethiopia, *internal* secession issues have been triggered a number of times. The most famous and successful one was the *Silte* case: here, the *Silte* ethnic group claimed a distinct identity from the *Guraghe* group to which it was attached and sought to secede from the latter to form its own local government as part of the Southern Nations, Nationalities and Peoples regional state. The HoF eventually recognized the *Silte* as a distinct group, allowing them to establish their own sub-region, after a referendum in 2000 where the majority of the *Silte* people voted for secession. The case was quite complex, especially because of the numerous parties involved (the *Silte* and *Guraghe* ethnic groups, the state parliament composed of the various ethnic groups, and the HoF) (Fiseha 2007).

understanding of federalism. Nonetheless, the *Reference* and the Ethiopian Constitution do share one striking feature: they both break away with a constitutional taboo by discussing secession in legal terms (Martinico 2019, this volume). In fact, the *Reference* overtly discusses the possibility to secede from the Canadian federation, while the Ethiopian Constitution bluntly entrenches it as an unconditional right for all the NNPs. Although the constitutional recognition of a right to secession as recognized under Article 39 is still rather exceptional in comparative perspective, the SCC in the *Reference* has somehow indirectly acknowledged it.

To conclude, similarly to other countries that have emerged out of colonialism or authoritarian rule, Ethiopia is also a country of sharp contrasts: in fact, the aspirations to quickly leave behind the past and fully embrace Western values stand in contrast with a culture that is still unfamiliar with the true meaning and implications of such values. For this reason, as Regassa and Mengie point out, there is still a gap between constitutional law (design) and practice, since most of the values it enshrines—like democracy—are imported, and the Ethiopian federation often works in a way that is far from what the Constitution dictates.

References

Abbay, Alemseged (2009), "Diversity and Democracy in Ethiopia", in *Journal of Eastern African Studies*, 3, 175–201.

Abbink, Jon (1997), "Ethnicity and Constitutionalism in Contemporary Ethiopia", in *Journal of African Law*, 41, 159–174.

Abbink, Jon (2006), "Ethnicity and Conflict Generation in Ethiopia: Some Problems and Prospects of Ethno-Regional Federalism", in *Journal of Contemporary African Studies*, 24, 389–413.

Abdullahi, Ahmednasir M. (1998), "Article 39 of the Ethiopian Constitution on Secession and Self-Determination: A Panacea to the Nationality Question in Africa?" in *Verfassung und Recht in Übersee*, 31, 440–455.

Bihonegn, Tesfa (2015a), "Federalization with a Constitutional Guarantee to Secession: Controversies, Paradoxes and Imponderables in Ethiopia", in *Regional and Federal Studies*, 25, 45–70.

Bihonegn, Tesfa (2015b). "The House of Federation: The Practice and Limits of Federalism in Ethopia's Second Federal Chamber", in *Journal of Eastern African Studies*, 9, 394–411.

Brietzke, Paul H. (1995), "Ethiopia's 'Leap in the Dark'": Federalism and Self-Determination in the New Constitution", in *Journal of African Law*, 39, 19–38.

Fessha, Yonatan T. and Van der Beken, Christophe (2013), "Ethnic Federalism and Internal Minorities: The Legal Protection of Internal Minorities in Ethiopia", in *Africa Journal of International and Comparative Law*, 21, 32–49.

Fiseha, Assefa (2007), "Constitutional Adjudication in Ethiopia: Exploring the Experience of the House of Federations (HoF)", in *Mizan Law Review*, 1, 1–32.

Henrard, Kristin and Smis, Stefaan (2000), "Recent Experiences in South Africa and Ethiopia to Accommodate Cultural Diversity: A Regained Interest in the Right to Self-Determination", in *Journal of African Law*, 44, 17–51.

Hessebon, Gedion and Idris, Abduletif (2017), "The Supreme Court of Ethiopia: Federalism's Bystander", in Nicholas Aroney and John Kinkaid (eds.), *Courts in Federal Countries: Federalists or Unitarists?* University of Toronto Press, Toronto, 165–192.

Medlock Wigger, Kimberly (1998), "Ethiopia: A Dichotomy of Despain and Hope", in *Tulsa Journal of Comparative and International Law*, 5, 389–411.

Mengie, Legesse T. (2015), "Ethnic Federalism and Conflict in Ethiopia: What Lessons Can Other Jurisdictions Draw?", in *African Journal of International and Comparative Law*, 23, 462–474.

Mengie, Legesse T. (2016), "Federalism as an Instrument for Unity and the Protection of Minorities: A Comparative Overview: Ethiopia, India and the US", in *Mizan Law Review*, 10, 265–295.

Regassa, Tsegaye (2004), "State Constitutions in Federal Ethiopia: A Preliminary Observation", in *federalismi.it*, 10, 1–15.

Regassa, Tsegaye (2010), "The Making and Legitimacy of the Ethiopian Constitution: Towards Bridging the Gap Between Constitutional Design and Constitutional Practice", in *Afrika Focus*, 23, 85–118.

Turton, David (2006), "Introduction", in David Turton (ed.), *Ethnic Federalism: The Ethiopian Experience in Comparative Perspective*, James Currey, Oxford.

Van der Beken, Christophe (2013), "Federalism in a Context of Extreme Ethnic Pluralism: The Case of Ethiopia's Southern Nations, Nationalities and Peoples Region", in *Verfassung und Recht in Übersee*, 46, 3–17.

Van der Beken, Christophe (2015), "Federalism, Local Government and Minority Protection in Ethiopia: Opportunities and Challenges", in *Journal of African Law*, 59, 150–177.

Vaughan, Sarah (2013), "Federalism in Ethiopia: Hybridity in Ambiguity?", in John Loughlin, John Kinkaid and Wilfried Swenden (eds.), *Routledge Handbook of Regionalism and Federalism*, Routledge, London, 428–441.

Vibhute, K.I. (2014), "Non-judicial Review in Ethiopia: Constitutional Paradigm, Premise and Precinct", in *African Journal of International and Comparative Law*, 22, 120–139.

Wheare, Kenneth (1963), *Federal Government*, Oxford University Press, Oxford.

Secessionist Impulses and the Italian Legal System: The (Non)Influence of the Secession Reference

Giacomo Delledonne and Matteo Monti

Introduction

Secessionist claims have characterised the Italian constitutional order since the fall of the Fascist regime and the Armistice of Cassibile, and the entry into force of the Constitution in 1948. The presence of distinct quasi-national identities and secessionist impulses influenced debates at the Constituent Assembly, most notably with regard

---

This paper is the result of joint reflections, however Matteo Monti wrote paragraph 2; Giacomo Delledonne wrote paragraph 3; while paragraphs 1 and 4 were elaborated on jointly.

G. Delledonne (✉) · M. Monti
Sant'Anna School of Advanced Studies, Pisa, Italy
e-mail: giacomo.delledonne@santannapisa.it

M. Monti
e-mail: matteo.monti@santannapisa.it

G. Delledonne and G. Martinico (eds.), *The Canadian Contribution to a Comparative Law of Secession*,
https://doi.org/10.1007/978-3-030-03469-6_9

to the issue of regional autonomy. In addition, during the life of the Republic, new secessionist movements have appeared (and others have disappeared). Recently, the attempts to secede from Italy have stemmed—above all—from Veneto, which tried to organise a referendum in order to demand secession from Italy. This failed attempt led to a major decision of the Italian Constitutional Court that declared the corresponding legislative provisions unconstitutional because they infringed and violated Article 5 of the Constitution, stating that the Republic "shall be one and indivisible".

The aim of this chapter is to analyse the impact of the *Reference Re Secession of Quebec* on the Italian legal system, looking at both the judgements of the Italian Constitutional Court and the strategies and narratives of the political actors. Italian comparative law scholarship has traditionally taken a keen interest in Canadian constitutionalism and its evolution (see Delledonne et al. 2017: 5). The Quebec Secession Reference is no exception, as it attracted the attention of a number of Italian commentators (Olivetti Rason 1999; Passaglia 1999; Poggeschi 1998). However, this chapter aims at looking beyond the scholarly debate in order to consider the influence of the Reference on the Italian constitutional system as a whole.

The analysis is divided into two sections.

First, Paragraph 2 will study the presence and the evolution of distinct national or quasi-national identities and secessionist impulses in the Italian legal system and how they influenced the writing of the Italian Constitution and its more recent reforms. That part shall focus in particular on the "traditional" forms of identity and secessionism, such as the Sicilian secessionist movements, the South Tyrolean one, and the occasional secessionist instincts in Val D'Aosta and Sardinia, as well as the new forms of quasi-national identity and secessionism in the so-called Padania and Veneto. In doing so, Paragraph 2 will shed some light on the strength of "contractualist" or "compact" arguments in the architecture of the Italian regional state (see La Pergola 1969).

Paragraph 3, in turn, will analyse the direct or indirect impact of the system designed by the Canadian Supreme Court on the Italian scenario, looking at the issues of the interpretation of Article 5 of the Constitution, the decisions of the Constitutional Court, and finally, the debates concerning the "secessionist laws" approved by the regional legislature of Veneto.

In the final remarks, some considerations about the influence of the Canadian Reference shall be developed, and the Italian approach to secession shall be underlined.

The Issue of the National and Quasi-national Identities and the Secessionist Movements in Italy

Like most European states, the Italian Republic is a multinational state (Toniatti 1994: 294–295) with many subnational identities. Only a few of them have forms of self-government developed in regions.

The rise of national and quasi-national identities and secessionist threats is a *leitmotiv* in the life of the Italian Republic, starting from the genesis of the Constitution of 1948 and continuing up to the present.

The asymmetry[1] granted to "special regions" was designed to avoid secession or—at least—riots in four regions, namely Sicily, Sardinia, Valle d'Aosta/Vallée d'Aoste and Trentino-Alto Adige/South Tyrol. Finally, a special statute was also provided for Friuli-Venezia Giulia.

The secessionist impulses were indirectly enhanced by the aggressive policy developed by the Fascist Regime, which tried to eliminate the traditional linguistic minorities through the imposition of the Italian language and some forms of Italianisation in the territories inhabited by minorities. After the downfall of Fascism and the end of WWII, secessionist and autonomist movements arose in the four aforementioned regions.

In the works of the Constituent Assembly, some traces of a sort of contractualism (see La Pergola 1969) can be found, which, in some ways, hint at the hidden danger of secession: In the Constituent Assembly, many deputies discussed the "facts" and the "political facts"

[1]The differences between the regions were generally accepted and highlighted since the first sessions of the 2nd Subcommittee of the Commission, which was deputised to write the Project for the Italian Constitution. This was also the thesis expressed by the President Mr. Terracini at the beginning of the workings of the 2nd Subcommittee of the Commission (Camera dei Deputati 1970–1971: 63—Session 31 July 1946, 63). Finally, the Agenda of the Day approved considered the special situations of the four aforementioned regions (Camera dei Deputati 1970–1971: 77—Session 1 August 1946), and the closed number of special regions was affirmed (Camera dei Deputati 1970–1971: 514—Session 15 November 1946). Finally, see the speeches of Mr. Persico, Mr. Perassi, and Mr. Ambrosini the day of the discussion of the Statute of Sardinia (Camera dei Deputati 1970–1971: 4049 and ff.—28 January 1948).

regarding the situation in the four aforementioned regions. It is noteworthy that the deputies elected in those regions created delegations and acted in one direction trying to gain and conserve the autonomy of their regions. The proto-contractualism and the secessionist fears are the two main arguments affecting the debate concerning the Special Statutes.

What do we mean by "contractualism" when we consider the constituent debates in 1946–1947? This idea was developed in relation to the statutes conceded before and during the Constituent Assembly and the idea of an autonomous region granted with special status as something that was, in some ways, untouchable, or more accurately, irrevocable. This concept was explicitly claimed by the Rapporteur of the 2nd Subcommittee, Gaspare Ambrosini[2] (Camera dei Deputati 1970–1971: 43—Session 30 July 1946), and by the President of the Subcommittee, Umberto Terracini, who also invited the constituents to consider the existence of the autonomies that had yet been granted (Camera dei Deputati 1970–1971: 74—Session 1 August 1946). This approach also seems to be expressed by Vittorio Emanuele Orlando in the General Discussion of the Project of the Italian Constitution (Camera dei Deputati 1970–1971: 4779—Session 13 June 1947). The minority of the Subcommittee, led by Luigi Einaudi (Camera dei Deputati 1970–1971: 75—Session 1 August 1946), accepted this idea, but it refused to consider the autonomy laws enacted as binding or untouchable; we will see that this idea was deeply contested. Finally, it must be stressed that this contractualist idea was strongly denied by the Italian Constitutional Court.[3]

The second relevant argument was the fear of secessionist impulses in some regions, and as we will explore, it was deeply connected to the idea of an irrevocability and an untouchability of the regimes of autonomy granted or promised: This fear was well expressed by the request (denied) of Emilio Lussu to diffuse the news that the 2nd Subcommittee of the Commission of the Constituent Assembly was working on the statutes of the Special regions and not only on the Sicilian one… "in order to avoid the rise of justifiable resentments" (Camera dei Deputati 1970–1971: 351—Session 15 October 1946).

[2] Gaspare Ambrosini, a constitutional law scholar who had theorised the emergence of "regional" states in the interwar years, went on to become a Judge (1955–1967) and the President (1962–1967) of the Constitutional Court.

[3] See *Corte costituzionale*, judgement no. 365/2007.

In this paragraph, the secessionist movements and the quasi-national identities shall be analysed in a diachronic way.

After the fall of Fascism, the first secessionist movement, based on its importance and strength, was probably the Sicilian Independence Movement (*in Italian*, Movimento Indipendentista Siciliano; *In the Sicilian dialect*, Muvumentu pâ Nnipinnenza râ Sicilia—MIS), a pro-independence movement that was launched after the Allies landed in Sicily (Ganci 1968: 262 and ff.).

Its goal was originally to secede from Italy under the protection of the Allies with a plebiscite in which only Sicilians would be entitled to vote.[4] It was one of the first attempts at unilateral secession by a territory of Italy. The MIS also had a small "army" (E.V.I.S.) that engaged in several uprisings against the Italian army. Remarkably, from the vantage point of international law, the MIS attempted to justify its position on the ground of the freshly drafted Charter of the United Nations and tried to influence the first General Assembly and the Allies by sending them messages and requests.[5] The MIS leader, Andrea Finocchiaro Aprile, did not exclude adherence, after the independence, to a European Confederation or an Italian one.[6]

After the downfall of the Fascist regime, while the war was still going on, in Sicily, a Consulta Regionale (see Giarrizzo 1975; Salemi 1961) established by the provisional Italian government drafted a Statute (a charter of regional autonomy which might be seen as a sort of subnational constitution). The Statute was finally enacted in 1946 by royal law

[4]This was clearly expressed in a flyer printed after the landing in which the "Committee for the Independence" made a demand to the Allied governments for the constitution of a Sicilian Provisional Government in order to hold a plebiscite for the independence of Sicily (Ganci 1966: 43) and in the speech entitled "The Sicily's Reasons", in which Finocchiaro Aprile claimed the democratic right of the Sicilian people to hold such a plebiscite (id.: 54–55).

[5]See Finocchiaro's speech about the Atlantic Charter made in Palermo on the 16th of January 1944 (Ganci 1966: 47); the speech "The Allies and Sicily" kept in Partinico on the 20 August 1944 (id.: 110–111); the flyer "Memorandum for the San Francisco Conference" (id.: 115); and the discourse "Sicilian secessionism in relation to the International situation" (id.: 136).

[6]He spoke about a federation, or more accurately, a confederation in the speeches "For the Independence of Sicily" in Palermo on the 13 February 1944 (Ganci 1966: 64–65) and in "The Allies and the Sicily" in Partinico on the 20 August 1944 (id.: 91). See also the document "Sicily in the Italian Federation" (id.: 112–113) and the documents from the Taormina Congress of the MIS (id.: 148 and ff.).

decree no. 455/1946. The MIS did not participate directly in the activities of the Consulta.[7]

At the Constituent Assembly election in 1946, the MIS obtained only 166.332 votes out of two million Sicilian voters, thereby gaining four seats. At the Constituent Assembly, Andrea Finocchiaro Aprile was a supporter of the confederation thesis (Camera dei Deputati 1970–1971: 19—Session 29 July 1946) and sometimes of the federative ones (the two terms were used in a very similar way by Finocchiaro). He explicitly affirmed acceptance of an autonomist solution as merely as a step towards secession (*ex pluribus* Camera dei Deputati 1970–1971: 507—Session 15 November 1946), and, in addition, he proposed a sort of *fictio iuris*: The creation of independent states, and meanwhile, the creation of a confederation (Camera dei Deputati 1970–1971: 71—Session 1 August 1946). Of course, this could not be done in the Constituent Assembly. Finocchiaro was also one of the main "unaware" supporters of a contractualism thesis by claiming that the Statute established for Sicily and its contents cannot be modified *in pejus* even by the Constituent Assembly (Camera dei Deputati 1970–1971: 508—Session 15 November 1946); Antonino Varvaro, another important member of MIS, although granting the unity of Italy, demanded the ratification of the Statute enacted in 1946 without any modifications (Camera dei Deputati 1970–1971: 447—Session 6 June 1947). This was a shared position in the Constituent Assembly, given the risks of the secessionist impulses.[8]

[7]The nearest—politically speaking—movement to MIS was the Movement for Autonomy (*in Italian*, Movimento per l'Autonomia) led by Duke Avarna di Gualtieri, whose project was not the most autonomist one between the different projects proposed (Ganci 1968: 387).

[8]This fear was expressed, for example, by Mr. Ambrosini, who spoke about the political commitments assumed in front of the Sicilian people, and by Mr. Patricolo, who suggested the Statute could have been modified only by the Sicilian constituents (Camera dei Deputati 1970–1971: 349—Session 15 October 1946). In addition, see the speech of Mr. Russo Perez, who exposed the secessionist risks (id.: 4551—Session 7 June 1947) and that of Mr. Terracini, President of the Assembly, who seemed to endorse a sort of contractualism by saying that the problem of the region of Sicily was not connected to the regionalism discussed in the Assembly (id.: 4694—Session 7 June 1947). See also the speeches of Mr. Gullo Rocco (id.: 4777—Session 13 June 1947). During the discussion concerning the Sicilian Statute, the *bagarre* was maximum. The opening discourse of the Rapporteur Mr. Cevolotto expressed a weak contractualism and the hidden risk of secession (id.: 4282–4283—Session 31 January 1948); Mr. Ambrosini led the attack against the Commission, affirming the political reason of the untouchable character of the Statute—politically

The Statute had to be "coordinated" with the Italian Constitution, as it was established before the enactment of the Constitution, but in the end, it was treated as a quasi-untouchable law. This idea was also deeply supported by almost all the Sicilian politicians (Tarli Barbieri 1998; Ganci 1968: 426), who believed that for "political" reasons, it would be impossible to change the Statute, and it only had to be coordinated with the Constitution with regard to "formal" issues.

Finally, the Constitution guaranteed a special regime of autonomy to Sicily, and this led to the political disappearance of MIS, which was undermined by the enactment of the Statute (Paci and Pietrancosta 2010). Indeed, at the regional election in 1947, MIS gained only 8.8% of the votes, and in the political election in 1948, only 2.1% in Sicily. The next regional elections in 1951 marked the end of MIS, which was not able to gain any seats. Thus, the identity issue was not very strong, and in some ways, it seemed to be overshadowed by questions linked to poverty and the mistreatment of the resources of the island by the Italian governments.

The issue of secession was also quite strong in the territories of the Alps, where the linguistic minorities are concentrated. In those territories, the Fascist regime had tried to destroy the national identities of the French, German and Slovenian populations by promoting an aggressive policy of Italianisation. In reaction to this, organised Anti-Fascist forces started seeing the protection of minorities as a fundamental goal of their action. Therefore, the Resistance Committees expressed the will to safeguard the different identities in the Chivasso Declaration of 1943 (Demuro and Louvin 2017; Peyronel and Giordano 2015), in which both the minorities' rights and the creation of a future federal state were required.

A dangerous problem for the unity of the State was the situation of Valle d'Aosta/Vallée d'Aoste, which was deeply affected by secessionist claims and French influence.

speaking—and the psychological risks of this process (id.: 4291 and ff.); following him, almost all the Sicilian constituents—although they were not alone—attacked the new Statute: Li Causi warned about the secessionist movements (id.: 4391); Mr. Gullo Rocco recalled the idea of the coordination as a formal coordination (id.: 4303); Mr. Musotto discussed an acquired right concerning the Statute (id.: 4313); and Mr. Lussu warned about the danger to the Republic (id.: 4319). In the end, the old statute was approved and the new one dismissed.

In particular, the French army tried to occupy the Valle and then to instigate the French minority of Valle d'Aosta to secede from Italy through a plebiscite. The idea of a plebiscite was a *leitmotiv* (see the numerous episodes and requests reported in Torrione [2010]) of the years before the Conference of Paris, in which the idea of the secession of the Valle from Italy was excluded.

After the fanciful attempt of some members of the French minorities to make a demand to join the Swiss Federation, the separatist movements decided to support the idea of the annexation to France, which was ambiguously kept alive by the French Government and supported by the French secret service, which helped the separatist movement (Lengereau 1975; Torrione 2010; Wildgen 1970).

In order to contain the secessionist impulses, the Italian Provisional Government set the basis for the special autonomy of Valle d'Aosta by enacting two laws concerning autonomy (laws no. 545 and 546 of 1945), starting with the creation of a Regional Council.

In September 1945, the Union Valdôtaine (Valdostan Union—UV) was founded as an association constituted in order to defend the French minority and to demand full autonomy for the Valle d'Aosta. Some of the members of this association were nominated in the first Regional Council in the lists of the national parties, and in 1948, a fully fledged party was created. The Union Valdôtaine wanted to require an international warranty (Zanotto 1985: 70) for the Valle d'Aosta that could guarantee the rights of the minorities and a cantonal regime for the Valle, as expressed in the guidelines of the movement on 26 July 1946 (Mannello 2006: 119) or in the proposal of the UV counsellors at the Regional Council in the session of 7 March 1946 (Torrione 2010: 31).

Under the new provisional Italian Government, there was a riot on 26 March 1946 (Torrione 2010: 39 and ff.) in Aosta, where the separatist movements comprised 5000 persons and tried to occupy the city, requiring a plebiscite for the annexation; the movement tried to force the President of the Regional Council, Federico Chabod, to enact the plebiscite by threatening him with defenestration. The position of UV was ambiguous. It is not clear historically whether the attempts at secession were merely a means of obtaining more autonomy, a real objective or a way to understand which of the states would have conceded more autonomy between France and Italy (Zanotto 1985: 25 and ff.). The first position seems to be the closest to the position of Emile Chanoux, the *maître-à-penser* of the UV (Mannello 2006: 89 and ff.).

At the election of the Constituent Assembly, the candidate for the national left-wing parties, Giulio Bordon, won the only seat available; the UV sought to invalidate the ballots by writing the word "plebiscite": 4444 ballots were invalidated out of 50,945 votes (plus 4308 white ballots). During the Constituent Assembly, Mr. Bordon,[9] but also other constituents, seemed to sustain a sort of proto-contractualism by affirming the "irrevocability" of the autonomy conceded to Valle d'Aosta[10] and by predicting that the unity of the State would be endangered in the case of the development of an autonomy not comparable (i.e. minor) to the one conceded in 1945.[11]

After realising the impossibility of obtaining an international warranty, the UV decided to concentrate its efforts on applying the Statute, and it tried to obtain a more complete autonomy governing the region with some Italian national parties and shifting alliances according to contingencies (Mannello 2006: 122 and ff.).

It seems possible to claim that from the end of 1949, the UV did not advance further requests for a referendum or a plebiscite for secession or annexation, but instead focused only on the matter of an international warranty for the French minorities and considering its future in Europe. Currently, the only reference to the identity of the Valle—in the form of external self-determination—is linked to the statute of UV, which affirmed the "political sovereignty of the Aosta Valley" (*souveraineté*

[9] See Mr. Bordon's speech at the 2nd Subcommittee (Camera dei Deputati 1970–1971: 74—Session 1 August 1946), in which Mr. Bordon affirmed that the Subcommittee must take into account the existence of the autonomy granted by laws no. 545 and 546 of 1945. In the 2nd Subcommittee, Session 14 November 1946 (Camera dei Deputati 1970–1971: 499), he talked about the "acquired rights" of the four special regions, and in particular, of Valle d'Aosta. Also, Mr. Lussu discussed the acquired rights for Sicily and Valle d'Aosta, and a "political right" for Sardinia (Camera dei Deputati 1970–1971: 505—Session 15 November 1946).

[10] See the speech of Mr. Lussu, Rapporteur of the Statute of Valle d'Aosta, during the debate about its approbation regarding the promises and commitments assumed by the State (Camera dei Deputati 1970–1971: 4210—Session 30 January 1948) and the need to respect the past laws (id.: 4263), and that of the President of the Assembly, Mr. Terracini, which affirmed the necessity of a simple coordination (id.: 4241). In this sense, see also the speech of Mr. Finocchiaro Aprile (Camera dei Deputati 1970–1971: 4296—Session 31 January 1948).

[11] See the speech of Mr. Chatrian, who recalled the risk of the irredentism of Valle d'Aosta (Camera dei Deputati 1970–1971: 4249—Session 30 January 1948).

politique du Val d'Aoste) and the aim of self-government in the frame of a Europe of populations.[12]

Another secessionist phenomenon was the South Tyrolean one; the phenomenon in the Italian-speaking territories of Trento was less problematic (Vadagnini and Piccoli 1988). Looking at the issue of South Tyrol, the particular situation and the chaos after WWII of the Province of Bolzano, i.e. the German and Ladino territory, must be stressed. The complexity was caused by the international uncertainty about the future of South Tyrol because the Austrian government was in favour of the reunification of Tyrolean lands and South Tyrolean irredentism.[13]

After the Liberation, the *Südtiroler Volkspartei* (South Tyrolian Peoples' Party—SVP) and the *Dolomiten* newspaper were founded; this German-speaking minority party demanded the freedom to self-determine the future of South Tyrol and eventually to secede from Italy.[14] In the case of South Tyrol, the issue of identity was quite clear, given the request for the revision of the Hitler-Mussolini pacts of 1939 regarding citizenship, and it can be seen the continuation up to the present of the SVP as the party of the Austrian minority in Italy (Holzer and Schwegler 2003).

Again, as in the Sicilian scenario, the possibility of a plebiscite for a unilateral secession under the protection of the Allies seemed to be possible. After the decision of the Allies to deny the right to self-determination through a plebiscite on 24 June 1946, the SVP decided to choose the path of autonomy, abandoning the goal of secession.[15]

[12]Statute of the UV, available at http://www.unionvaldotaine.org/datapage.asp?id=3&l=1 (accessed 20 July 2018).

[13]As reported by Vadagnini and Piccoli (1988: 31), in 1945, the autonomist solution was the second option after secession in the aims and intentions of the South Tyrol intelligentsia. On the same matter, see the document of the SVP reported by id. (1988: 35).

[14]The request for a self-determination referendum was made in point 3 of the SVP's programme in the newspaper "Dolimiten, 15th May 1945". The declaration is available at the following link as part of a larger documentation of the Austrian Parliament: https://www.parlament.gv.at/PAKT/VHG/XXIII/J/J_04105/fname_106708.pdf (accessed 20 July 2018).

[15]The abandonment of point 3—which is the one connected with irredentism—was formally declared at the first Congress of the SVP; "Im politischen Teil des Programms versicherte die Partei", sie werde tätig daran mitarbeiten, damit das italienischösterreichische Abkommen vom 5. September seinem Geist und Sinn nach durchgeführt werde. "Die unerlässliche Voraussetzung hierzu sei die Gewährung einer wirklichen Autonomie". Summary reported by the SVP website, available at https://www.svp.eu/de/partei/geschichte-937.html (accessed 20 July 2018); cf. Forcher (1984).

The De Gasperi-Gruber Agreement of 5 September 1946 regarding the autonomy of the territories that had been part of the Austrian-Hungarian Empire until 1918 (Trentino and South Tyrol) closed the issue of secession, only keeping open the issue of autonomy.

It must be remembered that South Tyrol's population was excluded from the voting process of the Constituent Assembly, but the Assembly carefully took its necessity into consideration, and the particular status of South Tyrol was recognised. After a complicated series of proposals and counter-proposals, the Statute for Trentino-Alto Adige/South Tyrol was approved, and the constitutional law no. 5 of 1948 was enacted. The statute was written with the Government's contribution, given the lack of constituents from South Tyrol, and it was considered quite untouchable in the debate in the Constituent Assembly,[16] in which Prime Minister Alcide De Gasperi significantly took a very pro-active stance.

In the regional election of 1948, the SVP stipulated an alliance with the Italian party DC; in 1957, the SVP, with the famous motto "Los von Trient!", abandoned the regional council and returned only after the approval of the so-called *Pacchetto per l'Alto Adige* (Package Agreement), i.e. a law granting a more complete autonomy to the Province of Bolzano. In the meantime, there were South Tyrolean terrorist attacks and riots between Italian speakers and German ones. In 1992, the international dispute between Italy and Austria was closed, and the De Gasperi-Gruber Agreement was considered to be completely respected.

Today, the identity of South Tyrol remains quite alive, as the recent issuance of a double passport has shown, but currently, the secessionist impulses seem to have been relegated to several right-wing parties; although the SVP continues to talk about self-determination, it has not made any significant legal efforts to obtain it,[17] and it currently governs the Province with the Democratic Party (PD).

[16] See the speech of Mr. Uberti, the Rapporteur of the Statute, who described the Statute as a fragile building that could fall if a stone were to be removed (Camera dei Deputati 1970–1971: 4146—Session 29 January 1948). Obviously, in this Statute, the influence of the DeGasperi-Gruber Pact was high. See the critics about the untouchability of Mr. Toniello (id.: 4162).

[17] There are plenty of declarations in this sense: The general Declaration of the SVP ("beschloß die Landesversammlung der Südtiroler Volkspartei") of 18 November 1983; the newspapers Volksblatt and Nürnberger Zeitung reported interviews of the leader of the SVP Durnwalder, who claimed to be in favour of self-determination and irredentism; the resolution adopted by the SVP on 21 November 1992 in favour of a unique and united Tyrol in the EU. Documents available at https://www.parlament.gv.at/PAKT/VHG/XXIII/J/J_04105/fname_106708.pdf (accessed 20 July 2018); cf. Pallaver (2006).

In fact, the secessionist parties, namely Die Freiheitlichen, Süd-Tiroler Freiheit and Bürger Union für Südtirol received about one-third of the votes in the election of 2013. In 2014, Eva Klotz's Süd-Tiroler Freiheit organised a sort of informal referendum to ask the South Tyrol people to express themselves on the matter of self-determination.

In addition, as we will see in the next paragraph, it must be highlighted that one of the most recent acts submitted to the Bozen Council is the final report of the "Commission for Autonomy", which proposed a modification of the Preamble of the Statute to make reference to the right of self-determination enshrined in the UN Charter.[18]

Among the stronger secessionist movements, the "weakest" was the Sardinian independence movement. Inside the Partito sardo d'azione (Sardinian Party of Action, PSd'Az), before the advent of Fascism, there were two different positions: The moderate-autonomist faction went hand in hand with a more radical one with sympathies for independence (Sechi 1969: 299 and ff.). One of the most important leaders of this second tendency was Emilio Lussu. After the war, the largest and most dominant position (Del Piano 1974: 25) in Sardinia was the anti-separatist one, which Lussu eventually supported as a member of the Constituent Assembly.[19]

After the creation of a Consultancy for the Statute, which failed to establish a provisional Statute, the Constituent Assembly enacted the Special Statute for Sardinia (Cardia 1992). The main *defensor* of the autonomy of the Sardinia region in the Constituent Assembly was Lussu, who also proposed a contractualist concept of the autonomy of Sardinia, and along with all the Sardinian constituents, defended the project elaborated by the Commission from attempts to weaken it.[20]

[18] Document available at http://www.consiglio-bz.org/it/attualita/cs-consiglio-attuali.asp?aktuelles_action=4&aktuelles_article_id=597517#accept-cookies (accessed 20 July 2018).

[19] In many speeches in the Assembly, he tried to stress that autonomy is something very different from separatism. See Camera dei Deputati (1970–1971: 527—Session 19 November 1946).

[20] See the debate on the Statute of Sardinia (Camera dei Deputati 1970–1971: 4082 and ff.—Session 28 January 1948). After the position assumed by the Sardinian constituents, the Statute proceeded quickly toward approbation without amendments. It is worthwhile to mention the affirmation of the Rapporteur of the Statute, Mr. Ambrosini, who claimed that it was necessary to consider the psychological answer of the Sardinian people (Camera dei Deputati 1970–1971: 4126–4127 and ff.—Session 29 January 1948).

In Sardinia, a separatist movement arose during the 1970s, and today, approximately 15–20% of the votes go to separatist and pro-independence parties (Pala 2013).

In 2012, the separatist movement Malu Entu tried to propose a referendum concerning the independence of Sardinia—as we will discuss in the next paragraph—and at the end of 2017, the Independent movement Meris also tried to collect signatures to have a referendum about Sardinian Independence.

Finally, more recently, a new secessionist movement has arisen in Italy: The Lega Nord—Padania (Northern League—Padania). The party has described itself as the only one that can defend the North of Italy (the richest part of the Peninsula) from the avidity of the Centre-South of Italy. The attempt to create a quasi-national identity failed (De Luna 1994; Ferraiuolo 2016: 108; Giordano 2000; Petrosino 1996: 76 and ff),[21] and today, the League is in the process of becoming a national party.

The original secessionist impulses, as stressed by De Fiores (1996: 100), who cited the main ideologue of the Northern League Gianfranco Miglio (1992), seemed to be subordinated to the absence of a federalist reform of the state. Within the Lega Nord, there were several different positions regarding the secessionist plan: Some wanted to negotiate the secession of Padania, and in case of the failure of such attempt, to use the legal instruments of a regional referendum[22]; others wanted to use the natural right as a foundation to secede.[23]

Finally, it must be stressed that since the aforementioned "nationalisation" of the Lega Nord, one of its regional branches, namely the *Liga Veneta* (Veneto League), has led the secessionist battle. The regional government of Veneto, where the electoral strength of Liga Veneta is huge, tried to call for a regional referendum in order to obtain

[21] As stressed, the Northern League was absent in some regions that were part of Padania, namely Emilia-Romagna, Liguria, Trentino and Piemonte (Cantaro 1996: 8).

[22] As claimed by the Lega Nord's Leader, Roberto Maroni, and reported by C. De Fiores (1996: 101).

[23] This seems to be the position sustained by Gianfranco Miglio in a book in which he engaged in a frank dialogue with Augusto Barbera, an eminent constitutional law scholar who has sat on the Constitutional Court since December 2015 (Miglio and Barbera 1997: 180).

independence through regional law no. 16/2014. As we will see, the regional law was declared unconstitutional by the Constitutional Court in its decision no. 118/2015.

As seen in this paragraph, some ideas promoted and popularised by the Quebec secessionist movement were shared by the Italian secessionist ones: The idea of the contractual nature of the relationship with the State (which has traditionally been quite weak in Italy: see Cassese [2011]); the attempt to call for a unilateral referendum; and the attention to the international level and the possibility of gaining legitimacy from it.

As a result, in Italy, there were presuppositions in favour of an evolution similar to the Canadian experience, focusing on the secessionist impulses and the idea of a contractualist relationship between some of the regional autonomies and the State; however, the solutions envisaged by the secessionist movements, and above all, the answers developed by the Constitutional Court, were very different from the Canadian ones. In the next paragraph, we will discuss the attempts at secession made after 1998—the year of the Reference Re Secession—and the possible influence of the Canadian Reference on the Italian legal system and on the political actors.

The *Reference Re Secession of Quebec* and Its Influence on the Italian Legal System

As Palermo (in this volume) has shown, the case of Quebec has been an important inspiration for regionalist and pro-independence movements in Italy—but only to a certain extent. This is particularly evident in the political and parliamentary debates which have marked the evolution of the Italian regional system over the last two decades. Furthermore, in spite of some interesting similarities, the Italian Constitutional Court has embraced a line of reasoning which is clearly distinct from the one followed by its Canadian counterpart in 1998. All these aspects were particularly evident in the case of an attempt to organise a secessionist referendum in the north-eastern (ordinary) region of Veneto.

The quest for greater autonomy has been a major issue in Venetian politics since the "white", Christian Democratic political subculture began its decline and the Venetian branch of the Northern League (*Liga Veneta*) became increasingly influential. As early as the 1990s, the

Regional Council, i.e. the regional legislature of Veneto, tried to organise regional consultative referendums to launch a revision of its own constitutional status. On both occasions, the Constitutional Court declared that those attempts were unconstitutional because they were improperly altering the entrenched procedure for amending the Constitution.[24] Moreover, the Court condemned a law empowering a distinct group of the Italian people—i.e., the voters residing in Veneto—to launch a procedure to modify the Constitution, "as if there were no single people under our Constitution, shaping the political unity of the Nation and, in turn, there were several peoples"[25] (see Conte 2015; Morrone 2012). In the light of this, the secessionist attempt of 2014–2015 was not completely unprecedented—all the more so if the relative interchangeability of "autonomy" and "independence" in the Italian political (not legal) discourse is duly taken into account.

In June 2014, the Regional Council of Veneto approved a law calling for a "consultative referendum on the independence of Veneto"[26] (see Fasone 2015). The wording of the question was as follows: "Do you want Veneto to become an independent and sovereign republic?" (Article 1(1)). For the Yes vote to prevail, the law required the turnout to be higher than 50%: In this way, a "clear majority" was necessary for the secessionist option to be formally recognised.[27] Everyone residing in a Venetian municipality was entitled to vote in the referendum. When the draft bill was introduced, its promoters stressed that referendums on independence had become a common practice for ascertaining the will of the affected peoples: Among the most important examples, they mentioned Catalonia and Scotland.[28] In a more recent draft bill, which

[24] *Corte costituzionale*, judgements no. 470/1992 and 496/2000.

[25] *Corte costituzionale*, judgement no. 496/2000 (our translation).

[26] Regional law of Veneto no. 16 of 19 June 2014. On the same day, the Venetian legislature also approved another law (regional law no. 15/2014) calling for a referendum "on the autonomy of Veneto". The referendum took place on 22 October 2017 and was followed by a bilateral negotiation to grant further autonomy to Veneto (see Arban 2018).

[27] This "double majority" requirement is a typical feature of the *Statuto*, the regional statute of Veneto, which strongly favours direct democratic participation (see Ferri 2013: 404–405).

[28] Regional Council of Veneto, Draft bill no. 342 (2010–2015 legislative term), available at ligavenetarepubblica.org/wp-content/uploads/2014/01/pdlr342-Referendum.pdf (accessed 20 July 2018).

tries to relaunch the secessionist process, reference is made in bulk to Scotland, Quebec, Montenegro, Catalonia, Greenland and Crimea.[29] In this respect, the supporters of a referendum on the independence of Veneto have proven to be conscious of the institutional evolution in Europe and North America over the last two decades: The organisation of a referendum seems to be the chief instrument for ascertaining the will of the affected peoples. The Quebec independence movement led by the Parti Québécois has been an obvious forerunner in this trend.[30] On the other hand, as it emerges from the text of the draft bill, the idea of a principled negotiation between the state government and the regional government of Veneto, with a key role played by the fundamental principles of the Italian constitutional order, is all but foreign to the concerns of the Venetian lawmakers (see also Serges 2015: 9–11). The emphasis is placed on a strong notion of democracy, clearly trumping the other constitutional values involved. On the other hand, unilateralism is another defining feature of this regional initiative: If the Yes option prevails, the state government is simply invited to acknowledge this result. Some scholars (Ferraiuolo 2014: 704) have remarked that the report submitted by the 1st Committee of the Venetian legislature conceived of the referendum as a vote on the ongoing "allegiance of the Venetian people to the Italian Republic": This wording recalls international law, but also the conception of the Constitution as a compact.

The Italian state government immediately decided to challenge this regional law of Veneto before the Constitutional Court.[31] In short, the state government argued that the Venetian legislature, by calling for a referendum on independence, was violating a fundamental

[29] Regional Council of Veneto, Draft bill no. 149 (2015–2020 legislative term), available at http://www.consiglioveneto.it/crvportal/pdf/pratiche/10/pdl/PDL_0149/1000_5Ftesto_20presentato.pdf (accessed 20 July 2018).

[30] See, e.g., the intervention by Senator Francesco Speroni during the meeting of the Senate on 1 April 1998, available at http://www.parlamento.it/japp/bgt/showdoc/frame.jsp?tipodoc=Resaula&leg=13&id=00005002&part=doc_dc&parse=no&stampa=si&toc=no (accessed 20 July 2018).

[31] According to Article 127(1) of the Italian Constitution, the state government "may challenge the constitutional compliance of a regional law before the Constitutional Court within sixty days of its publication, if it deems that such law exceeds the jurisdiction of the region".

principle of the Italian constitutional order and was trying to amend the Constitution surreptitiously by means of an alternative, illegal procedure.

Quite predictably, the Constitutional Court declared the impugned law unconstitutional and struck it down. The Court resorted to three main arguments in its reasoning. The first one is based on the allocation of competences: The consultative referendum on the independence of Veneto concerns "fundamental choices on [a] constitutional level, which are as such precluded from the scope of regional referendums".[32] The second one, in turn, is more radical: The regional law of Veneto "seeks to subvert the institutions in a manner that is inherently incompatible with the founding principles of the unity and indivisibility of the Republic laid down in Article 5 of the Constitution".[33] In the light of this, there is no room at all for referendums on the independence of the constituent units of the Republic, such as Veneto. Indeed, the unity of the Republic, which is a fundamental principle of the constitutional order, is "protected even against the power of constitutional amendment": Therefore, it would be innately illogical to allow Veneto to organise a referendum with this object. The third and final argument builds on well-established constitutional dogmatic and is used by the Constitutional Court in order to debunk the unilateralistic attitude underlying the Venetian attempt: Under the Italian Constitution, territorial "pluralism and autonomy do not permit the regions to classify themselves as sovereign bodies and do not permit their governmental organs to be treated as equivalent to the representative bodies of a nation (see Judgements no. 365 of 2007, no. 306 and no. 106 of 2002).[34] A fortiori, the same principles cannot be taken to extremes so as to result in the fragmentation of the legal order and cannot be invoked as justification for initiatives involving the consultation of the electorate ... concerning prospective secession with a view to the creation of a new sovereign body".[35]

[32] *Corte costituzionale*, judgement no. 118/2015 (English translation available at www.cortecostituzionale.it/documenti/download/doc/recent_judgements/S118_2015_en.pdf [accessed 20 July 2018]).

[33] Id.

[34] As the Court clearly put it in those judgements, even after the "federalising" constitutional reform of 2001, the constitutional position of the Italian regions can only be aptly described in terms of "autonomy", and not of "sovereignty" (see Delledonne and Martinico 2009: 224)

[35] *Corte costituzionale*, judgement no. 118/2015 (see above footnote 32).

As mentioned before, in its judgement no. 118/2015, the Italian Constitutional Court clearly followed a very different path from that followed by its Canadian counterpart in the 1990s. If constitutional legality is respected, there is no room for secessionist attempts in Italy. Leaving aside the unilateralistic attempt of the Venetian legislature, it would also be plainly unconstitutional to hold negotiations between the state government and one or more regions with secession as a possible outcome. On a different note, it is possible to find at least one similarity between the Italian judgement of 2015 and the *Quebec Secession Reference*: It has to do with the role of fundamental principles in the contemporary constitutional discourse. Fundamental principles are being called upon to shape the political sphere with increasing frequency: Of course, this should come as no surprise, as the normative force of constitutional provisions is a decisive component of present-day constitutionalism. At present, however, fundamental principles are invoked even with respect to the most important political decisions, regarding, e.g. the unity and survival of the state. In the Canadian Reference, the "underlying principles animating the whole of the Constitution" are supposed to shape a process of negotiation between the governments of Canada and Quebec. In the Italian case, in turn, relying on the principle of the unity and indivisibility of the Republic clearly limits the scope of admissible political action: Regional and local governments may well ask for greater autonomy[36]—but "these principles must be developed within the framework of the Republic alone".[37]

The Venetian attempt of 2014–2015 was the most important attempt to organise a regional secessionist referendum. For the purposes of this chapter, parallel developments in two special regions, Trentino-Alto Adige/South Tyrol and Sardinia (see above paragraph 2), deserve to be mentioned as well. In January 2012, the Sardinian pro-independence movement Malu Entu ("bad wind") submitted a petition to organise a consultative referendum on the independence of Sardinia. According to its proponents, the legal foundation for this attempt was to be found in the "international law of the United Nations". However, the Regional Office for Referendum (*Ufficio regionale per il referendum*) held that this request for a referendum was plainly illegitimate: In so doing, it mainly relied on

[36] As the Constitutional Court itself acknowledged in the very same judgement by recognising the Venetian regional law no. 15/2014 (see above footnote 26) as constitutional.

[37] *Corte costituzionale*, judgement no. 118/2015 (see above footnote 32).

arguments similar to those used by the Constitutional Court in its well-established case law.[38]

As mentioned before, in 2015, the provincial legislature of South Tyrol established a Convention for the Reform of the Statute of Autonomy (*Statuto di autonomia*) of Trentino-Alto Adige/South Tyrol, better known as the Autonomy Convention. The self-determination of South Tyrol was one of the main issues addressed during this interesting experiment in constitutional deliberative democracy (see Eerola and Reuchamps [2016] and, with regard to the South Tyrolean case, Happacher [2017]). In its final report for the provincial legislature, a majority of members of the Autonomy Convention suggested that the right of self-determination, as recognised by Article 1 of the UN Charter, be mentioned in the preamble of the regional statute of autonomy. In this regard, the two independence referendums in Quebec have always been an inspiration for the German-speaking right-wing parties. The representatives of the Italian-speaking parties have sometimes revealed a more careful reading of the institutional evolution in Canada over the last two decades, acknowledging the impossibility of recognising a right to self-determination in the absence of institutional oppression.[39]

Concluding Remarks

In conclusion, we think that our research questions should be answered in a nuanced way. On the one hand, it cannot be argued that the Quebec Secession Reference has directly influenced the Italian constitutional system. The Italian Constitutional Court has chosen a firm and strong approach against secessionist projects, closing every possible space of action for the secessionist movements. The Italian Constitution—or, more accurately, its unamendable fundamental principles—appears to be a "straightjacket" for the subnational units. Indeed, leaving aside Veneto, whose attempt was probably merely part of a more complex strategy to gain more competences and a more favourable fiscal regime from the state, and ultimately, to obtain a status closer to that of the special

[38]The deliberation of 6 June 2012 of the *Ufficio regionale per il referendum* is available at www.regione.sardegna.it/documenti/1_19_20120607105045.pdf (accessed 20 July 2018).

[39]See, e.g. the intervention by Councillor Vezzali (from the centre-right party Popolo della libertà) in the Council meeting of 8 May 2012.

regions (cf. Ferraiuolo 2016: 133 and ff.), no serious challenges have been posed by ethnic secessionist movements so far. Consequently, the relative weakness of the Venetian pro-secession arguments has probably made it possible for the Constitutional Court to sustain its intransigent line, which has avoided offering any kind of legitimation and recognition to secessionist movements and has not taken into account the possibility for a negotiated solution.

References

Arban, Erika (2018), "The Referenda for More Autonomy in Veneto and Lombardia: Constitutional and Comparative Perspectives", in *Perspectives on Federalism*, 10 (1), 242–267.

Camera dei Deputati ed. (1970–1971), *La Costituzione della Repubblica nei lavori preparatori della Assemblea Costituente*, Camera dei Deputati, Roma.

Cantaro, Antonio (1996), "Introduzione", in Claudio De Fiores and Daniele Petrosino (eds.), *Secessione*, Ediesse, Roma, 7–24.

Cardia, Mariarosa (1992), *La nascita della Regione autonoma della Sardegna 1943–1948*, Franco Angeli, Milano.

Cassese, Sabino (2011), *L'Italia: una società senza Stato?* Il Mulino, Bologna.

Conte, Francesco (2015), "La Corte costituzionale sui referendum per l'autonomia e l'indipendenza del Veneto. Non c'è due senza tre. Anche se…", in *Quaderni costituzionali*, 35 (3), 759–761.

De Fiores, Claudio (1996), "Secessione e forma di Stato", in Claudio De Fiores and Daniele Petrosino (eds.), *Secessione*, Ediesse, Roma, 89–133.

De Luna, Giovanni (1994), *Figli di un benessere minore. La Lega 1979–1993*, La Nuova Italia, Firenze.

Del Piano, Lorenzo (1974), *Lo Statuto sardo*, Edizioni della Torre, Sassari.

Delledonne, Giacomo and Martinico, Giuseppe (2009), "Handle with Care! The Italian Charters and Italian Constitutionalism's 'Grey Zone'", in *European Constitutional Law Review*, 5 (2), 218–236.

Delledonne, Giacomo, Martinico, Giuseppe and Pierdominici, Leonardo (2017), "Il costituzionalismo canadese a 150 anni dalla Confederazione. Riflessioni comparatistiche", in Giacomo Delledonne, Giuseppe Martinico, and Leonardo Pierdominici (eds.), *Il costituzionalismo canadese a 150 anni dalla Confederazione. Riflessioni comparatistiche*, Pisa University Press, Pisa, 5–13.

Demuro, Gianmario and Louvin, Roberto (2017), *La fondazione di un ordinamento federale per le democrazie regionali*, Le Château Edizioni, Aosta.

Eerola, Aleksi and Reuchamps, Min (2016), "Constitutional Modernisation and Deliberative Democracy: A Political Science Assessment of Four Cases", in *Revue interdisciplinaire d'études juridiques*, 77, 319–336.

Fasone, Cristina (2015), "Il tentativo secessionista 'all'italiana' e la semi-indifferenza della politica nazionale", in *Diritti comparati*, March 5, 2015, available at www.diritticomparati.it/il-tentativo-secessionista-allitaliana-e-la-semi-indifferenza-della-politica-nazionale.

Ferraiuolo, Gennaro (2014), "Due referendum non comparabili", in *Quaderni costituzionali*, 34 (3), 703–706.

Ferraiuolo, Gennaro (2016), *Costituzione federalismo secessione. Un itinerario*, ES, Napoli.

Ferri, Giampietro (2013), "Gli istituti di partecipazione popolare", in Paolo Cavaleri and Gianfrancesco Eduardo (eds.), *Lineamenti di diritto costituzionale della Regione del Veneto*, Giappichelli, Torino, 399–406.

Forcher, Michael (1984), *Tirols Geschichte in Wort und Bild*, Haymon, Innsbruck.

Ganci, Massimo (1966), *Andrea Finocchiaro Aprile. Il Movimento Indipendentista siciliano*, Edizioni Libri Siciliani, Palermo.

Ganci, Massimo (1968), *L'Italia antimoderata*, Guanda, Parma.

Giarrizzo, Giuseppe (1975), "Sicilia politica 1943–1945. La genesi dello statuto regionale", in Consulta regionale siciliana (ed.), I, *Saggi introduttivi*, Edizioni della Regione siciliana, Palermo, 7–116.

Giordano, Benito (2000), "Italian regionalism or 'Padanian' Nationalism—The Political Project of the Lega Nord in Italian Politics", in *Political Geography*, 19 (4), 445–471.

Happacher, Esther (2017), "La Convenzione per l'Autonomia: Spunti per un'autonomia dinamica e partecipata dell'Alto Adige/*Südtirol*", in *Osservatorio sulle fonti*, 10 (3), 1–14, available at www.osservatoriosullefonti.it.

Holzer, Anton and Schwegler, Barbara (2003), "The Südtiroler Volkspartei: A Hegemonic Ethnoregionalist Party", in Lieven De Winter and Huri Tursan (eds.), *Regionalist Parties in Western Europe*, Routledge, London, 158–173.

La Pergola, Antonio (1969), *Residui "contrattualistici" e struttura federale nell'ordinamento degli Stati Uniti*, Giuffrè, Milano.

Lengereau, Marc (1975), *La France et la question valdotaine au cours et à l'issue de la 2ème guerre mondiale*, Société d'histoire alpine et italienne, Grenoble.

Mannello, Antonio Eugenio (2006), *L'Union Valdôtaine e il federalismo. La riforma dello Stato tra storia e politica del movimento autonomista*, Musumeci, Quart.

Miglio, Gianfranco (1992), *Come cambiare*, Mondadori, Milano.

Miglio, Gianfranco and Barbera, Augusto (1997), *Federalismo e secessione: un dialogo*, Mondadori, Milano.

Morrone, Andrea (2012), "Avanti popolo… regionale!", in *Quaderni costituzionali*, 32 (3), 615–618.

Olivetti Rason, Nino (1999), "A proposito della secessione del Québec: Tre quesiti e quattro risposte", in *Diritto pubblico comparato ed europeo*, 1 (3), 889–902.

Paci, Deborah and Pietrancosta, Fausto (2010), "Il separatismo siciliano (1943–1947)", in *Diacronie*, 3 (2), 1–27.

Pala, Carlo (2013), "La Sardegna tra indipendentismo e autonomia finanziaria", in Demuro Gianmarco, Mola, Francesco, and Ruggiu, Ilenia (eds), *Identità e autonomia in Sardegna e Scozia*, Maggioli, Sant'Arcangelo di Romagna, 156–179.

Pallaver, Günther (2006), "The Südtiroler Volkspartei: From Irredentism to Autonomy", in Lieven De Winter, Margarita Gómez-Reino, and Peter Lynch (eds.), *Autonomist Parties in Europe: Identity, Politics and the Revival of the Territorial Cleavage*, Aleu, Baecelona, 161–188.

Passaglia, Paolo (1999), "La Corte suprema del Canada definisce le regole mediante cui procedure alla secessione", in *Il Foro italiano*, 122(6), part IV, 271–277.

Petrosino, Daniele (1996), "Democrazie di fine secolo. L'epoca delle secessioni?", in Claudio De Fiores and Daniele Petrosino (eds.), *Secessione*, Ediesse, Roma, 25–87.

Peyronel, Susanna and Giordano, Filippo Maria (2015), *Federalismo e Resistenza. Il crocevia della Dichiarazione di Chivasso (1943)*, Società di studi valdesi Torre Pellice, Torino.

Poggeschi, Giovanni (1998), "Il diritto di secessione del Québec secondo la Corte suprema del Canada", in *Le istituzioni del federalismo*, 19 (6), 1173–1197.

Salemi, Giovanni (1961), *Lo Statuto della Regione siciliana*, Cedam, Padova.

Sechi, Salvatore (1969), *Dopoguerra e fascismo in Sardegna. Il movimento autonomistico nella crisi dello Stato liberale (1918–1926)*, Fondazione Luigi Einaudi, Torino.

Serges, Giovanni (2015), "Autodeterminazione, diritto a decider, indipendenza, sovranità (notazioni a margine della Legge regionale del Veneto, n. 16 del 2014)", in *federalismi.it*, 13 (1), 1–16, available at www.federalismi.it.

Tarli Barbieri, Giovanni (1998), "Il regionalismo prima della Costituzione repubblicana: La sofferta genesi dello statuto siciliano", in Nicola Antonietti and Ugo De Siervo (eds.), *Ambrosini e Sturzo. La nascita delle Regioni*, Bologna, Il Mulino, 195–242.

Toniatti, Roberto (1994), "Minoranze e minoranze protette: Modelli costituzionali comparati", in Tiziano Bonazzi and Michael Dunne (eds.), *Cittadinanza e diritti nelle società multiculturali*, Il Mulino, Bologna, 1994, 273–307.

Torrione, Gianni (2010), *Tàppa lo ba: 1946, Valle d'Aosta tra autonomia e annessionismo: Cronaca giornalistica di un anno difficile*, Musumeci, Quart.

Vadagnini, Armando and Piccoli, Paolo (1988), *Il cammino dell'autonomia nei progetti per lo statuto speciale del 1948*, Regione Trentino-Alto Adige, Trento.

Wildgen, John K. (1970), "The Liberation of the Valle d'Aosta, 1943–1945", in *The Journal of Modern History*, 42 (1), 21–41.

Zanotto, André (1985), "Il lungo cammino verso lo Statuto d'autonomia", in Consiglio regionale della Valle d'Aosta (ed.), *Le origini dello Statuto speciale*, Musumeci, Aosta, 9–94.

Secession Reference and Its Intellectual Legacy: Sceptical Notes from the European Peripheries

Zoran Oklopcic

Introduction

Reference Re Secession of Quebec (hereinafter Secession Reference, or simply the Reference) is probably one of the most, if not *the* most important judgement in the history of Canadian constitutional law. Over the years, a variety of scholars from a number of disciplines—from comparative constitutionalism and international law, to constitutional and political theory—explored the (potential) relevance of this decision to a number of lingering disputes over territorial sovereignty and ultimate constitutional authority: from Taiwan Sri Lanka, and Tibet, to Montenegro, Kosovo, Scotland, and Catalonia. Wherever it "migrated", this (technically advisory), 1998 opinion of the Supreme Court of Canada, aroused keen interest among the lawyers and the laymen alike,

Z. Oklopcic (✉)
Department of Law and Legal Studies, Carleton University,
Ottawa, ON, Canada

G. Delledonne and G. Martinico (eds.), *The Canadian Contribution to a Comparative Law of Secession*,
https://doi.org/10.1007/978-3-030-03469-6_10

and was appreciated even by those who considered its forthcoming attitude towards secessionist aspirations for whatever reason inadvisable.

Twenty years on, we are in a better position to evaluate its intellectual and political legacy. Should it be celebrated, and for what achievements? Who benefited from it, and in what way? Is it true, as Giuseppe Martinico argues in this volume, that "the greatest contribution to constitutionalism as a philosophical movement given by the Canadian Supreme Court [in the Secession Reference] consists in its broad concept of democracy, understood as a star in a constellation of values that need to be preserved and balanced by guaranteeing the evolution of the legal system" (Martinico 2019, this volume)? While I ultimately agree with Martinico about the centrality of the principle of democracy in the argumentative structure of the Secession Reference, its chief accomplishment—lending intellectual dignity to a highly responsive brand of foundational constitutionalism—can only be appreciated if we look behind the Court's ongoing references to democracy and popular sovereignty. Put differently, the only way to reconcile the Court's understanding of the "unwritten" principle of democracy with its understanding of the remaining three unwritten principles is to challenge the very imaginary that makes the idea of democracy intelligible and sensible.

If my diagnosis is correct, Secession Reference offers not an attractive new conception of democracy, but rather an opportunity to re-examine what we mean by it in the first place. Theoretically interesting in its own right, this question is also practically important, especially against the backdrop of the claims of those, who, as Errol Mendes in this volume, argue that the Reference "should also be viewed as a vital authoritative precedent for liberal democracies around the world facing secessionist challenges" (Mendes 2019, this volume). More on this issue later. What's more important to register at this point are other, equally suspicious gifts of the Secession Reference. In addition to what Martinico calls "broad conception of democracy", the international legacy of this judgement includes two other things as well: an account of the right to self-determination that offers qualified support for secession as an international legal *remedy* for state oppression; and an argument that makes the legitimacy of sovereignty referendums conditional on their conformity with the standards of *clarity*.

Democracy, remedy, clarity: this, in shortest terms, is the dubious international legacy of the Secession Reference. In this essay, my aim is to confront its legacy from the perspective of the periphery of the European Union: its external (Kosovo and Montenegro) and its internal (Catalonia and Spain) periphery. My conclusion—as it will hopefully become apparent by the end of this essay—will be different from Martinico's. The main gift of Secession Reference to contemporary constitutional theory is not a broader understanding of democracy, but an opportunity to look at democratic constitutions from the perspective of institutional responsiveness. From that, more granular perspective, the main domestic achievement of the Secession Reference was not a more democratic, but a more selectively responsive Canada.

Superficially, the Reference reconnected that Canada with its foundational commitments. On closer look, however, it also did something even more remarkable. It accepted the political dignity of unqualified secessionist aspirations. It is this institutional *attitude*—which still has no theoretical name—that ought to be recognized as the true contribution of the Secession Reference to constitutional theory. If so, the central message that the Supreme Court of Canada sent to its Quebecois audience was, simple, but profound: *You want it, because you want it. We get it. If you really want it, then you want it—and we respect that. No need to explain yourselves. No need to defend the dignity of your aspiration. Rest assured,* if *you really want it, we won't ignore it. Once you've figured out what it is specifically, let's get together to see what can we do to make it happen.* The vocabulary of democracy, self-determination, popular sovereignty, and the clarity of a winning majority doesn't allow us to convey this message fully and explicitly, without, at the same time, dramatically raising everyone's level of political anxiety.

If that's the case, it might not be unreasonable to uphold the scholarly conspiracy of silence, and keep quiet about the contours of a conceptual vista that would inevitably occur appears once we looked beneath the Reference's references to self-determination, democracy, federalism, and popular sovereignty. Perhaps. What we must talk about, however, are the political side effects of relying on secession as an institutional *remedy* for ethico-political depravity; the blind spots that appear once we allow the criteria of *clarity* to guide our evaluations of referendum legitimacy, and the disappointments destined to follow once *democracy* reveals itself in its fully conceptual ambiguity. With the help of the examples drawn from the East and West of Europe's Southern periphery, it is the aim of this essay to show why.

Secession (Reference): A Remedy for Oppression?

Secession Reference addresses one of the most important, if not the most important, existential challenge of modern constitutional government: secession. For the most part, naturally, it focuses on Canada: on its constitutional history, on the specific precedents that give rise to unwritten constitutional principles, on the potential issues that might arise in the negotiations, should a referendum on the independence of Quebec show that a clear majority of voters favours secession, and so on. Confronted not only with the question of constitutionality, but also with the question of international legality of the secession of Quebec, the Reference also addresses the question of the right to self-determination. Over time, this account of self determination achieved a fair amount of persuasive authority among the scholars of international law, and was—as we will soon see—prominent in actual legal disputes over the international legality of unilateral secession, such as in the case of Kosovo. But before this interpretation of the Supreme Court of Canada migrated to the outer periphery of the European Union in the mid-2000s, the interpretations of the right to self-determination from that periphery arrived to Canada first.

In 1992, the National Assembly of Quebec commissioned a report from five reputed international jurists asking them to interpret the current state of international law as it relates to state formation who heavily relied the Badinter Committee, whose opinions on the constitutional and international legal aspects of the constitutional crisis in Yugoslavia, guided the policy of the European Community towards that country's dissolution. The Five Experts applied this analysis to the Canadian context, arguing that the principle of self-determination is of limited applicability to the issue of secession, that the creation of a new state is a matter of fact, and that the provincial boundaries of an independent Quebec would be protected by international law (Bayefsky 2000).

The most intellectually fascinating rejoinder to their report arrived in 1997, in the form of an extensive and polemical academic treatise, titled *Sovereign Injustice*, written in support of the self-determination rights of the James Bay Crees in Quebec. In response to the Five Experts, and by implication, the Badinter Opinion arguments. One of their most potent arguments was a simple claim: if Canada is divisible, so is Quebec. If "the people of Quebec" have a right to self-determination, other peoples on the territory of Quebec have a sovereign right to remain in Canada.

The Secession Reference implicitly positioned itself between these two arguments. It agreed with the Five Experts that self-determination is largely inapplicable in the case of the secession of Quebec, but it rejected their claim that international law approves of unilateral secessions. It argued that "the international law right to self-determination only generates, at best, a right to external self-determination in situations … where a people is oppressed … where a definable group is denied meaningful access to government to pursue their political, economic, social and cultural development … because they have been denied the ability to exert internally their right to self-determination" (*Reference Re Secession of Quebec* 1998, paragraph 138).

As I've shown in an earlier article on the subject, the Supreme Court's interpretation of the law of self-determination and territorial integrity attracted remarkable attention during the preliminary stage of the proceedings in the Kosovo case. Though most interested parties made a reference to that interpretation, their own understandings of it differed, sometimes dramatically. In the first, smaller group were those that opposed the independence of Kosovo, and interpreted the Secession Reference's international legal argument not for its understanding of the right to self-determination, but for its principled re-affirmation of the principle of territorial integrity. The Chinese submission, for example, made no mention of the Secession Reference's stance on self-determination. It paraphrased the Reference only in the part where it argues that modern international law evolved in a framework of respect for the territorial integrity of existing states. In the second group were the countries which, while opposing Kosovo's UDI, more fully acknowledged that the Secession Reference ought to be interpreted as supporting the idea of remedial secession outside of the colonial context. Russia—the only country among powers states to quote the Secession Reference—argued that self-determination "evolved within a framework of respect for the territorial integrity of existing states" and that there is no incompatibility between territorial integrity of states and self-determination. Russia took notice of the Reference's formulation of remedial, external self-determination but went on to interpret it restrictively, as applying only in cases where there is an "outright armed attack by the parent state threatening the very existence of the people in question". For Russia, Kosovo Albanians didn't have a right to self-determination, because no threat of attack existed in 2008 or after, in the case of Kosovo.

Relying on the purported stance of the Canadian Supreme Court on remedial self-determination countries in a third group argued that Kosovo's UDI doesn't violate international law. Finland's position was particularly interesting: it argued that the Secession Reference's interpretation of remedial self-determination was not an example of (possible) evolution of international law (as the Canadian Supreme Court argued), but rather the correct interpretation of self-determination that has been in effect since the emergence of self-determination as a dominant political and legal principle of polity formation. For Martti Koskenniemi, the Finnish legal advisor, this trajectory is what the Supreme Court of Canada "had in mind" when it stated that "when a people is blocked from the meaningful exercise of its right of self-determination internally, it is entitled, as a last resort, to exercise it by secession" (Oklopcic 2011).

Acknowledging the remarkable interest aroused by the Secession Reference among the parties participating in the proceedings, the Advisory Opinion on Kosovo independence only did so in order to preemptively deflect criticism about the failure of the Court to address the question of the right to self-determination squarely. Unlike the Supreme Court of Canada, which could not evade answering a point-blank question—"[I]s there a right to self-determination under international law that would give … Quebec the right to effect the secession of Quebec from Canada unilaterally?"—the International Court of Justice was only tasked with answering whether Kosovo's unilaterally declared independence was "in accordance with" international law. In answering this question, according to the ICJ, "[t]he Court is not required by the question it has been asked to take a position on whether international law conferred a positive entitlement on Kosovo unilaterally to declare its independence or, *a fortiori*, on whether international law generally confers an entitlement on entities situated within a State unilaterally to break away from it".

What emerges against the backdrop of this analysis is a soberer picture of the persuasive authority of Secession Reference in international law. Most of those who engaged with it in the case of Kosovo implicitly or explicitly accepted its relevance for the development of the international law of self-determination. But when it came to making use of what the Secession Reference had to say about self-determination, they either ignored its interpretation altogether (like the ICJ itself), or chose to apply it *mechanically*—plugging it into their doctrinal arguments with no consideration for the conceptual conundrums that accompany the idea of remedial secession,[1] and with no appreciation for its *conceptual* contribution to the debates about the right to self-determination.

Secession Reference intervenes into the debates about the right to self-determination in two ways. The first, discussed above, is interpretive and doctrinal: what it offers is support for already developed ethical *justification* of secession—or, from the perspective of international legal doctrine, the expansion of the right to external self-determination to a limited set of situations. On closer inspection, the Supreme Court tackles the right to self-determination not only by addressing it explicitly—in the part of the opinion devoted to the question about the international legality of a unilateral secession of Quebec—but also when it speaks to it obliquely: in the part of the judgement devoted to Canadian constitutional law. Its contribution there is conceptual—not doctrinal. It consists not in justification for remedial secession, but in the explanation of how democracy, constitutionalism, and popular sovereignty relate to two aspects of self-determination which remain analytically undistinguished from the perspective of international law: the *initiation* of the process (intended to result in secession); and the *delineation* of the boundaries of a unit, whose "people" claims the right to external self-determination. In speaking to these aspects in the language of Canadian constitutional law, the Secession Reference may also be read as a contribution to a debate about the content of the right to internal self-determination.

Secession Reference and the Meaning of Clarity

According to the Supreme Court, "[t]he continued existence and operation of the Canadian constitutional order cannot remain indifferent to the clear expression of a clear majority of Quebecers that they no longer wish to remain in Canada" (*Reference Re Secession of Quebec* 1998, paragraph 92). What are the implications of this? "The clear repudiation by the people of Quebec of the existing constitutional order would confer legitimacy on demands for secession, and place an obligation on the other provinces and the federal government to acknowledge and respect that expression of democratic will by entering into negotiations and conducting them in accordance with the underlying constitutional principles already discussed" (*Reference Re Secession of Quebec* 1998, paragraph 88).

[1] For a discussion see Oklopcic (2009).

At this point, many, if not most international lawyers will simply presume that the same "democratic will" that legitimately initiates the process that may lead to secession is the same will that has the final say when it comes to possible alterations of Quebec's boundaries. Without its decision to the contrary, Quebec will maintain its territorial integrity. The Supreme Court saw things differently. In what could be read as an indirect warning, the Court rejected the proposition that Canada's "national existence, seamless in so many aspects, could be effortlessly separated along what are now the provincial boundaries of Quebec". The meaning of these allusions remains unclear, and their credibility—if read as threats—untested.

That is important to notice. The evaluative standards of clarity could only gain prominence in an environment that either bracketed, or suppressed, or resolved the question of territorial boundaries. The Constitution of the former Yugoslavia never addressed this question. Nor did it contain a mechanism for the resolution of conflicts over territorial sovereignty. What was left of that Yugoslavia in the early 2000s, however, did.

In contrast with Yugoslavia's 1974 constitution—notorious for the ambiguities in its principled affirmation of the right of every Yugoslav nation to self-determination—the 2003 Charter of the short-lived State Union of Serbia and Montenegro contained an explicit provision about the right of each unit to secede from the Union, *unilaterally*. Secession Reference became relevant for the secession of Montenegro as it became apparent that the Montenegrin government wouldn't abandon its previously announced decision to organize the referendum on independence by 2005. Passive during the initial stages of the dissolution of Yugoslavia in 1991, this time around, the European Union was determined to sit idly. After a request by the Parliamentary Assembly of the Council of Europe, the European Commission for Democracy through Law (the Venice Commission) publicized its opinion on the compatibility of Montenegro's referendum legislation with international standards.

The Commission concentrated on the issues of the wording of the referendum question, the required turnout, majority, and eligibility criteria to vote. Discussing the issue of the wording of the referendum question, the Venice Commission stated, without expressly referring to Canadian experience, that a question submitted to the electorate must be clear, not be misleading, and that it must not suggest an answer. Concerning the issue of minimum voter turnout, the Venice Commission claimed that while there are no indisputable international standards on what is an acceptable minimum, the Montenegrin *Law on Referendums* requiring that the minimum voter turnout be the majority of citizens with voting rights was approved.

In suggesting that Montenegro amend its referendum legislation, the Commission relied not only on the *Secession Reference* but also on the *Clarity Act* that the Canadian parliament adopted in 2000. While quoting the first part of §1 §§5 of that act—which stated that in making a decision on a clear majority, the views of all political parties represented in the legislature of the seceding entity should be considered—the Commission made no mention of the part that refers to the inclusion of other political stakeholders *outside* of the province. In the Montenegrin context, faithful adoption of the approach of the *Clarity Act* would have required considering the opinions of the Serbian government on the definition of a clear majority as well.

Following the suggestions of the Venice Commission, the proposal of the EU mediator excluded from the franchise those Montenegrin citizens who at that time outside of Montenegro; a clear concession to the pro-independence forces and the Montenegrin government. The compensation for their opponents came in the form of a turnout requirement—more than 50% of registered voters—and a "clear majority" benchmark for victory: 55%. Grudgingly accepted, this proposal allowed the Montenegrin government to organize the referendum under the patronage of the EU. Mindful of the Canadian experience, and keeping with the recommendations of the Venice, the referendum question read: "Do you want the Republic of Montenegro to be an independent state with full international and legal responsibility?" As in the Quebecois referendum eleven years earlier, the margin of victory was razor-thin: without 2300 "yes" votes Montenegro would have remained in the union with Serbia. Back in Canada, the old questions about the legitimacy of supermajority requirements, resurfaced again.

On the one hand, the opponents of Quebecois independence argued that the Montenegro precedent would almost certainly shape international response to a unilateral declaration of independence by Quebec, arguing that "if the Secession Reference and the Clarity Act are good enough for Montenegro ... they will likely be good enough for Quebec" (Choudhry 2007). On the other hand—predictably—Quebecois sovereigntists saw no connection between Montenegro and Canada: "every case is a specific case and needs to be adapted ... to geopolitical realities which are appropriate for different societies", and "if one accepted a 55% rule that would mean that minorities would decide for majorities", and "that doesn't make sense"—especially in the light of the cases to the contrary where no one disputed the legitimacy of referendums that produced only absolute majorities in favour of full state sovereignty (Dutrisac 2006).

One deeper, conceptual issue remained ignored. While the language of clarity has a technical purpose—to guide those who legislate sovereignty referenda, at home, and to assist those who come to judge their legitimacy from abroad—it also embodies a certain normative ideal. What that ideal is, however, remains unclear. In fact, the "clarity" of a referendum majority may be seen as an evidence of three separate aspects of popular support: (1) its sufficient *magnitude*; (2) its sufficient *intensity*; and (3) its sufficient *constancy*. The language of popular sovereignty discourages us from approaching this question analytically. That way, our intuitions about clarity remain intact—unclear and unexamined. Do we only think of clarity as an indicator of (1)? Or do we think that (1) matters only because it is an indicator of (2) and (3)? If 95% voted in favour of secession, they *really* want to secede, or so we think. If that many of them voted in favour, it is *highly* unlikely that they will change their minds in the foreseeable future.

These are not academic questions. But we can only appreciate that now—after Brexit, and after Catalonia. In Montenegro, the language of clarity worked as intended: in proceduralizing a conflict that was in its essence political, it made the legitimacy of the referendum outcome indisputable. In Britain, however, the same standard of clarity turned into a farce. Not because 52% of those who voted to leave the European Union are not strong enough numerically, but because too many of them changed their minds too soon. In the case of Brexit, to put it differently, the size of the winning majority provided no clarity—both about the intensity of popular aspirations, as well as the stability of popular intentions. This raises an interesting question. If "[t]he continued existence and operation of [a] constitutional order cannot remain indifferent to the clear expression of a clear majority [of voters] that they no longer wish to remain [in the European Union]", how soon—or how often—should the institutions of that order show its sensitivity? Every time when it becomes apparent that "the people" in question changed its mind? As soon as there is an indication that a substantive portion of some "people" intensely desires something which cannot be obtained easily—or quickly—by going through the motions of a procedure reserved for constitutional amendment? How intense should that desire be, in order to override regular amendment procedures, and trigger the process of a more easily achievable constitutional change? Finally, who is to say that extant provisions that regulate constitutional change are not already sensitive enough to the desires of clear majorities?—whatever that may mean.

Our conceptions of democracy and popular sovereignty answer these questions—furtively. Once we pose them openly, what confronts us is the reverse side of popular sovereignty: the relief of constitutional democracy institutional responsiveness in the multiplicity of its dimensions. At that point, instead of justification, our problem becomes calibration: how *frequently*, how *sensitively*, how *reliably*, how *amply*, and how *speedily* should those institutions register, respond, engage, and accommodate ever-changing popular aspirations? The language of popular sovereignty keeps these questions meaningless. Though Secession Reference uses the same language, it nonetheless poses a striking challenge to the prevailing conceptions of constitutional government popularly summarized in an old formula: *of the people, for the people, by the people.* On that view, a sovereign people retains the authority to transform its constitution either through a revolutionary exercise of constituent power, or through a constitutionally prescribed amendment procedure. Such constitutional change must under no circumstances damage that people's unity, nor should it violate the territorial integrity of its state.

From the perspective of the Secession Reference, however, all this is negotiable—in Canada. The duty to negotiate secession in good faith follows from the interplay of four unwritten principles which themselves derive from Canadian constitutional history—not from a free-standing moral argument about the value democracy, federalism, popular sovereignty or the consent of the governed. What is more, the Supreme Court made very clear that any possible act of secession has to occur in conformity with (some) amending formula, specified in the Constitution Act 1982. All this becomes important once we devote our intention to another secessionist crisis, this time in Catalonia, Spain—at the internal, not external, periphery of the European Union.

Secession Reference and the Limits to Persuasive Authority

Though no state can reasonably hope to endure forever, most of them anxiously seek to assure themselves of their earthly immortality. In most of them, constitutions are seen as vehicles for the political self-determination of sovereign peoples, not "suicide pacts". The constitution of Spain is no exception. Like most constitutions in modern liberal democracies, it looks at secession with hostility. Some scholars, such as Francesco Palermo in this volume, find it surprising. According to Palermo, "one would expect that most of the countries experiencing secessionist requests would have adopted a similar complex legal framework to encapsulate secession into a sophisticated procedural shell". What happened instead, as he rightly notes, is the "proliferation of referendums on sovereignty, very often unofficial and thus contested" (Palermo 2019, this volume).

Both in terms of the repressive reactions it provoked from the Spanish government, as well the escalation of conflict to which it contributed, Catalan referendum easily fits into this enduring pattern of acrimony, instability and violence that has historically accompanied most bids for sovereign statehood. And yet. Though the 1, October 2017 referendum appears quite unremarkable within this wider historical plane, its striking features become obvious when approached from a more parochial, Eurocentric perspective. What made 1 October—together with the events that preceded and followed it—remarkable was not the fact of a referendum, or the violent reaction of the Spanish police, but rather that it was not supposed to happen—not there, not like that.

Events like those on 1 October were supposed to occur in the external, not internal peripheries of liberal democratic constitutionalism—in Eastern, not Western Europe—in the 1990s, not 2010s. From that perspective, Catalan referendum is a Black Swan—an event which students of secession, self-determination, minority nationalism, multinational federalism, and constitutional pluralism not only failed to anticipate, but which they also implicitly deemed inconceivable. Before 1 October, the Secession Reference indeed seemed to offer an attractive constitutional framework for responding to secessionist aspirations. The expectations behind it could perhaps be best summarized in the following formula: *negotiation as a constitutional obligation + formal criteria of evaluation > domestication of secession > no need to invoke the right to "self-determination"*. 1 October shattered those expectations.

What explains such a colossal indifference of those on the ground towards scholarly expectations? Why couldn't the Spanish government realize that the "path to a peaceful, orderly, and good governance secession framework" offered by the Supreme Court of Canada may not only be attractive to secessionist groups, such as the Catalans, but also to national governments that face secessionist groups, such as themselves. In Canada, this approach seems to be paid off (even though we will never know for sure whether those who took part in the crafting of the Secession Reference did indeed intend to contribute to the deflation of nationalist passions through the risky embrace of their dignity). But one thing is clear enough: no interpretation of democracy—either in isolation, or in tandem—could ever hope to achieve that purpose.

Democracy belongs to nobody in particular. It demands that constitution-makers organize a responsive system of government, but it doesn't tell them how. It is a *scale-*, *frequency-*, and *size-agnostic* concept. Though various adjectival accounts of democracy seek to persuade us to believe otherwise, democracy, on its own, simply doesn't care—how often it will be exercised, within which boundaries, in relation to which political objectives. To make it appear partial (towards us) democracy will either need to be ideologically *qualified* ideologically (as liberal, radical, socialist, cosmopolitan), or conceptually *supplemented* (with pluralism, subsidiarity, originalism, multinationalism). Only then will democracy become capable of discriminations; a concept that allows us to perform polemical incisions: to insist on this not that, here not there, now not later.

We ignore the constitutive role of these supplements in our conceptions of democracy because we remain focused on the perennial questions constitutional theory: Who is the people? What is the meaning of the right to self-determination? At what level of government, and where, may constituent power be legitimately exercised? Those who take these questions seriously assume that they can be answered persuasively. The problem, however, is that they can't. If nothing else, the crisis in Catalonia offers a vivid reminder of just that: that Catalan sovereigntists have no reason to accept the ultimate authority of a polity that exists only in virtue of performative contradiction—just as the Spanish defenders of constitutional status quo have no reason to be impressed by the arguments that identify Catalans as a demos, vested with constituent power. Why would they? Especially if this demos owes its very existence (not to say anything about "sovereignty") to the provisions of the Spanish constitution, and if even the most cursory look at the political map of Catalonia reveals desperately polarized—and in some cases even territorially clustered—citizenry? For the most part, contemporary constitutional theory ignores these polemic, situational questions. In doing so, it misses an opportunity to rethink the relationship between democracy and constitutionalism without resorting to the vocabulary of popular sovereignty.

Constitutional Democracy and (Un)responsive Constitutions

What we encounter at the intersection of democracy and constitutionalism are two things: constitutional democracy (as a particular form of legitimate government) and democratic constitutionalism, as its ideology. That constitutionalism is foundational, not just democratic. In the eyes of those captivated by its imagery, we govern ourselves collectively in conformity with the ideals of political equality. Once we approach secession from the perspective of institutional responsiveness and not democratic self-government, or popular sovereignty foundational constitutionalism presents itself in three different guises: as unresponsive, quasi-responsive, and responsive.

The central figure of unresponsive foundational constitution is a particular kind of political community—not only the holder of sovereignty, and the source of ultimate authority, but also a political body intended to last in perpetuity. Unreflectively, we tend to associate this figure with unitary, not federal, or quasi-federal states. On closer inspection, the image of the people as sovereign, authoritative, and perpetual transcends the unitary—federal binary. Consider the USA, for example. According to Michael Paulsen

> An overriding principle of constitutional and national self-preservation that operates as a meta-rule of construction for the document's specific provisions and that may even, in cases of extraordinary necessity, trump specific constitutional requirements. The Constitution is not a suicide pact; and, consequently, its provisions should not be construed to make it one, where an alternative construction is fairly possible. (Paulsen 2004)

The USA is an "indestructible union made of indestructible states" (Texas v. White 1869). Though the American Supreme Court didn't further specify what is meant by this "indestructibility", it is reasonable to assume that it refers to three things: the *perpetuity* (of the existence of the state), the *integrity* (of territory), and the *unity* (of the American nation). Variations of these three commitments—perpetuity, integrity, unity—may also be found in the constitutions of Algeria, Angola, Benin, Burkina Faso, Burundi, Cameroon, Chad, Congo, Gabon, Equatorial Guinea, Guinea-Bissau, India, Madagascar, Mali, Rwanda, Somalia, Azerbaijan, Kazakhstan, Moldova, Romania, Tajikistan, El Salvador, Honduras, Portugal, Turkey, and a number of other countries as well.

At first sight, Spanish constitution belongs in this group. Its Article 1 states: "National sovereignty belongs to the Spanish people, from whom all State powers emanate", followed by the notorious Article 2: "The Constitution is based on the indissoluble unity of the Spanish Nation, the common and indivisible homeland of all Spaniards". At the same time, the Spanish Constitutional Tribunal seems to have subtly rejected the idea of the Spanish people as a collective sovereign which must remain spatiotemporally integral in perpetuity. In a judgement delivered in early 2014, the Tribunal stated that

> [a]ny approach that intends to change the very grounds of the Spanish constitutional order is acceptable in law, as long as it is not prepared or upheld through an activity that infringes democratic principles, fundamental rights or all other constitutional mandates, and its effective achievement follows the procedures foreseen for constitutional reform, given that these procedures are inexcusable. (Opinion No. 42/2014)

There seems to be a principled difference between the constitutions that are fully unresponsive to secessionist aspirations—such as American, or Indian—and those, such as Spanish, or Canadian, that can fathom the possibility of accommodating them. From that perspective, the Canadian and the Spanish approaches to secession don't appear all that different. Both affirm the sovereignty of the (entire) people (of the state), and both profess their commitment to the rule of law. The difference lies elsewhere. While the Spanish constitutional order conforms to the template of responsive foundational constitutionalism in principle, seceding from Spain constitutionally remains virtually impossible, in practice. Impossible, that is, unless Catalans manage to achieve something almost unimaginable: persuade the qualified majority in the Spanish Cortes to initiate the process of constitutional change—which, in order to result in secession—would need to be approved by the majority of all Spaniards.

And herein lies the difference between Spain and Canada. While the Spanish constitution allows legal and political officials to ignore Catalan attempts to trigger constitutional change that contravene the modality provided by Articles 87 and 166, the Canadian constitution imposes the duty on "all participants" in the federation to negotiate, in good faith, the Quebecois plebiscitary demand for secession, under the condition that such preference is manifested as a response to a "clear question" by a "clear majority" of voters in a province-wide referendum. In other words, the responsiveness of the Canadian constitution is more sensitive as it registers not only the impulses it has anticipated at the time of adoption, but also those that were not anticipated earlier—such as the ones manifested in a provincial referendum.

Federalism and Democracy: Calibrating Responsiveness, Quietly

On a closer look, however, three of those four principles do nothing to generate the responsiveness to the Quebecois demand to secede. The principle of federalism, for example, is justified as the vehicle of collective self-government capable of accommodating national diversity where different but equally legitimate majorities coexist at the central and substate levels. Nothing in federalism explains what would justify the triggering of a constitutional process that might sanction the departure from the existing, federal status quo. Equally, constitutionalism and the rule of law are justified by their role in structuring the exercise of democratic will and by providing a stable set of rules that enables purposive, predictive behaviour, and additionally, do not explain why an entire constitutional order would have to respond to a radical demand for its reconstruction—especially in a way that goes beyond what has already been entrenched in that constitution's amending formula. The same applies for the principle of the protection of minorities.

What opens the conceptual space for a more radical responsiveness is a more granular vision of "the consent of the governed" as the ideal behind the Canadian "understanding of a free and democratic society". The system, as the Court said, "must be capable of *reflecting the aspirations* of the people" (*Reference Re Secession of Quebec* 1988, paragraph 67). But what could "reflecting" possibly mean in a situation where, notionally, sovereignty belongs to the entire people of Canada, where different segments of that people disagree about secession, and where both "popularly elected levels of government are equally legitimate", each in its own sphere? These utterances make sense only if we reintroduce the idea of ***constituent attachments*** and understand "the consent of the governed" as another name for them. Here, the "capacity to reflect the aspirations" should be seen as the capacity to respond *tendentially* towards changes in the aggregate satisfaction of constituent attachments.

The system, then, must be capable of adjusting itself so that it increases that aggregate in relation to the status quo ante. Or, to put it a bit more concretely, there would be comparatively more individuals who would wilfully submit to the situation "Rest-of-Canada + independent Quebec" than to "Canada-including-Quebec". This doesn't mean—as David Haljan suggested in his monograph on the Secession Reference—that "20 to 25 percent of the total of the Canadian population" could decide the future of the entire Canada (Haljan 2014: 379). What it means that more people would see their most meaningful political preferences satisfied. While it is true that the first preferences of many Canadians—to live in a particular Canada—would not be satisfied, they would still end up in a country which they can wilfully, even affectively, endorse.

What follows from this? The only way in which we may understand the duty to negotiate—as something that exists over and above regular channels of constitutional change—is if we postulate the existence of a meta-constitutional orientation of institutional responsiveness—*tendential* towards achieving the increased satisfaction of the constituent attachments *behind* the interplay of the four unwritten principles of the Canadian constitutional order. This casts a different light not only on the principle of democracy, but also the principle of federalism. From that perspective, federalism can be seen as another cognitive therapy for the anxieties of peoplehood on the one hand, and as a mechanism of preemptive quality control in the process of polity formation on the other.

At the initial stage, it *modulates* the strength of a political "signal"—the size of a popular desire for secession—that sets in motion the deliberative machinery of constitutional change. Its function is to contribute to *plausible deniability* of tendential responsiveness: both as an ideal of constitutional government that is selectively operative, and as an ideal that informs all forms of democratic constitutional change: constitutional and extra-constitutional.

In the Secession Reference, the principle of federalism constrains the principle of democracy. Its vocabulary of self- and shared government allows the institutions of respond to large, and ignore the small. Otherwise, Canadian government would be obliged to respond to secessionist demands in good faith indiscriminately: from frivolous and fleeting ones, to those that are supported by provincial majorities, and verified by a referendum. At the same time, the language of federalism offers assurances against the political risks of sovereign existence. If you've already been a highly autonomous unit in a relatively decentralized federation, surely you'll be able to cope as an independent state. Once federal, always viable. From that perspective, federalism offers a temporary reprieve to a deeper set of anxieties that undergird the modern social imaginary of popular sovereignty and foundational constitutionalism.

The success of that endeavour, however, depends on secrecy. By this point, its principal advantage should be clear: to allow a radically challenged constitutional order to continue its active effort to increase the degree of satisfied constituent attachments—within *all of Canada*—with less anxiety about territorial fragmentation, political disfunction, or external domination. From the perspective of comparative constitutionalism, however, that solution comes at a price: by finding an untapped reservoir of responsiveness in its constitutional roots, responsive foundational constitutionalism is rather inert, and has trouble reaching distant constitutional destinations.

The Poverty of Persuasive Authority

In Canada, the Secession Reference had a therapeutic effect (Des Rosiers 2000). In lending democratic legitimacy to the secessionist aspirations of the Quebecois, it also seems to have diminished the attractiveness of resorting to the self-righteous and indignant language of historical grievances and nationalist particularity. If true, this is no small feat. What often inflames passions and destroys goodwill in disputes over territorial sovereignty are not nationalist aspirations but their insultingly hypocritical justifications. The main achievement of the Reference is to make such justifications unnecessary. What the Reference cannot do, however, is to offer abstract generalizations: about the spatiotemporal extent of constituent power, the limits to its legitimate exercise, or the locus of ultimate authority.

From both the perspective of contemporary democratic theory and that of comparative law—and this is something which Catalan sovereigntists, secessionists, and nationalists prefer not to hear—Spain is right. There is nothing, either in currently prevailing conceptions of democracy or popular constitutionalism, which would justify the migration of the attitude with which the organs of the Canadian and the British constitutional order approached the prospective secessions of Quebec and Scotland.

And yet, Catalan sovereigntist movement achieved one important victory. Though its leaders wrongly assumed that the scenes of confrontation and violence would suffice to mobilize international public opinion (that would then successfully pressure powerful states to step into the conflict in Spain on the side of Catalonia) they nonetheless successfully framed the issue of the referendum with that of the freedom of expression and association. Within that frame, the principled attitude of the Spanish government appears not only insensitive, petty, and inhumane, but also unreasonable and unethical.

But if violence and police repression are not the way to respond to democratic aspirations, what is? Why can't Catalan secessionist not engage in clearly unconstitutional activities in the first place? A cynical defender of the Spanish constitutional authority would most likely say that the Catalans brought that violence and repression onto themselves. In the context of the constitutional crises such as the one in Spain—where both parties enjoy more or less equal democratic credentials—the ideals of constitutionalism, self-determination, and popular sovereignty—have no way of arbitrating between the conflicting positions. From the second half of the eighteenth century onwards, the secessionists who invoked these ideals—until, roughly, the last quarter of the twentieth century—invoked them against colonial empires, not constitutional democracies.

Spain, of course, is not an empire, and 1 October didn't change that. The citizens of Catalonia have equal rights to exercise their democratic freedoms at all levels of government, from municipal to regional and central. Those rights include the freedom of speech and the freedom of association—just not in the form of an unconstitutional independence referendum officially organized by a regional government. For our purposes, it is nonetheless productive to ask what exactly might Catalan sovereigntists mean when they denounce Spanish imperialism? This is a salient question because those who make that association never really explain what would be constitutional duties of the Spanish government, were it accept the existence of the alleged "right to decide" (*dret a decidir*) vested in a sovereign Catalan people:

(1) To (only) *tolerate* a referendum on secession?
(2) To *enter* into negotiations *over* the secession of Catalonia?
(3) To negotiate *towards* the secession of Catalonia?
(4) To *not obstruct* the formation of an independent Catalan state (should negotiations end without agreement)?

To the third question, the Secession Reference answered with an oblique *yes*. To the fourth, it's answer was a more resounding *no*. But the duty to negotiate good faith which the Supreme Court deduced from the interplay of four unwritten principles has its origins in Canadian constitutional history—not from a free-standing moral argument about the value democracy, federalism, popular sovereignty—or, for that matter, the consent of the governed. If so, why should those whose job is to defend the integrity of the Spanish constitutional order not take advantage of that? Invited by those who'd have them be inspired by Canada and Britain, they have responded—directly or indirectly—with a more elaborate version of "That's different!"—the cheapest and the most popular in the history of argumentative comebacks. To this there are no good comebacks themselves, only further questions: different in what way, when, and how much?

Final Remarks

To those who critique its adamant refusal to take the Catalan aspirations seriously, the defenders of the Spanish constitution respond solemnly: but we are taking them seriously—just as it was intended by the established rules of our constitutional democracy! In alleging that the refusal of the (otherwise unimpeachably democratic) Spanish constitutional order to be responsive towards their secessionists aspirations constitutes the reason to apply the "remedy" of external self-determination, Catalan secessionists seem to have started from the assumption that the moral, political, and institutional appeal of the ideal of responsiveness thus understood, is obvious—or at least intuitive. No it's not. In asking for more sensitivity towards secessionist aspirations, the Secession Reference encourages us to approach our democratic intuitions—whatever they may be—more reflectively and systematically. That—not the internationally influential language of clarity and remedy—is its most important, yet still unrecognized, intellectual legacy.

References

Bayefsky, Anne F. (2000), "Self-Determination", in *International Law: Quebec and Lessons Learned*, The Hague, London, and Boston, Kluwer Law International.

Choudhry, Sujit (2007), "Referendum? What Referendum?", in *Literary Review of Canada*, 15 (3), 7–9.

Des Rosiers, Nathalie (2000), "From Telling to Listening: A Therapeutic Analysis of the Role of Courts in Minority-Majority Conflicts", in *Court Review*, 37, 54.

Dutrisac, Robert (2006), *Référendum—Québec fixe la barre à 50% plus un*, Montreal, Le Devoir, 16 March 2006.

European Commission for Democracy through Law (2005), *On the Compatibility of the Existing Legislation in Montenegro Concerning the Organization of Referendums with Applicable International Standards*, Opinion No. 343/2005.

Grand Council of the Crees (1995), "Sovereign Injustice: Forcible Inclusion and Cree Territory into a Sovereign Quebec", available at http://www.gcc.ca/gcc/querelations.php.

Haljan, David (2014), *Constitutionalising Secession*, Oregon and Portland, Hart Publishing.

International Court of Justice (2010), *Accordance with International Law of the Unilateral Declaration of Independence in Respect of Kosovo*, 22 July 2010.

Oklopcic, Zoran (2009), "Populus Interruptus: Self-Determination, the Independence of Kosovo, and the Vocabulary of Peoplehood", in *Leiden Journal of International Law* 22 (4), 677–702.

Oklopcic, Zoran (2011), "The Migrating Spirit of the Secession Reference in Southeastern Europe", in *Canadian Journal of Law & Jurisprudence*, 24 (2), 347–376.

Paulsen, M. (2004), "The Constitution of Necessity", *Notre Dame Law Review*, 79, 1257–1297.

Spanish Constitutional Tribunal, Opinion No. 42/2014.

Texas v. White (1869), 74 U.S. 700.

A Political Theory Perspective on the Reference

Roberto Castaldi

Introduction

The *Quebec Secession Reference*[1] (from now on just *Reference*) received much wider attention from the legal scholarly community than within the political theory literature. However, the *Reference* offers some important perspectives with regard to the various issues that dominate the discussion about secession within both political philosophy and political science.

Political philosophy and theory investigated the issue mainly from a normative perspective. More specifically the main debate regards if, and/ or under what conditions, secession can be considered a legitimate right (see Baer 2000; Castellino 1999; Catala 2013, 2017; Costa 2003; Glaser

[1] *Reference Re Secession of Quebec*, [1998] 2 S.C.R. 217-297.

R. Castaldi (✉)
eCampus University, Novedrate, Italy
e-mail: roberto.castaldi@uniecampus.it; roberto.castaldi@cesue.eu

R. Castaldi
International Centre for European and Global Governance, Pisa, Italy

G. Delledonne and G. Martinico (eds.), *The Canadian Contribution to a Comparative Law of Secession*,
https://doi.org/10.1007/978-3-030-03469-6_11

2003; Lee 2005; Lefkowitz 2008; Margiotta 2005; Moore 2000; Patten 2002; Rubin 2000; Shorten 2014; Tideman 2004; Weinstock 2001; Wellman 2005) or its relationship with globalization (see Kolers 2006; Pavkovic and Radan 2008).

Political science literature adopts an analytical perspective and focuses mainly on specific case studies. On more general terms, the main issues discussed are the role of referenda and the dynamics in the decision-making processes related to secessions and on the impact of the issue of secession on the affected political systems, with particular reference to the emergence and role of autonomist and/or secessionist parties and on the possibility for them to use the request of more autonomy as a step towards secession (see Bartkus 1999; Courtois 2004; Dardanelli 2005; Lynch 2005; Meadwell 2009; Pavkovic and Radan 2007, 2008; Qvortrup 2012, 2014, 2016; Schmucker 2010; Usher 2000). This is hardly surprising as in the last thirty years all secession attempts and claims have exploited one form or another of referenda, with the exception of the break-up of Czechoslovakia. Within International Relations attention is given to the international dimension of secession and of preventing it, and the possible role of secession within conflict-resolution mechanisms (see Anderson 2013; Griffiths 2014; Ker-Lindsay 2012; McGarry 2001; Meadwell 1999; Pavković and Radan 2003).

An important debate focuses on secession with regard to the EU member states and as such, which was further boosted recently with regard to the Brexit process, and the issue of seceding from the European Union (see Closa 2016, 2017; Connolly 2013; Schäfer 2003; Vaubel 2013; Waters 2016), a multi-level polity usually compared with federal states, but still considered as not being a fully fledged federation (see Burgess 2000, 2006; Dobson and Follesdal 2004; Dosenrode 2007; Fabbrini 2005, 2007; Filippov et al. 2004; Follesdal and Koslowski 1998; Karmis and Norman 2005; Hesse and Wright 1996; Hueglin and Fenna 2006; Longo 2006; McKay 1996, 1999, 2001; Nicolaidis and Howse 2001).

Max Weber distinguished three levels of political struggle: community, regime, and government. It is safe to observe that political science has devoted more attention to those related to regime and government than to the community. The latter is approached mainly within the literature on nationalism and federalism, and to a small extent within the IR literature (see Anderson 2004; Bauböck 2000; Burgess and Gagnon 2010; Cameron 2009; Choudhry and Hume 2011; Dahbour 2009; Erk 2007; Erk and Swenden 2010; Gagnon 2009; Gagnon et al. 2015;

Guibernau 2006; Harbo 2008; Keating 2004; Norman 2006; Rector 2009; Requejo 2001, 2017; Requejo and Badia 2012; Rodrigues 2010; Seymour and Gagnon 2012). The literature on federalism was originally biased by the experience of the American federation. The attempt to secede brought there to the Civil war. And the Supreme Court *Texas v. White*[2] judgement stated the illegality of secession. From then onwards, the vast majority of the political theory literature has assumed that secession was not allowed even within federal states until recently. Obviously, it is a political possibility, but it implies a rupture of the established legal order. Indeed, historically secessions have often taken place after violent struggles. Peaceful secession is an exception rather than the norm, with the break-up of Czechoslovakia being the most prominent example.

Political science is an empirical discipline. The complex legal negotiated procedure for secession mandated by the Reference has never been applied in Canada, nor elsewhere. The first instance of a similar, but different, procedure is the current negotiation between the EU and the UK, based on Article 50 TEU. And this eventually leaves it open the possibility of a unilateral secession, the so-called no-deal scenario.

All this helps to explain the reasons why the Quebec Secession Reference has not spurred a wide debate within political theory, except within the Canadian scholarly community and few others (see Aronovitch 2006; Bautista-Beauchesne 2015; Brown 2009; Buchanan 2003a, b; Cameron 2009; Choudhry and Howse 2000; Connolly 2013; Closa 2016; Ford 2001; Kymlicka 2000; Kymlicka and Norman 2000; Jovanovic 2007; Leslie 1999; MacLauchlan 1997; Moore 2000; Pavković 2004; Radmilovic 2010; Rocher 2002; Wiltanger 1999). This chapter thus attempts to sketch the contribution that the Reference can bring to the political theory debates. First, with regard to the relationship between federalism and secession, and the definition of a legal procedure to secede and how it can be exercised, especially within a federal system. Second, with regard to the decision-making processes linked to secession, and particularly on the use of referenda. Third with regard to the EU and the Brexit experience, which are a sort of experiment of a negotiation on secession and thus provide useful insights into the matter.

[2] *Texas v. White*, 74 US 700 (1869).

A Possibility to Secede Anchored to the Principle of Federalism?

The first fundamental contribution of the Reference to the political theory debate is about federalism and secession. Essentially, the Court considers that the Canadian Constitutional order is based on 4 interlinked principles or shared values: "federalism, democracy, constitutionalism and the rule of law, and respect for minorities" (p. 220). For the Court: "Federalism was the political mechanism by which diversity could be reconciled with unity" (p. 245). Both these approaches can be easily applied to basically all democratic federal systems in the world.[3]

On that basis the Court rejects the possibility of a legal form of unilateral secession, very much in line with established literature (this point is also stressed by Wiltanger 1999). However, it also innovates decisively, by recognizing that if a clear majority on a clear question in Quebec was in favour of secession this would have to be taken into account and negotiations between Quebec and Canada should start. They shall find ways to guarantee the rights of all Canadians (including the Quebecois) in Quebec and in the rest of Canada, with a particular focus on the rights of the minorities, that are constitutionally protected.

Essentially the Court links secession and federalism, by recognizing the impossibility for a federal system to give absolute permanent prevalence to the federal majority over the majority of one of its members, and vice versa: "The relationship between democracy and federalism means, for example, that in Canada there may be different and equally legitimate majorities in different provinces and territories and at the federal level. No one majority is more or less 'legitimate' than the others as an expression of democratic opinion" (p. 255). If there was a clear majority in Quebec for secession, this would not be enough to give a legal right for unilateral secession because that would mean that the Quebec majority prevails over the Canadian one. At the same time as each Province

[3] Historically there have been non-democratic federal states, such as the USSR, Yugoslavia, and several others. But the literature has generally recognized that their communist or authoritarian regime de facto void their federal features of any real significance and thus does not consider them as really federal systems: see, for example, Burgess (2006) and Burgess and Gagnon (2010).

can start constitutional amendment, such a clear majority would imply a legal obligation by the other components of the Canadian federation and the federal government to negotiate with Quebec over secession, which implies a constitutional change.

This idea recalls Wheare's famous definition of federal government as being "the method of dividing powers so that the general and regional governments are each within a sphere co-ordinate and independent" (Wheare 1963: 11). The Court has found a way to ensure this principle also with regard to the ultimate issue of the participation to the federation as such. While previously that principle was usually considered by the literature to apply to the various competences, but not to the federal compact as such, considered to be irreversible. For the Court, "The Constitution is the expression of the sovereignty of the people of Canada. It lies within the power of the people of Canada, acting through their various governments duly elected and recognized under the Constitution, to effect whatever constitutional arrangements are desired within Canadian territory, including, should it be so desired, the secession of Quebec from Canada" (p. 264).

The *Reference* thus opens a theoretical question that needs to be addressed more directly by the literature on federalism, within both political theory and political science. This is relevant for the future of federalism—which is an increasingly used tool to create multi-level system of government—notwithstanding the fact that currently only a few constitutions explicitly provide for a right of secession. The debate has both a theoretical and an empirical significance. At the theoretical level, the issue is if the irreversibility of the federal pact and polity should be considered an essential defining feature necessary to ensure stability to polities which usually encompass a wide range of diversity (otherwise a unitary or decentralized system of government rather than a federal one would be in place). At an empirical level, the issues are at least two: Does the possibility of a legal way to secede actually make members of federal system feel less constrained and thus less inclined to actually activate secession? A similar discussion was held in the Convention drafting the Treaty establishing a Constitution for Europe, which for the first time include the right to withdraw from the EU (see Schäfer 2003). This was then enshrined in Article 50 TEU, eventually activated by the UK after the Brexit Referendum.

What Decision-Making Process About Secession?

Referenda have become a most common feature in secession processes. They can be used as a decision-making procedure ex-ante, or as a legitimacy-providing tool ex-post. Their use is very much linked to an extremely simple and simplistic vision of democracy, which characterizes especially the new wave of populism (for an excellent overview see Mény and Surel 2002). The Canadian Court squarely rejects such a perspective with effective arguments. "It would be a grave mistake to equate legitimacy with the 'sovereign will' or majority rule alone, to the exclusion of other constitutional values" (p. 256). "The argument that the Constitution may be legitimately circumvented by resort to a majority vote in a province-wide referendum is superficially persuasive, in large measure because it seems to appeal to some of the same principles that underlie the legitimacy of the Constitution itself, namely, democracy and self-government" (p. 259). By emphasizing the linkage between the four principles of "federalism, democracy, constitutionalism and the rule of law, and respect for minorities" (p. 220) the Court also stresses that none of them is enough alone to provide adequate legitimacy to the constitutional order.

A referendum on secession can be a tool to assess if there is a wide and clear majority in favour of secession in a given province. But by itself it is not enough as a basis for secession. "The secession of a province from Canada must be considered, in legal terms, to require an amendment to the Constitution, which perforce requires negotiation. The amendments necessary to achieve secession could be radical and extensive" (p. 263). The Court provided for a legal and multilateral avenue to secession. At the same time, it was careful not to predetermine the results of the negotiations, placing the burden squarely on the political and institutional actors, not the judges: "the content and process of the negotiations will be for the political actors to settle. The reconciliation of the various legitimate constitutional interests is necessarily committed to the political rather than the judicial realm precisely because that reconciliation can only be achieved through the give and take of political negotiations. To the extent issues addressed in the course of negotiation are political, the courts, appreciating their proper role in the constitutional scheme, would have no supervisory role" (pp. 221–222).

It was a balanced view, and a way not to take on itself a huge burden. The process of substituting politics with rules and legal means has limits (see Craven 1999; Hirschl 2006). There are clear political issues that can only be settled by political negotiations. This provides politics with a distinct and elevated role. Negotiation and compromise are not bad things: they are the essence of politics and of democracy too, provide it is interpreted in a complex and comprehensive manner, and not simplistically as the rule of the majority without any other constraint.

Some more considerations about the decision-making process about secession will be offered at the end of this chapter, also on the basis of the discussion of the EU and the process of withdrawal by the UK, the so-called Brexit.

The EU and Brexit

Article 50 TEU for the first time explicitly included in the EU legal framework the possibility of withdrawal. In the public debate, this was often considered as a sort of nuclear option never to be used. An article aimed at reassuring public opinion in the various member states that they were still in charge and had a way out. A way to curtail the propaganda against the EU as a sort of prison, especially in the UK after the birth of the UK Independence Party led by Nigel Farage. It turned out very differently.

However, it is worth recalling that the possibility to withdraw was implicitly admitted much earlier, in the 1970s. The UK first asked to join the European Economic Community in 1962, due to the fact that the EEC proved much more effective than the UK-led European Free Trade Area in providing economic growth. De Gaulle's veto twice prevented the first enlargement, which eventually took place after he lost power in France. The UK thus joined the EEC on 1 January 1973, together with Denmark and Ireland. The Labour party won the 1974 elections in the UK, including in its Manifesto a pledge to hold a referendum on the continued participation of the UK to the EEC. The referendum took place on 5 June 1975. About 2/3 of the voters endorsed continued membership in the EEC. Even if the referendum was not binding, just like the Brexit one, there could be little doubt that if a majority had voted against continued membership the UK would have quitted the EEC, even in the absence in the Rome Treaties of an explicit withdrawal clause and procedure. It may have been a complex process to be invented. But after just one year and a half of UK membership it would probably be a manageable process.

Exploiting the existence of Article 50 TEU the Tories under David Cameron made the same pledge of holding a referendum on EU membership in 2015. This choice had several reasons. One was similar to the 1974 Labour one: to keep united a party highly divided on the European issue, postponing the internal fight to the referendum. The second reason was to win back anti-EU voters that may otherwise vote the UKIP, which in the 2014 European election had raised to be the first British party, even if in an election with a low turnout. The third was that Cameron did not expect the Tories to get a majority, but to continue the coalition government with the Liberal Democrats, fiercely opposed to the referendum, thus making it impossible. It was a miscalculation. The Tories did obtain a majority and this eventually brought to the Brexit referendum, to the end of Cameron's political career, and to the activation of Article 50 TEU and the start of the negotiation of the withdrawal agreement.

The Brexit negotiation somehow resembles the negotiation process sought by the Canadian Court. And it shows how difficult it is to disentangle a member state from the EU. Interdependence is a defining feature of the contemporary world. As Pascal Lamy pointed out: "Brexit is like trying to get an egg out of an omelette" (http://www.france24.com/en/20180115-talking-europe-pascal-lamy-brexit-egg-out-omelette-wto-rules-trade-no-deal). Probably even more so for a member state of a fully fledged federal system, which may not have managed certain competences for an even longer period of time than the UK with regard to the EU. The debate about the UK participation in a number of European agencies which manage technical but essential issues, such as nuclear, aviation, or food safety is just an example.

The Brexit negotiation shows the huge number and relevance of the issues that need to be dealt with. One of the most prominent is the protection of the rights of citizens of both sides which have legitimately settled with the expectation of enjoying certain rights. Media paid less attention to the crucial issue of the possibility to exploit certain federal agencies or programme, at least during a transition period, with regard to many issues for which there is no administrative system already in place able to immediately fill the gap. Finally, the future relationship with regard to trade, market access, free circulation of people, security cooperation, and defence. The Brexit negotiations are amazingly complex, and still relatively easy from a comparative perspective. The EU does not enjoy exclusive competence on foreign and defence policies, as it happens in most federal polities. This makes it much easier to withdraw.

Furthermore, the EU as such has no public debt. Therefore, there is no need to define which share of it should be burdened on the UK. If Quebec was to secede from Canada, or other member entities from most other federal polities, these kinds of issues would probably have a crucial role in the negotiations of secession mandated by the *Reference*.

There are three further lessons to be drawn by the Brexit process. The first regards what the Court called "a clear majority vote in Quebec on a clear question in favour of secession" (p. 220; on the issue see also Ford 2001). The Brexit referendum provided a clear if very small majority. But a relevant group of citizens, actually the most affected group in case of withdrawal could not vote: the British residents in other European country for more than 5 years, and the EU citizens resident in the UK. Their rights have been a major issue in the negotiations, but they could not have a say on the very decision of the UK withdrawal. And this should be an issue to be taken into account in future referenda on such topics in any federal polity. Following the logic and the principles set out by the *Reference*, it would be coherent to let the people most affected by the decision participate in that decision.

The second regards the fact that the decision about secession, as in the Brexit case, does not really say anything about the future relationship with the federal polity which is abandoned. Brexit can be made anything from a complete secession with no agreement nor transition period, to a complex trade agreement (like CETA between the EU and Canada), to the participation in the EU Custom Union (like Turkey), to the participation to the Single Market (like the participants to the European Economic Area). Each of these scenarios has specific costs and benefits and entails very different relationships with the EU. In itself, the Brexit referendum did not say anything about the desired future relationship with the EU. This has made almost impossible for the UK to define its desired outcome of the negotiations, making them particularly difficult. The split in the Tory party and in the British government, and the extremely frequent substitution of its ministers in this legislature are objectively an obstacle. Often to find a compromise able to keep the party and the government going the position taken seems to contain contradictory stands or to ignore the basic principles set out by the EU from the very first day of the negotiation. Such a situation is likely to occur in similar other secession processes.

The third regards the logic of referenda and the decision-making process about secession. In the UK, there is a growing demand for a new referendum to take place at the end of the negotiation. The underlying idea is that the citizens should have a final say on the basis of the real options on the table. These vary according to the proponents, but usually include the deal that will hopefully be reached between the EU and the UK, a complete no-deal exit, remaining in the EU, or remaining in the Single Market. Such proposals are based on the idea that democracy is not about always taking the right decision, but about the possibility to change course. The people who voted for Brexit could not really know what this would entail. The negotiation has brought to light the many issues and the real costs of Brexit, contrary to many of the promises of the Brexiteers during the referendum campaign. At the end of the negotiation, the citizens will be more aware of the real options and therefore will be able to take the final decision. This is an element that was not present in the Reference, but that would be fully coherent with its underlying logic and complex vision of the Canadian democratic constitutional order.

Conclusion

The Reference sketches a rich and complex constitutional framework for Canada, that can be widely extended to other federal democracies. Already 20 years ago, it provided an effective counter-narrative to the populist simplified version of democracy which is now threatening the constitutional order in many countries. From this perspective, it is very much relevant to the current debate on populism and on democracy.

The Canadian Court offers a theoretical linkage between federalism and secession, contrary to much established political theory and political science literature. It thus requires adequate theoretical attention to assess if this choice has intrinsic theoretical merit, or if it was the result of the specific situation of the time in Canada, tailored at effectively tampering the Quebec secessionist movement, while theoretically opening a very difficult legal pathway to secession. Federalism has many different forms and varieties in different contexts. It may well be that different solutions may be appropriate in different cases also with regard to the recognition of secession.

The *Reference* finds a delicate balance between law and politics, by providing a legal pathway to secession while recognizing the dominant role of politics and political actors along that path. A similar procedure is to some extent currently being experimented in the Brexit process.

This allows to draw some useful lessons and considerations in the light and in the perspective of the *Reference*. Essentially, Brexit shows that a particularly vulnerable and most affected group by a secession are the citizens of the potentially seceding entity resident in the rest of the federation, and the citizens of other member states resident in the potentially seceding entity. This suggests that they should have the right to vote in the referendum on the secession, which will impact on their lives more than on anybody else. This process also shows that secession may mean very different things to different people, and that the most important issue is actually the definition of the future relationship between the seceding entity and the federal polity. Therefore, a clear majority on a clear issue is actually unattainable ex-ante. It would be coherent with the complex view of democracy put forward by the Court to include a clear majority on the final outcome of the negotiation of secession as the end point of that process. And it is essential to ensure that the most vulnerable groups of citizens affected by such a decision can take part in the decision.

References

Anderson, Glen (2013), "Secession in International Law and Relations: What Are We Talking About?", in *Loyola of Los Angeles International and Comparative Law Review*, 35 (1), 343–388.

Anderson, Lawrence M. (2004), "Exploring the Paradox of Autonomy: Federalism and Secession in North America", in *Regional & Federal Studies*, 14 (1), 89–112.

Aronovitch, Hilliard (2006), "Seceding the Canadian Way", in *Publius*, 36 (4), 541–564.

Baer, Josette (2000), "Who, Why and How: Assessing the Legitimacy of Secession", in *Swiss Political Science Review*, 6 (3), 45–69.

Bartkus, Viva Ona (1999), *The Dynamics of Secession*, Cambridge University Press, Cambridge and New York.

Bauböck, Rainer (2000), "Why Stay Together? A Pluralist Approach to Secession and Federation", in Will Kymlicka and Wayne Norman (eds.), *Citizenship in Diverse Societies*, Oxford University Press, Oxford.

Bautista-Beauchesne, Nicholas (2015), "Rethinking the Future of Quebec: Towards a Quiet Secession?", in *Canadian Journal of Political Science/Revue Canadienne De Science Politique*, 48, 3.

Brown, Blake R. (2009), "One Version of History: The Supreme Court of Canada's Use of History in the Quebec Secession Reference", in Penny E.

Bryden (ed.), *Framing Canadian Federalism: Historical Essays in Honour of John T. Saywell*, Toronto University Press, Toronto, 15–50.

Buchanan, Allen (2003a), "The Quebec Secession Issue: Democracy, Minority Rights, and the Rule of Law", in *Nomos*, 45, 238–271.

Buchanan, Allen (2003b), *Justice, Legitimacy, and Self-Determination*, Oxford University Press, Oxford.

Burgess, Michael (2000), *Federalism and European Union: The Building of Europe 1950–2000*, Routledge, London and New York.

Burgess, Michael (2006), *Comparative Federalism in Theory and Practice*, Routledge, London.

Burgess, Michael and Gagnon, Alain-G. eds. (2010), *Federal Democracies*, Routledge, London.

Cameron, David (2009), "The Paradox of Federalism: Some Practical Reflections", in *Regional & Federal Studies*, 19 (2), 309–319.

Castellino, Joshua (1999), "Order and Justice: National Minorities and the Right to Secession", in *International Journal on Minority and Group Rights*, 6 (4), 389–416.

Catala Amandine (2013), "Remedial Theories of Secession and Territorial Justification", in *Journal of Social Philosophy*, 44 (1), 74–94.

Catala Amandine (2017), "Secession and Distributive Justice", in *Philosophical Studies*, 174 (2), 529–552.

Choudhry, Sujit and Howse, Robert (2000), "Secession: Constitutional Theory and the Quebec Secession Reference", in *Canadian Journal of Law and Jurisprudence*, 13 (2), 143–169.

Choudhry, Sujit and Hume, Nathan (2011), "Federalism, Devolution and Secession: From Classical to Post-conflict Federalism", in Tom Ginsburg and Rosalind Dixon (eds.), *Research Handbook on Comparative Constitutional Law*, Edward Elgar, Cheltenham, 356–384.

Closa, Carlos (2016), "Secession from a Member State and EU Membership: The View from the Union", in *European Constitutional Law Review*, 12, 240–264.

Closa, Carlos ed. (2017), *Secession from a Member State and Withdrawal from the European Union: Troubled Membership*, Cambridge University Press, Cambridge.

Connolly, Christopher K. (2013), "Independence in Europe: Secession, Sovereignty, and the European Union", in *Duke Journal of Comparative & International Law*, 24 (1), 51–125.

Costa, Josep (2003), "On Theories of Secession: Minorities, Majorities and the Multinational State", in *Critical Review of International Social and Political Philosophy*, 6 (2), 63–90.

Courtois, Stéphane (2004), "Démocratie délibérative et secession", in *Canadian Journal of Political Science/Revue canadienne de science politique*, 37 (4), 811–838.

Craven, Greg (1999), "The Quebec Secession Reference: The Law of Politics or the Politics of Law?", in *Murdoch University Electronic Journal of Law*, 6 (1).

Dahbour, Omar (2009), "Nationalism, Self-Determination and Secession", in Patrick Hayden (ed.), *The Ashgate Research Companion to Ethics and International Relations*, Ashgate, Aldershot, 393–406.

Dardanelli, Paolo (2005), "Democratic Deficit or the Europeanisation of Secession? Explaining the Devolution Referendums in Scotland", in *Political Studies*, 53 (2), 320–342.

Dobson, Lynn and Follesdal, Andreas eds. (2004), *Political Theory and the European Constitution*, Routledge, London and New York.

Dosenrode, Sören (2007), *Approaching the European Federation?* Ashgate, Aldershot.

Erk, Jan (2007), "Comparative Federalism as a Growth Industry", in *Publius*, 37 (2), 262–278.

Erk, Jan and Swenden, Wilfried eds. (2010), *New Directions in Federalism Studies*, Routledge, London.

Fabbrini, Sergio ed. (2005), *Democracy and Federalism in the European Union and the United States*, Routledge, London and New York.

Fabbrini, Sergio (2007), *Compound Democracies: Why the United States and Europe are Becoming Similar*, Oxford University Press, Oxford.

Filippov, Mikhail, Ordeshook, Peter C. and Shvetsova, Olga (2004), *Designing Federalism: A Theory of Self-Sustainable Federal Institutions*, Cambridge University Press, Cambridge and New York.

Follesdal, Andreas and Koslowski, Peter eds. (1998), *Democracy and the European Union*, Springer, Berlin.

Ford, Cristie L. (2001), "In Search of the Qualitative Clear Majority: Democratic Experimentalism and the Quebec Secession Reference", in *Alberta Law Review*, 39 (2), 511–560.

Gagnon, Alain G. (2009), *The Case for Multinational Federalism: Beyond the All-Encompassing Nation*, Routledge, London.

Gagnon, Alain-G., Keil, Soeren and Mueller, Sean eds. (2015), *Understanding Federalism and Federation*, Routledge, London.

Glaser, Daryl J. (2003), "The Right to Secession: An Antisecessionist Defence", in *Political Studies*, 51 (2), 369–386.

Griffiths, Ryan (2014), "Secession and the Invisible Hand of the International System", in *Review of International Studies*, 40, 559–581.

Guibernau, Montserrat (2006), "National Identity, Devolution and Secession in Canada, Britain and Spain", in *Nations and Nationalism*, 12 (1), 51–76.

Harbo, Florentina (2008), "Secession Right—An Anti-federal Principle? Comparative Study of Federal States and the EU", in *Journal of Politics and Law*, 1 (3), 132–148.

Hesse, Joachim Jens and Wright, Vincent (1996), *Federalizing Europe? Costs, Benefits, and Preconditions of Federal Political Systems*, Oxford University Press, Oxford.

Hirschl, Ran (2006), "The New Constitutionalism and the Judicialization of Pure Politics Worldwide", in *Fordham Law Review*, 75 (2), 721–753.

Hueglin, Thomas O. and Fenna, Alan (2006), *Comparative Federalism: A Systematic Enquiry*, Broadview Press, Canada.

Jovanovic, Miodrag (2007), *Constitutionalizing Secession in Federalized States: A Procedural Approach*, Eleven International Publishing, Utrecht.

Karmis, Dimitrios and Norman, Wayne eds. (2005), *Theories of Federalism: A Reader*, Palgrave Macmillan, New York and Basingstoke.

Keating, Michael (2004), *Plurinational Democracy: Stateless Nations in a Post-sovereignty Era*, Oxford University Press, Oxford.

Ker-Lindsay, James (2012), *The Foreign Policy of Counter Secession: Preventing Recognition of Contested States*, Oxford university Press, Oxford.

Kolers, Avery (2006), "Subsidiarity, Secession, and Cosmopolitan Democracy", in *Social Theory and Practice*, 32 (4).

Kymlicka, Will (2000), "Federalism and Secession: At Home and Abroad", in *Canadian Journal of Law & Jurisprudence*, 13 (2), 207–224.

Kymlicka, Will and Norman, Wayne eds. (2000), *Citizenship in Diverse Societies*, Oxford University Press, Oxford.

Lee, Steven (2005), "Globalization and Secession", in *Journal of Philosophical Research*, 30 (9999).

Lefkowitz, David (2008), "On the Foundation of Rights to Political Self-Determination: Secession, Nonintervention, and Democratic Governance", in *Journal of Social Philosophy*, 39 (4), 492–511.

Leslie, Peter (1999), "Canada: The Supreme Court Sets Rules for the Secession of Quebec", in *Publius*, 29 (2), 135–151.

Longo, Michael (2006), *Constitutionalising Europe: Processes and Practices*, Ashgate, Aldershot.

Lynch, Peter (2005), "Scottish Independence, The Quebec Model of Secession and the Political Future of the Scottish National Party", in *Nationalism and Ethnic Politics*, 11 (4), 503–531.

MacLauchlan, H. Wade (1997), "Accounting for Democracy and the Rule of Law in the Quebec Secession Reference", in *The Canadian Bar Review*, 76 (1–2), 155–185.

Margiotta, Costanza (2005), *L'ultimo diritto. Profili storici e teorici della secessione*, Il Mulino, Bologna.

McGarry, John (2001), *Minority Nationalism and the Changing International Order*, Oxford University Press, Oxford.

McKay, David H. (1996), *Rush to Union: Understanding the European Federal Bargain*, Clarendon Press, Oxford.

McKay, David H. (1999), *Federalism and European Union: A Political Economy Perspective*, Oxford University Press, Oxford.

McKay, David H. (2001), *Designing Europe: Comparative Lessons from the Federal Experience*, Oxford University Press, Oxford.

Meadwell, Hudson (1999), "Secession, States and International Society", in *Review of International Studies*, 25 (3), 371–387.

Meadwell, Hudson (2009), "The Political Dynamics of Secession and Institutional Accommodation", in *Regional & Federal Studies*, 19 (2), 221–235.

Mény, Yves and Surel, Yves (2002), *Democracies and the Populist Challenge*, Palgrave, Basingstoke.

Moore, Margaret (2000), "The Ethics of Secession and a Normative Theory of Nationalism", in *Canadian Journal of Law & Jurisprudence*, 13 (2), 225–250.

Nicolaidis, Kalypso and Howse, Robert eds. (2001), *The Federal Vision: Legitimacy and Levels of Governance in the United States and the European Union*, Oxford University Press, Oxford.

Norman, Wayne (2006), *Negotiating Nationalism: Nation-Building, Federalism, and Secession in the Multinational State*, Oxford University Press, Oxford.

Patten, Alan (2002), "Democratic Secession from a Multinational State", in *Ethics*, 112 (3), 558–586.

Pavković, Aleksandar (2004), "Secession as Defence of a Political Liberty: A Liberal Answer to a Nationalist Demand", in *Canadian Journal of Political Science/Revue canadienne de science politique*, 37 (3), 695–713.

Pavković, Aleksandar and Radan, Peter (2003), "In Pursuit of Sovereignty and Self-Determination: Peoples, States and Secession in the International Order", in *Macquarie Law Journal*, 3, https://www.mq.edu.au/public/download/?id=16205.

Pavkovic, Aleksandar and Radan, Peter (2007), *Creating New States: Theory and Practice of Secession*, Ashgate, Aldershot.

Pavkovic, Aleksandar and Radan, Peter eds. (2008), *On the Way to Statehood: Secession and Globalization*, Routledge, London.

Qvortrup, Matt (2012) "The History of Ethno-National Referendums 1791–2011", in *Nationalism and Ethnic Politics* 18 (1), 129–150.

Qvortrup, Matt (2014), "Referendums on Independence, 1860–2011", in *Political Quarterly*, 85 (1), 57–64.

Qvortrup, Matt (2016), "Referendums on Membership and European Integration 1972–2015", in *The Political Quarterly*, 87 (1), 61–70.

Radmilovic, Vuk (2010), "Strategic Legitimacy Cultivation at the Supreme Court of Canada: Quebec Secession Reference and Beyond", in *Canadian Journal of Political Science/Revue canadienne de science politique*, 43 (4), 843–869.

Rector, Chad (2009), *Federations: The Political Dynamics of Cooperation*, Cornell University Press, Ithaca and London.

Requejo, Ferran (2001), *Democracy and National Pluralism*, Routledge, London.

Requejo, Ferran (2017), "Plurinational Democracies, Federalism and Secession: A Political Theory Approach", in *Revista Catalana de Dret Públic* (54), 62–80.

Requejo, Ferran and Badia, Miquel Caminal (2012), *Federalism, Plurinationality and Democratic Constitutionalism: Theory and Cases*, Routledge, London.

Rocher, François (2002), "The Evolving Parameters of Quebec Nationalism", in *International Journal on Multicultural Societies*, 4 (1), http://www.unesco.org/most/vl4n1rocher.pdf.

Rodrigues, Daniel (2010), "Fédéralisme, conflit ethnique et sécessionnisme: Le fédéralisme comme instrument de sécession non-violente", in *Fédéralisme Régionalisme*, 10, https://popups.uliege.be:443/1374-3864/index.php?id=903.

Rubin, Alfred P. (2000), "Secession and Self-Determination: A Legal, Moral, and Political Analysis", in *Stanford Journal of International Law*, 36 (2), 253–270.

Schäfer, Wolf (2003), "Withdrawal Legitimised? On the Proposal by the Constitutional Convention for the Right of Secession from the EU", in *Intereconomics*, 38 (4), 182–185.

Schmucker, R (2010), "Secession and Democracy", in *Deutsche Zeitschrift Fur Philosophie*, 58 (5), 827–833.

Seymour, Michael and Gagnon, Alain G. eds. (2012), *Multinational Federalism: Problems and Prospects*, Palgrave, Basingstoke.

Shorten, Andrew (2014), "Constitutional Secession Rights, Exit Threats and Multinational Democracy", in *Political Studies*, 62 (1), 99–115.

Tideman Nicolaus (2004), "Secession as a Human Right", in *Journal of Moral Philosophy*, 1 (1), 9–19.

Usher, Dan (2000), "The Referendum Papers: Essays on Secession and National Unity", in *Canadian Public Policy-Analyse De Politiques*, 26 (2), 266–271.

Vaubel, Roland (2013), "Secession in the European Union", in *Economic Affairs*, 33 (3), 288–302.

Waters, Timothy William (2016), "A World Elsewhere: Secession, Subsidiarity, and Self-Determination as European Values", in *Revista d'Estudis Autonòmics i Federals*, 23 (1), 11–45.

Weinstock, Daniel (2001), "Constitutionalizing the Right to Secede", in *Journal of Political Philosophy*, 9 (2), 182–203.

Wellman, Christopher Heath (2005), *A Theory of Secession: The Case for Political Self-Determination*, Cambridge University Press, Cambridge.

Wheare, Kenneth C. (1963), *Federal Government*, 4th ed. Oxford University Press, London.

Wiltanger, Elizabeth L. (1999), "Sound the Trumpets! Quebec Is Shouting, 'Victory!' Despite the Canadian Supreme Court's Denial of Unilateral Secession", in *Penn State International Law Review*, 17 (3), 505–529.

"A Message of Hope": A Legal Perspective on the Reference

Giuseppe Martinico

Why Are We Celebrating the Reference?

If in 2017 the academic community celebrated the Sesquicentennial of the Canadian Confederation (Albert and Cameron 2017), 2018 marks another important anniversary: 20 years of the seminal Reference of the Canadian Supreme Court on the secession of Québec. For many years after the American Civil War, secession was understood as a sort of "constitutional taboo" (Mancini 2012), at least until 1998 when the Canadian Supreme Court broke the taboo, delivering its famous Reference regarding the secession of Québec. That was a crucial decision, because on that occasion the Canadian Supreme Court dealt frontally with the issue, going beyond a formalist reading of its constitutional text(s), i.e. rejecting the argument according to which secession was banned since no written provision provided for that in the Canadian legal system. It did so by identifying the untouchable core of its constitution and reading the issue in the light of the principles belonging to such a hard nucleus (federalism, democracy,

G. Martinico (✉)
Sant'Anna School of Advanced Studies, Pisa, Italy
e-mail: giuseppe.martinico@santannapisa.it

G. Delledonne and G. Martinico (eds.), *The Canadian Contribution to a Comparative Law of Secession*,
https://doi.org/10.1007/978-3-030-03469-6_12

constitutionalism and rule of law, protection of minorities). When offering its view, the Canadian Supreme Court did not limit its attention to domestic law only but, on the contrary, accepted the need to take international law into account. For all these reasons, this Reference has become a turning point.[1] Since then a new debate has started about how to constitutionalise secession (Haljan 2014) and how to tame something which had been considered for a long time as a sort of "beast" hard to domesticate. That Reference also gave the Supreme Court the chance to deal with the broader issue of the Canadian constitutional identity based on the coexistence of different languages and cultures. In this sense, this Reference should be seen as a link of a longer chain including the veto and the patriation References.[2]

Indeed, secession, as Mancini among others pointed out, is a sort of two-faced Janus, having both a revolutionary and conservative nature (Margiotta 2005) and this explains why it has been a sort of "f-word" in constitutional studies for many years:

> Secession is at once the most revolutionary and the most institutionally conservative of political constructs. Its revolutionary character lies in its ultimate challenge to state sovereignty; its conservative side, in the reinforcement of the virtues of the latter. This inherent duality is reflected in the legal regulation surrounding secession. With very limited exceptions, secession is prohibited both by international law as well as, albeit often implicitly, by the overwhelming majority of state constitutions. Nevertheless, a state born out of a successful secessionist project, is likely to be recognized both by international organizations and by the community of states. Often though, in that connection the term 'secession' is substituted by 'dissolution' (Yugoslavia) or 'voluntary disassociation' (Bangladesh, Eritrea, Czechoslovakia, the Soviet Union). Thus, it becomes apparent that legal regulation of secession tends to run counter and to dissimulate its revolutionary character, while legitimizing its conservative dimension, through state building in the context of a new sovereign entity (Mancini 2012: 481).

[1] On the increasing importance of references in Canadian constitutional law, see McKay-Panos (2014).

[2] Canadian Supreme Court, Patriation Reference Re: Resolution to amend the Constitution [1981] 1 SCR 753, https://scc-csc.lexum.com/scc-csc/scc-csc/en/item/2519/index.do; Canadian Supreme Court, Quebec Veto Reference [1982] 2 S.C.R. 793, https://scc-csc.lexum.com/scc-csc/scc-csc/en/item/5530/index.do. On this, see Russell (2011).

More recently, looking at the Spanish case, it is possible to find evidence of the importance acquired by Supreme and Constitutional Courts in this ambit: it is sufficient to think of decisions like judgement no. 42/2014 of the Spanish Constitutional Court.[3] When commenting upon this judgement, Ferreres Comella wrote that "the Constitutional Court is eager to speak" (Ferreres Comella 2014: 579) and stressed its will to remind political actors about the "the constitutional framework within which political decisions may ultimately be made" (to quote the Canadian Supreme Court, *Reference Re Secession of Quebec*, [1998] 2 S.C.R. 217, paragraph 100) and how a secession procedure should develop. For the purpose of this chapter, I shall limit myself to two points: first, I shall try to highlight the importance of the legal reasoning developed in the Reference on that occasion and second, I shall also stress its important anti-populist potential.

Without denying or neglecting the political side of secession, this chapter (but the same can be said with this book in general) maintains that it also presents legal aspects, and indeed over the years Courts (especially Constitutional and Supreme Courts) have devised a set of techniques in order to cope with it (Castellà Andreu 2016; Martinico 2017). In order to tackle secession, the Canadian Supreme Court first contextualised it in a legal scenario, avoiding easy choices and facing the preliminary objections concerning the lack of legal relevance of the challenged acts or of the raised questions (Dumberry 2015). This strategy was perceived as necessary in order to compensate the passivity of the relevant political actors or to try to facilitate a dialogue which had not yet started between the central and regional levels. Second, the Canadian Court gave a complex notion of democracy which cannot be reduced to the mere majority rule. This is a very important point as we will see later, which also makes this Reference a powerful tool against populism. Third, it reconstructed the core of Canadian constitutional identity by recalling the untouchable principles that make the Canadian Constitution special. Finally, it is important to recall that, on that occasion, the Canadian Supreme Court did not recognise a proper right to secession; rather it treated secession as an option that may be tolerated only in the presence of some important safeguards.

[3] Spanish Constitutional Court, Judgement no. 42/2014, available (in English) at http://www.tribunalconstitucional.es/es/jurisprudencia/restrad/Paginas/STC42-2014.aspx.

In order to make this point, the Canadian Court came up with a sort of "exit related conditionality" as we will see in the next section. This way, it guaranteed the respect of the constitutional identity of Canada.

Exit-Related Conditionality and Secession

Comparative lawyers have analysed the provisions concerning the possibility of secession (Mancini 2014) and also legal and political theorists have dealt with the issue of how to justify the option of secession, even in legal systems whose constitutions say nothing about that, including the Canadian one (*ex multis* Norman 2006; Buchanan 1991; Weinstock 2001). Without recalling the very huge debate already mentioned, I would like to briefly mention an element that in my view could justify the constitutionalisation of secession in some federal/regional contexts. It is linked to constitutional homogeneity: legal systems[4] tend to ensure a virtuous connection between diversity and unity with a series of mechanisms aimed at preserving loyalty and adhesion to the fundamental values of the national system. Evidence of this can be found in Article 28 of the German Basic Law[5]

[4] Recently on this, see Delledonne (2017).

[5] Article 28 of the German Basic Law:

1. The constitutional order in the Länder must conform to the principles of a republican, democratic and social state governed by the rule of law, within the meaning of this Basic Law. In each Land, county and municipality the people shall be represented by a body chosen in general, direct, free, equal and secret elections. In county and municipal elections, persons who possess citizenship in any member state of the European Community are also eligible to vote and to be elected in accord with European Community law. In municipalities a local assembly may take the place of an elected body.
2. Municipalities must be guaranteed the right to regulate all local affairs on their own responsibility, within the limits prescribed by the laws. Within the limits of their functions designated by a law, associations of municipalities shall also have the right of self-government according to the laws. The guarantee of self-government shall extend to the bases of financial autonomy; these bases shall include the right of municipalities to a source of tax revenues based upon economic ability and the right to establish the rates at which these sources shall be taxed.
3. The Federation shall guarantee that the constitutional order of the Länder conforms to the basic rights and to the provisions of paragraphs (1) and (2) of this Article.

and in Article 51 of the Swiss Constitution which conditions, for example, the contents of the cantonal constitutions.[6]

Similar examples can be found even at supranational level. Here, it is sufficient to recall the criteria employed for the accession of new Member States. Reasons connected to homogeneity can always suggest forms of control and monitoring and even the possibility of activating forms of centripetal intervention in case of departure from the fundamental values of the constitutional pact. This is the case of Article 155 of the Spanish Constitution and above all Article 37 of the German Basic Law.[7]

How is this connected with the possible introduction of a secession clause? Even the clauses on exit/withdrawal from a federal union can be read as forms of "exit related conditionality", by ensuring an axiological continuity between the new order and the old one. This might appear paradoxical, but it is actually a process in which the old system accepts the detachment of the seceding entity by making it conditional upon the adhesion to its fundamental values. According to this scheme, the constituent phase of the seceding legal system is partly guided and influenced by the values of the old constitution. This way the revolutionary character of secession is partly "exorcised". To understand what I mean by exit-related conditionality, it is useful to recall the Canadian Reference, according to which, in case of activation of the negotiations with Québec, "the conduct of the parties in such negotiations would be governed by the same constitutional principles which give rise to the duty to negotiate: federalism, democracy, constitutionalism and the rule of law, and the protection of minorities" (Canadian Supreme Court, *Reference Re Secession of Quebec*, [1998] 2 S.C.R. 217, paragraph 90).

[6]Article 51 of the Swiss Constitution: "Each Canton shall adopt a democratic constitution. This requires the approval of the People and must be capable of being revised if the majority of those eligible to vote so request.

Each cantonal constitution shall require the guarantee of the Confederation. The Confederation shall guarantee a constitution provided it is not contrary to federal law".

[7]Article 37 of the German Basic Law:

1. If a Land fails to comply with its obligations under this Basic Law or other federal laws, the Federal Government, with the consent of the Bundesrat, may take the necessary steps to compel the Land to comply with its duties.
2. For the purpose of implementing such coercive measures, the Federal Government or its representative shall have the right to issue instructions to all Länder and their authorities.

This axiological continuity would guarantee the rights of that population residing in the territory of the new State which had not voted for the independence. A possible argument against the constitutionalisation of a secession clause is linked to the threat of constantly exposing a legal system to the blackmail of the exit, in a sort of game to negotiate further forms of autonomy. Actually, the Spanish scenario shows that a risk like this exists even in the absence of a secession clause. In this sense, the lack of a provision like this has led to the explosion of a constitutional crisis in the absence of constitutional paths other than the constitutional amendment. Scholars have already explored the question of how to design a norm concerning the exit from the federal entity. Moreover, examples that could be taken into account are not missing and many of the models recalled by comparative lawyers have acknowledged an important role to referendums (Ziegler et al. 2014; Gökhan Şen 2015; Frosina 2017; Qvortrup 2014).

In this sense, the Canadian case shows how even in the absence of explicit constitutional clauses it is possible to attempt to proceduralise this phenomenon, by contributing to its domestication and in that the Canadian Supreme Court has indeed sent a message of hope: law—especially constitutional law—can and must have a role, avoiding delegating this issue to violence or politics only.

As Norman recalled: "the perceived advantages of handling secessionist politics and secessionist contests within the rule of law rather than as 'political' issues that lie outside of, or are presumed (by the secessionists) to supersede, the law" (Norman 2006: 189).

The Idea of Democracy Endorsed in the Reference

Concerning the anti-populist potential of the Reference, it is important to recall the idea of democracy endorsed by the Canadian Supreme Court.

On that occasion, the Court also presented the referendum as an instrument which needs to be mediated and which should not be considered as a source of automatic political or legal truth.

This responds to an important feature of populism: as political scientists (Mény and Surel 2002) pointed out, populism does not accept the compromise which representative democracy is based on. This also explains the emphasis over instruments of direct and participatory democracy portrayed as a form of appeal to the people.

This explains the deference that characterises the Reference, which is also clear in giving political actors the task "to determine what constitutes a clear majority on a clear question" (Canadian Supreme Court, *Reference Re Secession of Quebec*, [1998] 2 S.C.R. 217, paragraph 153). This way the Canadian Court avoided treating the referendum as something alternative to representative democracy.

While referendums are normally seen by populist movements as a kind of "catch all" appeal to the people which should be used to react against the corruption or passivity of the institutions, constitutional lawyers tend to handle referendums with care, looking upon them as a noble instrument whose compatibility with representative democracy must be guaranteed. This perspective can be justified in the light of the political risks connected to a massive use of referendum, in other words referendums, if used as a full alternative to the instruments and institutions representative of democracy, risk creating parallel channels of legitimation which could destabilise and delegitimise parliaments.

In order to prevent this, constitutions generally come up with solutions designed to divide the labour so to say between representative and direct/participatory democracy (depending on how scholars understand referendums, on this see Luciani 2008).

In the light of these considerations, the legacy of the Canadian Reference is also helpful to challenge the constitutional counter-narrative advanced by populists. In an important article, Corrias tried to go beyond a conflictual analysis (constitutionalism versus populism) by showing that—to a certain extent at least—even populism "contains a (largely implicit) constitutional theory" (Corrias 2016: 8).[8] Even more recently Fournier defined this relationship by relying on a "parasite analogy", saying that: "the relation between populism and constitutional democracy is comparable to a process of parasitism where constitutional democracy would be the host and populism the parasite" (Fournier 2018).

In fact, one could say that the real aim of populist movements is to alter the axiological hierarchies that characterise constitutional democracies, for instance by presenting democracy (understood as the rule

[8] "Constitutional theorists have not devoted a lot of attention to the phenomenon of populism [...] There may be two interpretations of this silence. Either constitutional theory has nothing to say about populism, in which case the silence is justified, or constitutional theory does have something to say, in which case the silence is unjustified and (potentially) problematic" (Corrias 2016: 7).

of majority) as a kind of "trump card" which should prevail over other constitutional values (Fournier 2018). To question this argument, one could recall one of the most important "lessons learned" thanks to the Canadian Reference, which instead proposed a richer understanding of democracy—i.e. not limited to its formal or procedural sense.

As Fournier recalled, "Populist rhetoric argues that the rule-of-law is used for a specific agenda by non-elected (and so non-representative) bodies. Populism turns the original equilibrium of constitutional democracy into a balance of power in which the majority no longer sits alongside the rule of law, but rather is constrained by it" (Fournier 2018).

To impede such an alteration of the fragile equilibrium characterising constitutional democracy, it is necessary to embrace a complex (i.e. non-reductionist) notion of democracy. In this respect throughout the text of the Reference, the Canadian Supreme Court clarified the relationship between democracy and majority. Here are some key passages.

> Democracy, however, means more than simple majority rule. Constitutional jurisprudence shows that democracy exists in the larger context of other constitutional values… Canadians have never accepted that ours is a system of simple majority rule. Our principle of democracy, taken in conjunction with the other constitutional principles discussed here, is richer [….] While it is true that some attempts at constitutional amendment in recent years have faltered, a clear majority vote in Quebec on a clear question in favour of secession would confer democratic legitimacy on the secession initiative which all of the other participants in Confederation would have to recognize. (Canadian Supreme Court, *Reference Re Secession of Quebec*, [1998] 2 S.C.R. 217, paragraph 63).

These words confirm the strong counter-majoritarian nature of constitutionalism as such and imply the necessity to understand democracy as a mosaic where the will of majority cannot be treated as a trump card against other constitutional values. This is also confirmed by the artificial concept of majority:

> A majority is not something you will find in nature. It is an artifact of law. You need legal rules to determine who counts, and in which way. You need legal safeguards of liberty, equality and diversity of opinion. You also need legal rules to determine what the majority will be able to do, which necessarily implies that the majority gets told what she is not allowed to do. In short, you need constitutional law (Steinbeis 2017).

It is possible to find confirmation of this in comparative law. Both the *Clarity Act* in Canada and Schedule I of the *Good Friday Agreement* give political actors an important role in detecting the existing majorities. The Clarity Act was a follow-up to the secession Reference in the part in which the Canadian Supreme Court had said that: "In this context, we refer to a 'clear' majority as a qualitative evaluation. The referendum result, if it is to be taken as an expression of the democratic will, must be free of ambiguity both in terms of the question asked and in terms of the support it achieves" (Canadian Supreme Court, *Reference Re Secession of Quebec*, [1998] 2 S.C.R. 217, paragraph 87).

In the light of this, the *Clarity Act* listed some factors that should be taken into account by the House of Commons to verify a posteriori the existence of a majority:

> Factors for House of Commons to take into account (2) In considering whether there has been a clear expression of a will by a clear majority of the population of a province that the province cease to be part of Canada, the House of Commons shall take into account (a) the size of the majority of valid votes cast in favour of the secessionist option; (b) the percentage of eligible voters voting in the referendum; and (c) any other matters or circumstances it considers to be relevant.[9]

This has caused a harsh reaction in Québec as we know. A similar role, but to be played in the phase before the celebration of a referendum, is acknowledged to the Secretary of State by Schedule I of the *Good Friday Agreement*[10]:

[9] An Act to give effect to the requirement for clarity as set out in the opinion of the Supreme Court of Canada in the Quebec Secession Reference S.C. 2000, c. 26, http://laws-lois.justice.gc.ca/eng/acts/c-31.8/page-1.html.

[10] "ANNEX A 1.

1. It is hereby declared that Northern Ireland in its entirety remains part of the United Kingdom and shall not cease to be so without the consent of a majority of the people of Northern Ireland voting in a poll held for the purposes of this section in accordance with Schedule 1.
2. But if the wish expressed by a majority in such a poll is that Northern Ireland should cease to be part of the United Kingdom and form part of a united Ireland, the Secretary of State shall lay before Parliament such proposals to give effect to that wish as may be agreed between Her Majesty's Government in the United Kingdom and the Government of Ireland". The Northern Ireland Peace Agreement. The Agreement reached in the multiparty negotiations 10 April 1998, http://peacemaker.un.org/sites/peacemaker.un.org/files/IE%20GB_980410_Northern%20Ireland%20Agreement.pdf.

1. The Secretary of State may by order direct the holding of a poll for the purposes of Section 1 on a date specified in the order.
2. Subject to paragraph 3, the Secretary of State shall exercise the power under paragraph 1 **if at any time it appears likely to him that a majority of those voting would express a wish that Northern Ireland should cease to be part of the United Kingdom and form part of a united Ireland.**
3. The Secretary of State shall not make an order under paragraph 1 earlier than seven years after the holding of a previous poll under this Schedule.

These two examples show that the majority is not a neutral or easy concept; on the contrary, it is an artificial one which can be constructed through political and legal decisions, by excluding or including someone from the right to vote, for instance. That is why procedural caveats are important since they contribute towards ensuring the preservation of that core of untouchable values that is up to constitutionalism to defend. When applied to referendums—frequently recalled by populists as a *mantra*—this means that the good reasons for the introduction of participation and direct democracy must be balanced with other values that are connected to the need to protect the untouchable core of a legal system.

The Important Counter-Majoritarian Dimension of Constitutionalism

The last point I would like to make is about what we can learn from this Reference to tackle the rise of independentist populism.[11] As said, one of the greatest lessons of this Reference consists in accepting a complex (i.e. non-reductionist) vision of democracy, and this is crucial to find objections to the constitutional counter- narrative advanced by populists.

Scholars have traditionally pointed out the ambiguities of referendum and the risks connected to an appropriate use of the instrument. It is a very long debate and, for instance, Max Weber had already recalled such risks and stressed how it can be used to deresponsibilise the political forces:

[11] On the ambiguity of the concept see, among others, Berlin (1967), Mény and Surel (2004) and (Müller 2016). On Canada and populism see also Mendes (2017).

> The referendum does not know the compromise, upon which the majority of all laws is based in every mass state with strong regional, social, religious and other cleavages [...] Moreover, the plebiscitary principles weaken the autonomous role of the party leader and the responsibility of the civil servants. A disavowal of the leading officials through a plebiscite which rejects their proposals does not and cannot enforce their resignation, as does a vote of no-confidence in parliamentary states, for the negative vote does not identify its reasons and does not oblige the negatively voting mass, as it does a parliamentary majority voting against a government, to replace the disavowed officials with its own responsible leaders (Weber 1922).

These are considerations that have inspired generations of social scientists and that are highly topical nowadays. More in general "politics of immediacy", "politics of announcements" and "identity politics" are at the heart of the populist agenda. As Pinelli wrote, "Populism, to the contrary, claims immediate responses to the 'people's will', denying the good reasons of a longer time perspective of politics" (Pinelli 2011). The obsession of populist movements with the "politics of immediacy" (Corrias 2016) inevitably results in questioning many of the instruments of representative democracy. This explains why one of the pillars of many constitutional democracies, namely the prohibition of the imperative mandate, has been questioned by populists. Indeed, populists tend to depict Parliaments as one of the fora of those *élite* that are frequently portrayed as detached from the real needs of the people.

Identity politics consists of presenting majority as a monolithic entity vested with moral superiority as opposed to the *élite* frequently depicted as corrupted. "Populists combine anti-elitism with a conviction that they hold a superior vision of what it means to be a true citizen of their nation" (Marchlewska et al. 2017). Here, we can see again the reductionist attitude of populism which tends to depict all those who cannot be traced back to the majority as the "others". If the majority is "the people", thus its will must prevail at all costs and immediately. This dichotomic approach and this need for the enemy have led Müller to stress the Schmittian flavour of populism. As Abromeit pointed out when commenting on Müller, populism appeals to a "mythical *Volksgemeinschaft*" and constructs "imagined communities" (Abromeit 2017; Anderson 1983) by searching for political enemies. This also explains the bombastic approach that frequently characterises the populist rhetoric. Populists need "walls" to mark a border between what they claim to be the "real" people and the others and construct identity by excluding the political competitors from the circle of legitimacy.

This again confirms that populism has its own constitutional theory and aims to construct a constitutional counter-narrative by using concepts of constitutional theory.

How can we challenge this? By recalling the need to protect what the Canadian Supreme Court called the "underlying constitutional principles" (Canadian Supreme Court, *Reference Re Secession of Quebec*, [1998] 2 S.C.R. 217, paragraph 49), that is that set of values whose violation would create a revolution understood in a technical sense, understood as the break of the chain of validity (Kelsen 1945).

> Underlying constitutional principles may give rise to very abstract and general obligations, or they may be more specific and precise in nature. The principles are not merely descriptive, but are also invested with a powerful normative force, and are binding upon both courts and governments. 'In other words', as this Court confirmed in the Manitoba Language Rights Reference, supra, at p. 752, 'in the process of Constitutional adjudication, the Court may have regard to unwritten postulates which form the very foundation of the Constitution of Canada'. It is to a discussion of those underlying constitutional principles that we now turn. (Canadian Supreme Court, *Reference Re Secession of Quebec*, [1998] 2 S.C.R. 217, paragraph 54)

Although on that occasion, as I recalled at the beginning of this chapter, the Court identified these principles to make a potential exit conditional upon the respect of its basic values, this kind of reasoning can be applied to find powerful counter-arguments against any type of populism. Within the principles recalled by the Canadian Court, there is also the protection of minorities. Although the Canadian Court focussed on linguistic minorities on that case, the language used throughout the Reference allows this reference to be connected to a broader concept of minority as clarified by the Court itself by insisting on the distinction between democracy and majority rule (paragraph 63). From that and other passages, we can understand how democracy cannot be used as a "trump card" to alter the untouchable core that characterises (liberal) constitutional systems, since there are values that cannot be decided by the majority in democratic systems.

Something similar has been argued even in Europe where this idea is frequently associated with the nature of post-World War II constitutionalism and to what philosophers have called a "memory of evil"

(Veca 2012; Todorov 2010). In the selection of the emotions operated by national constitutions, a key role is of course played by the history of each legal system: the horror, the conflicts, the past. In other words, everything that has led to the rupture with the previous legal regime and to the creation of the new system of norms.

In conclusion, I think that the greatest contribution to constitutionalism as a philosophical movement given by the Canadian Supreme Court consists in its broad concept of democracy, understood as a star in a constellation of values that need to be preserved and balanced by guaranteeing the evolution of the legal system.

References

Abromeit, John (2017), "A Critical Review of Recent Literature on Populism", in *Politics and Governance*, 5 (4), 177–186.

Albert, Richard and Cameron, David eds. (2017), *Canada in the World Comparative Perspectives on the Canadian Constitution*, Cambridge University Press, Cambridge.

Anderson, Benedict (1983), *Imagined Communities: Reflections on the Origin and Spread of Nationalism*, Verso, London.

Berlin, Isaiah (1967), "To Define Populism", http://berlin.wolf.ox.ac.uk/lists/bibliography/bib111bLSE.pdf.

Buchanan, Allen (1991), *Secession: The Morality of Political Divorce from Fort Sumter to Lithuania and Quebec*, Routledge, Abingdon.

Castellà Andreu, Josep Maria (2016), "Tribunal constitucional y proceso secesionista catalán: Respuestas juriídico-constitucionales a un conflicto político-constitucional", in *Teoría y Realidad Constitucional*, (37), 561–592.

Corrias, Luigi (2016), "Populism in a Constitutional Key: Constituent Power, Popular Sovereignty and Constitutional Identity", in *European Constitutional Law Review*, 12 (1), 6–26.

Delledonne, Giacomo (2017), *L'omogeneità costituzionale negli ordinamenti composti*, Editoriale Scientifica, Napoli.

Dumberry, Patrick (2015), "The Secession Question in Quebec", in *Diritto Pubblico Comparato ed Europeo*, 17 (2), 357–380.

Ferreres Comella, Victor (2014), "The Spanish Constitutional Court Confronts Catalonia's 'Right to Decide' (Comment on the Judgment 42/2014)", in *European Constitutional Law Review*, 10 (3), 571–590.

Fournier, Théo (2018), *From Rhetoric to Action: A Constitutional Analysis of Populism*, EUI Working Paper 2018/08, http://cadmus.eui.eu/handle/1814/51725.

Frosina, Laura (2017), "Profili giuridici e aspetti problematici del referendum di secessione. Un'analisi comparata", in *Nomos*, 3, 1–37.

Gökhan Şen, İlker (2015), *Sovereignty Referendums in International and Constitutional Law*, Springer, Heidelberg.

Haljan, David (2014), *Constitutionalising Secession*, Hart, Oxford.

Kelsen, Hans (1945), *General Theory of Law and State*, Russell and Russell, New York.

Luciani, Massimo (2008), "Il referendum: questioni teoriche e dell'esperienza italiana", in *Revista catalana de dret públic*, 38, 157–182.

Mancini, Susanna (2012), "Secession and Self-Determination", in Michel Rosenfeld and Sajó Andras (eds.), *The Oxford Handbook of Comparative Constitutional Law*, Oxford University Press, Oxford, 481–500.

Mancini, Susanna (2014), "Costituzionalismo, federalismo e secessione", in *Le Istituzioni del federalismo*, 779–805.

Marchlewska, Marta, Cichocka, Aleksandra, and Panayiotou, Orestis (2017), "Populism as Identity Politics: Perceived Ingroup Disadvantage, Collective Narcissism and Support for Populism", in *Social Psychological and Personality Science*, 9 (2), 151–162.

Margiotta, Costanza (2005), *L'ultimo diritto. Profili storici e teorici della secessione*, Il Mulino, Bologna.

Martinico, Giuseppe (2017), "Identity Conflicts and Secession Before Courts: Three Case Studies", in *Revista General de Derecho Público Comparado*, 21, 1–30.

McKay-Panos, Linda (2014), "The Increasing Importance of Reference Decisions in Canadian Law", http://www.lawnow.org/increasing-importance-reference-decisions-canadian-law/.

Mendes, Errol ed. (2017), *Canada's Constitutional Democracy: The 150th Anniversary Celebration*, Lexis Nexis, Toronto.

Mény, Yves and Surel, Yves eds. (2002), *Democracies and the Populist Challenge*, Palgrave, Basingstoke.

Mény, Yves and Surel, Yves (2004), *Populismo e democrazia*, Il Mulino, Bologna.

Müller, Jan Werner (2016), *What Is Populism?* University of Pennsylvanian Press, Philadelphia.

Norman, Wayne (2006), *Negotiating Nationalism: Nation-Building, Federalism, and Secession in the Multinational State*, Oxford University Press, Oxford.

Pinelli, Cesare (2011), "The Populist Challenge to Constitutional Democracy", in *European Constitutional Law Review*, 7 (1), 5–16.

Qvortrup, Matt (2014), *Referendums on Independence, 1860–2011*, in *Political Quarterly*, 85 (1), 57–64.

Russell, Peter (2011), "The Patriation and Quebec Veto References: The Supreme Court Wrestles with the Political Part of the Constitution", *The Supreme Court Law Review: Osgoode's Annual Constitutional Cases Conference*, http://digitalcommons.osgoode.yorku.ca/cgi/viewcontent.cgi?article=1209&context=sclr.

Steinbeis, Maximilian (2017), *Majority Is a Legal Concept*, *Verfassungsblog*, http://verfassungsblog.de/majority-is-a-legal-concept/.

Todorov, Tzvetan (2010), *Memory as a Remedy for Evil*, Seagull Books, Kolkata.
Veca, Salvatore (2012), *La priorità del male*, Feltrinelli, Milano.
Weber, Max (1922), *Economy and Society*, https://archive.org/stream/MaxWeberEconomyAndSociety/MaxWeberEconomyAndSociety_djvu.txt.
Weinstock, Daniel (2001),"Constitutionalizing the Right to Secede", in *Journal of Political Philosophy*, 9 (2), 182–203.
Ziegler, Ruvi, Shaw, Jo and Bauböck, Rainer eds. (2014), *Independence Referendums: Who Should Vote and Who Should Be Offered Citizenship?* European University Institute, RSCAS 2014/90, http://cadmus.eui.eu/bitstream/handle/1814/32516/RSCAS_2014_90.pdf.

Towards a Comparative Constitutional Law of Secession?

Francesco Palermo

Introduction: What Is Left of the Quebec Secession Reference 20 Years Down the Road?

The Supreme Court of Canada's 1998 *Reference Re Secession of Québec*[1] has opened the door to the establishment of a comparative constitutional law of secession. Until then, the overwhelmingly prevailing constitutional thought assumed that constitutions are based on an inherent principle of self-preservation (Sunstein 1991: 633), as epitomized in the US Supreme Court most famous post-Civil War case, *Texas v. White*.[2] The Canadian Reference inaugurated a functional and procedural approach to secession. As experience shows, secession takes place irrespective of its

[1] *Reference Re Secession of Quebec*, [1998] 2 S.C.R. 217.

[2] *Texas v. White*, 74 US 700 (1869). It is worth recalling that independence referendums took place in the US Confederate States of Texas, Virginia, Tennessee and Arkansas, where narrow majorities voted for independence in 1861.

F. Palermo (✉)
Faculty of Law, University of Verona and Eurac Research,
Bolzano/Bozen, Italy
e-mail: Francesco.Palermo@eurac.edu

G. Delledonne and G. Martinico (eds.), *The Canadian Contribution to a Comparative Law of Secession*,
https://doi.org/10.1007/978-3-030-03469-6_13

constitutional permissibility: about 30 new states have been created since 1990 (with a particularly high number following the fall of the iron curtain), almost 60 in the last 50 years and 129 since 1941 (Baldacchino and Hepburn 2012). A functional approach as the one clearly followed by the Canadian Supreme Court aims at rationalizing the otherwise extremely politicized and emotional issue of secession and at channelling it into a legal framework (Weinstock 2001). After all, as advocates of the functional approach argue, "demonizing secession, turning it into a constitutional taboo, often adds fuel to secessionist claims" (Mancini 2012: 482). In fact, the Canadian trajectory after the Reference and the following Clarity Act (2000) seems to support this conclusion, as do several cases of denied secession, which have by no means eradicated the claims (Weller 2008). Thus, one would expect that most of the countries experiencing secessionist requests would have adopted a similar complex legal framework to encapsulate secession into a sophisticated procedural shell.

However, twenty years after, this has not been the case. Rather than establishing procedural and substantive checks and balances regulating secession—maybe even taming it by means of law—what has happened is a proliferation of referendums on sovereignty (Mendez and Germann 2018), very often unofficial and thus contested. The Canadian Supreme Court's call for balanced rules that take into account the principles of rule of law, federalism and protection of minorities in determining the legal framework for possible negotiations over secession remained confined within the Canadian borders. Elsewhere, such principles, while occasionally referred to in judicial rulings on secession claims[3] (Martinico 2017a), have been trumped by the use of the referendum as (if not the only by far) the dominant means for constitutional change, or rather for constitutional challenge, i.e. for secession claims.

This chapter first looks at the comparative state of the art and at what has happened so far with regard to referendums on sovereignty[4] (2.). Then it considers what, based on the current status of constitutionalism and on comparative experience, might become a set of rules for a

[3] See in particular, the ruling by the Spanish Constitutional Tribunal no. 42/2014 and 259/2015.

[4] The category is of course contested in itself. As pointed out by Mendez and Germann (2018: 143) the term "sovereignty referendum" usually includes referendums on territorial issues, plebiscites, ethnonational referendums, referendums on the boundary/identity question.

comparative constitutional law of secession following the principles laid down in the 1998 Reference (3.).

Referendums as Exclusive Means to Address Sovereignty Claims and the Risk of Plebiscitary Constitutionalism

Following the predominant approach, the overwhelming majority of constitutions does not provide for a right to secession and very often they rule it explicitly out by calling for eternity, unity, indivisibility, indestructibility of the state (Novic and Priya 2016). In very rare and exceptional cases, constitutions do contain provisions allowing for secession. These can provide for an undefined right to freely secede—such as in the case of Article 72 of the Soviet constitution of 1977[5] or of (the purely on paper provision of) Article 74 of the Uzbek constitution in the case of Karakalpakstan—or for a conditional although equally unspecified right to do so, like for Gagauzia in Moldova "in case of a change of the status of the Republic of Moldova as an independent state" (Article 1 law on the special legal status of Gagauzia, 1994). Only in the case of Ethiopia, the 1995 constitution (Article 39) lays down procedural rules on how to achieve independence by some subnational unit, which also include a referendum (Habtu 2005). In a handful of islands autonomies, specific provisions have been inserted in the course of time to allow for referendums on independence (or quasi-independence), such as in Greenland, Faroe Islands, Bougainville, Falkland Islands, New Caledonia (Ellis 2018).

In a comparative perspective, it results that *all* the few explicit—general or ad hoc—provisions on the possible separation of a territory from the state it belongs to provide for a referendum. Only in Ethiopia some additional procedural provisions are included, notably the initiative by a two thirds majority of the subnational legislature (Article 39, paragraph 4 lit a const.), although the referendum (which is to be organized within three years from the initiative) does not require any entrenched majority ("supported by a simple majority vote in the referendum", Article 39, paragraph 4 lit c const.). From a historical perspective, the last separation that took place without a referendum was the split of Czechoslovakia in

[5] This article was specified by a law as late as in 1990, when the dissolution of the Soviet Union was already in place (Bowring 2015).

1992—and interestingly enough, a referendum was possible there too[6] but it was not held, also because according to opinion polls at that time, the majority in both parts of the then Czechoslovak federation opposed dissolution.[7] Since then, all attempts—both successful and failed—to achieve independence resorted to a referendum, with the sole (and partial) exception of Kosovo due to its peculiar situation of (then) international protectorate.[8]

It can thus be said that since the post-1989 wave of constitution-making (for the concept, see Elster 1995) the referendum has become not only the main but often the exclusive means to address sovereignty claims (Şen 2015) irrespective of the typology of constitutional referendum (for a categorization of constitutional referendums, see Tierney 2012). More specifically, secession and territorial referendums have been different in scope, functions and procedure, as well of course in outcome (Qvortrup 2014). Most of the referendums held in nearly all former Soviet and former Yugoslav republics between 1991 and 1992 were plebiscitary moments of a process that was already in unstoppable motion (Kössler 2018). In some case, they just rubber-stamped the already achieved statehood, like in Georgia, Ukraine Uzbekistan (where the referendum took place three days after the official dissolution of the UdSSR) and in the more contested cases of Latvia, Estonia, and Lithuania. In other cases, more nuanced issues emerged, either in terms of participation (in the 1992 independence referendum in Bosnia and Herzegovina, the Serbian community boycotted the vote) or of threshold: for instance, in Slovenia, the referendum in December 1990 was subject to a threshold set at 50% of the whole electorate, which was easily

[6]If so requested by the Federal Assembly or by one or both subnational parliaments: Article 1 Constitutional Act 327/1991.

[7]According to a poll taken for the government in summer 1992, "only 37 percent of Slovaks and 36 percent of Czechs said they would vote for a split in a referendum, but more than 80 percent said that they considered a break inevitable" https://www.nytimes.com/1992/10/09/world/at-fork-in-road-czechoslovaks-fret.html.

[8]It must be recalled that the Provincial Assembly of Kosovo declared independence in 1991, and immediately after a referendum was called, in which 99% of the voters (by a turnout of 87%) supported independence. The whole process was blocked by Serbia. After the NATO military intervention in 1999 and the following international protectorate, Kosovo unilaterally declared independence in February 2008.

reached.[9] Other referendums simply remained without any consequence, at least in terms of international recognition of the formally proclaimed statehood, such as in Nagorno-Karabakh in 1991 and in Somaliland in 2001.

Referendums that took place after the immediate post-1989 and post-communist turmoil represented the real turning point for the countries concerned. In some case, they were held under international supervision, like in Eritrea in 1993, in East Timor in 1999, in Montenegro in 2006 or in South Sudan in 2011. While no specific requirements were provided for in East Timor, in Montenegro, after long disputes on the rules for the referendum, the European Union was eventually successful in imposing a double entrenched majority for the approval of the quest for independence: 55% of votes in favour, with a minimum turnout of 50% of the electorate.[10] Also in South Sudan, the validity of the referendum was subject to a specific threshold, i.e. 60% turnout. In both cases, the thresholds have been successfully met.

Several other independence referendums took place in recent years or are scheduled in a number of islands or other territories already enjoying autonomy from the mainland, normally agreed between the central government and the affected territory. Both in the Falkland Islands (2013) and in Gibraltar (2002), referendums were called in order to reiterate the expected support in favour of the territories' belonging to the UK and did not require any special majority as landslide support for the status quo was known. In Bougainville, a (consultative) referendum is scheduled for 2019 on independence from Papua New Guinea, although the situation remains in a state of flux and a second referendum is not ruled out (Regan 2013). In New Caledonia, an independence referendum took place in November 2018 as agreed in the Nouméa Accord from 1998.[11] The same referendum was held already in 1988, resulting in less than 20% of the votes in favour of independence from France. Another referendum based on mutual agreement between the concerned

[9] The total support for independence was 88.5% of eligible voters, 94.8% of those participating. Independence was accordingly proclaimed in 1991.

[10] Referendum Bill, 2006. The then Prime Minister Milo Đukanović promised that he would declare unilateral independence if the votes passed 50%, irrespective of the double majority requested by the law mediated by the European Union. The double threshold was however reached, albeit barely.

[11] See French Organic law No. 99-209 (1999).

parties was scheduled for spring 2018 in the Faroe Islands; however, not on full independence from Denmark but on a new constitution granting a sort of quasi-independence, but it was indefinitely postponed.

No doubt, the best-known example of an agreed referendum on independence has been the one that took place in Scotland in September 2014. After a complex set of negotiations following the seize of power in Edinburgh by the Scottish National Party (2007–2011) (Mitchell 2014), the so-called Edinburgh agreement (2012) provided for a referendum on just two options: independence or status quo, although the political promise from London was further devolution of powers in case of a vote against independence (Tierney 2013). Especially, noteworthy for the purposes of this paper are the absence of any entrenchment for the referendum, the scope of the right to vote and the exclusion of a third legal option between independence and status quo. As to the first aspect, the very concept of entrenched majorities is alien to the political nature of the British constitution[12] and it was never really considered as an option. As to the right to vote, Article 2 of the Scottish Independence Referendum (Franchise) Act 2013 extended it to persons aged 16 or over, resident in Scotland and citizen of the Commonwealth, of the Republic of Ireland or of the European Union, thus de facto increasing the chances for a "no" vote. Not least, no third option between independence and status quo was legally provided for by the Scottish Independence Referendum Act 2013, although this was initially considered (Devo Plus Group 2012), subsequently politically promised in case of a "no" vote and eventually realized with the adoption of the Scotland Act 2016.

Several other independence referendums took place in recent years illegally, i.e. without having been agreed between the affected territory and the central government or even informally. Among them the unofficial, privately organized online consultations in Catalonia and Veneto in 2014, and the more official, albeit contested, referendums in Iraqi Kurdistan in 2017[13]

[12]See however High Court, *Thoburn v. Sunderland City Council* (2003), in Common Market Law Reports, 50 and Leyland (2016).

[13]Despite the fact that the Iraqi Federal Supreme Court ordered the suspension of the referendum, the President of Iraqi Kurdistan went ahead with the vote on 25 September 2017. By a turnout of 72/, 92.7 of the voters were in favour of independence. The Federal Supreme Court declared the vote unconstitutional the same day and reiterated in November 2017 that Article 1 of the Iraqi constitution prevents any region from seceding (decision in Arabic https://www.iraqfsc.iq/krarat/1/2017/89_fed_2017.pdf).

and in Gagauzia in 2014.[14] In 2014, a referendum was held in Crimea on the separation of the peninsula from Ukraine and its access to the Russian Federation. The referendum was held despite the fact that its call had been declared illegal by the Ukrainian Constitutional Court,[15] and the Crimean Parliament had unilaterally declared independence three days before the vote. The referendum resulted in a plebiscite for secession from Ukraine and annexation to the Russian Federation (95.7% by a turnout of 82%, although the referendum was boycotted by Tatar and Ukrainian minorities) and was immediately followed by Russian annexation, regardless of its illegality under both international and Ukrainian constitutional law (Venice Commission 2014; Bílková 2016). In the Bosnian Entity of Republika Srpska, a referendum on independence has been often announced as a threat but never realized so far, while several identity-driven referendums took place. Common to all these unofficial referendums is their political nature: while legally irrelevant, they are used as instruments for political pressure (sometimes they are organized by political parties)[16] and/or to make the cause for independence more popular and always result in plebiscites in favour of independence, even when the turnout is low.[17]

The most significant and best known among the unofficial referendums of this kind is the consultation that was took place in Catalonia on October 1, 2017. The "referendum on self-determination" was

[14]With a turnout of more than 70%, 98.9% of the voters supported the declaration of independence of Gagauzia if Moldova eventually lost its sovereignty, a scenario that could imply the merger of Moldova and Romania into a single sovereign state, an option that is provided for in the Law on the Special Legal Status for Gagauzia from 1994. Similarly, 98.4% of voters said they prefer to tighten ties with Russian-led Customs Union rather than moving towards EU integration.

[15]Decision no. 2-rp/2014, case no. 1-13/2014.

[16]In 2013, an independentist political party in South Tyrol that currently enjoys support of 7.2% of the electorate organized a referendum on independence from Italy, to which less than 15% of the electorate participated and which resulted in a 92% "yes" vote for independence. In Iraqi Kurdistan, an informal independence referendum was organized by the Kurdistan Referendum Movement, producing an outcome of 99% of votes for independence.

[17]Normally, the turnout is low when informal referendums are organized by political parties or movements, while it tends to be high when they are called by subnational governments, such as in the case of Gagauzia (footnote 13) and Iraqi Kurdistan (72.6% turnout, 92.7%). High turnouts were achieved also in the illegal but equally locally organized referendums in Somaliland (2001) and in the Serb enclave of Kraijna in Croatia (1992).

called by a law of the regional parliament adopted less than one month before in a contested procedure[18] and was immediately suspended by the Constitutional Court, which subsequently declared it unconstitutional.[19] The referendum was held anyway, which led to harsh confrontation with the Spanish government and also to cases of violence and repression. The Catalan Government officially announced the results of the referendum[20] and on that basis the Catalan Parliament proclaimed, in a contested, majority vote, a unilateral declaration of independence.[21] In response, the Spanish Senate enacted coercive measures de facto suspending Catalan autonomy (Article 155 Spanish constitution) and called for early regional elections. After the elections, the legal situation was "normalized" but political tensions remained (Poggeschi 2018).

A final, *sui generis* example of independence referendum is represented by the UK's vote to leave the European Union (so-called Brexit) in 2016. The Treaty on the European Union lays down the procedure for withdrawing from the Union (Article 50 TEU), although it refers to "its own constitutional requirements" as to how a state may decide on the withdrawal. The British political constitution did not contain a provision on the "own constitutional requirements" although it was clear that a decision on leaving the EU was possible only by referendum, as the British membership in the EU, provided for by the European Communities Act 1972, was confirmed by referendum in 1975 (67.2% in favour by a turnout of 64.6%). Accordingly, the European Union Referendum Act 2015 provided for a consultative referendum on "whether the United Kingdom should remain a member

[18] Law no. 19/2017, of 6 September, "on the referendum of self-determination". Together with law no. 20/2017 ("on juridical transition"), the law was adopted following a special procedure that cuts debate and amending proposal to just one day. For more details Castellà Andreu (2017).

[19] STC 114/2017. Subsequent ruling STC 124/2017 outlawed also the Law on transition. For the Court, both laws violated the rights of participation of the minority in parliament and introduced a new legal order against the foundations of the Spanish Constitution without following the procedures for constitutional amendment.

[20] According to the Catalan government (22 October 2017), the turnout was 43.03% of the electorate and the support for independence was 92.01% of those who participated in the vote http://www.govern.cat/pres_gov/govern/ca/monografics/303541/govern-traslada-resultats-definitius-referendum-1l-doctubre-parlament-catalunya.html.

[21] Resolution 27 October 2017.

of the European Union". Like for the referendum on Scottish independence, no entrenched majority was required, nor an alternative was offered between leaving or remaining, although the government had already negotiated with Brussels a new treaty redefining the terms of UK membership in the Union, that should have entered into force in case the referendum was in favour of "remain" (Martinico 2017b). The Referendum Act 2015 also defined the electorate in a significantly different manner as compared to the Scottish referendum: only persons aged 18 or over, no citizens of EU countries residing in the UK and no UK citizens residing abroad for more than 15 years. The referendum took place in June 2016 and 51.9% of the voters (by a turnout of 72.2%) supported the withdrawal from the EU, leading to the approval of the European Union (Withdrawal) Act 2018 and to negotiations with the EU according to Article 50 TEU.

All these examples testify of a remarkable constitutional acceleration (Blokker 2018) with regard to secession claims over the past two decades and the resort to referendums with no exception as the main—in most case only—instrument to decide on or (in case of illegal referendums) to support the claim for independence. This is because the political impact of plebiscites trumps that of any other source of law, as is confirmed by the fact that almost no difference exists in practice between consultative and legally binding referendums, since all consultative referendums have been considered as politically binding.[22] The democratization of contemporary constitutionalism has gone as far as to consider a referendum unavoidable to establish a new legal order. In fact, as the Catalan case exemplarily shows, the so-called right to decide has functionally replaced the "right to self-determination" (see Levrat et al. 2017 and the arguments by the Spanish constitutional court in ruling STC 259/2015). Knowing that the advocates of an independence referendum always support independence, the battlefield on the (rather theoretical) right to self-determination has been moved to the much more pragmatic and prima facie less contentious right to decide (Ferraiuolo 2016). This way, constitutional checks and balances are subordinated to the sovereign will of people (Martinico 2018).

[22] See the interesting arguments put forward in the UK Supreme Court's landmark "Brexit" case *R (Miller) v. Secretary of State for Exiting the European Union* (2017) UKSC 5.

Beyond Plebiscitarianism: Constitutionalizing and Pluralizing Secession Procedures: The Legacy of Constitutionalism—And of the Quebec Secession Reference—In a Few Procedural Steps

The spreading of referendums as a means to channel secession claims has the great merit to institutionalize challenges that so far have been left outside the realm of law and thus decided either politically or on the battleground (Elster 2012). In this perspective, independence referendums represent an important step on the evolutionary path of constitutionalism, which ultimately means to regulate political processes with legal instruments (Hayek 1960: 176). Furthermore, referendums are also a manifestation of the democratic principle, at least when they are agreed and regulated by legal procedures. Against this background, it can be concluded that the post-1989 constitutional wave has represented a major step forward for constitutionalism with regard to secession, one of the areas so far immune from legal regulation.

The limit of referendums, however, is that they are too simplistic and 'trivial', especially when deciding on existential issues like secession and statehood and even more if they are not supported by procedural entrenchments or by additional procedures. The independence referendum held in Quebec in 1995 did not require any special majority. It was rejected by a narrow majority of 50.58%, fewer than 55,000 votes, and following the vote, there was significant controversy relating to the counting of the ballots, the enumeration of eligible voters and other concerns. The outcome of the referendums on Scottish independence in 2014 and on Brexit in 2016 were largely determined by the definition of the eligible voters. Furthermore, the question of structural minorities is always a challenge for referendums. If decisions are to be made by a majority (majoritarian constitutionalism), especially if simple, without a quorum and extemporary (plebiscitarian constitutionalism), how can the rights of minorities be respected, even more if such minorities are territorial majorities? In the Brexit, referendum 62% of the votes in Scotland and 55% in Northern Ireland were for "remain", representing a much more consistent support than the 51.9% for "leave" in the whole of UK. Beside ethnocultural minorities, should other minorities be considered, and how? In the London, metropolitan area 59.9% of votes have been for "remain", and so were 73% in Cambridge and 95.9% in Gibraltar. In Catalonia, both the (unreliable) referendum and the results of elections (especially, the one held in December 2017 after the dissolution of the Catalan Parliament by the Spanish Government, which has been politically considered an equivalent to a referendum on independence) show support for independence by little less than 50% of the electorate,[23] with uneven geographical distribution (more support in the periphery, less in the metropolitan areas): can a fundamental decision be made by a tiny majority where society is split? More generally, if referendums aim at legitimizing constitutional discontinuity, they fail to do so when legitimacy is conferred by simple majority.

To reduce the risk of majoritarian and even plebiscitary referendums (Sáenz Royo and Garrido López 2017), the Canadian Supreme Court's Quebec Secession Reference (followed by the parliament with the Clarity Act) has taken the natural step suggested by constitutionalism: it designed a legal framework for secession claims. These must include a referendum as unavoidable democratic expression by the people, but its shortcomings make the referendum unfit to represent the only decisional moment, especially if not assisted by some procedural entrenchment.

Moving from the Canadian experience, legal scholars have started to pay growing attention to this phenomenon and also to put forward proposals on how to combine constitutionalism and secession (among others Haljan 2014; Martinico 2018). The common denominator of any formula in this regard cannot but be the combination of procedures producing an effect that goes beyond rudimentary, plebiscitary majoritarianism and combines popular decision-making with the rule of law, including respect for minorities. Based on some of the greatest achievements of constitutionalism such as federalism, constitutional amending procedures and participatory democracy, on comparative case-law on secession and constitutional amendment, and on the "soft-jurisprudence" of international bodies such as the Venice Commission, a few elements for a comparative procedural framework on how to address secessionist claims can be sketched.

The *first* and simplest entrenchment is the provision of quorums both for the turnout and for the approval in a referendum on independence, as was provided for in the 2006 referendum for Montenegrin

[23]The support is constantly monitored by the poll center of the Catalan Government (Barómetro de Opinión Pública del Centre d'Estudis d'Opinió) which shows support ranging from 43 to 48% in 2018: see http://ceo.gencat.cat/ca/inici. See also López-Basaguren (2018).

independence. While quorums are generally problematic in referendums as they can easily be misused by opponents to torpedo the vote by encouraging abstention (as suggested by the Venice Commission's Code of Good Practices on Referendums 2006),[24] the situation is different when it comes to existential issues such as secession and statehood. In these cases, abstention is unlikely and not due to lack of interest or of information, and the criterion of the "clear majority" put forward in the Quebec Secession Reference is of utmost importance and can be ascertained only if entrenched majorities are provided for.

A *second* and related factor to dilute the rudimentary, black-and-white logic of referendums is the time element. Especially, if no requirement is made as regards (turnout and/or approval) quorums, it might be advisable to repeat a referendum at least one more time within a given time frame, in order to better ascertain the real will of voters and not making it conditional upon occasional variables. This might be of course the wiser the tighter the outcome is. While there is no guarantee that the result changes remarkably especially if the voters are split, there have been several precedents of repeated referendums where the outcome was different due to a broader information, or to changes adopted following further negotiations. One may think of the referendums held in some European countries on issues pertaining to the European Union (Mendez et al. 2014). Ireland has been the "champion" of repeated European referendums. In 2001, voters rejected the Treaty of Nice (53.9% against by a turnout of 34.8%), but the referendum was repeated in 2002, after some changes in the treaty concerning the Irish position on the common defence policy, and was approved by 62.9% of the voters (turnout 49.5%). In 2008, Ireland was the only EU Member State to call a referendum on the ratification of the Lisbon Treaty: ratification was initially rejected by a 53.2% majority (turnout 53.1%) and subsequently approved (unchanged) in a second referendum in 2009 (67.1% in favour, turnout 59%). Denmark held two referendums on the ratification of the Maastricht Treaty: the first was rejected in 1992 by 50.7% (turnout 83.1%), the second—after renegotiating the opt-out from significant policies such as the Economic and Monetary Union, the Union Citizenship, Justice and Home Affairs and Common Defence—was approved in 1993 by 56.7% of the voters (turnout 86.5%). Several examples also exist of

[24]CDL-AD(2007)008, esp. paragraphs 51 and 52. See also the Compilation of Venice Commission opinions and reports concerning referendums, CDL (2017)002.

provisions limiting the call for a referendum before a certain time has elapsed from a previous one.[25]

A *third* way to balance the majoritarian attitude of a referendum is to put more than just two options to the vote, thus allowing for a more nuanced deliberation, as it was initially proposed in Scotland (so-called Devolution-max) and eventually realized with the Scotland Act 2016. In fact, a referendum is a black-and-white instrument only if it is made one such, but can be more nuanced if more alternatives are offered.

A *fourth* element of a procedural framework for secession is to avoid that independence referendums be the only decisional instruments. In fact, for every (legal) referendum on independence or secession an act of parliament is required, but it often merely reflects political agreements made elsewhere. The involvement of parliament could, however, be made more "resistant" to possible abuses by occasional majorities. Article 39 of the Ethiopian constitution requires a request for starting the procedure by at least a two thirds majority of the legislature of the entity concerned. The referendum is not subject to entrenched majority (Article 39.4 lit c), but the constitution requires a subsequent law that inter alia transfers assets to the "nation, nationality or people which has opted for secession" (Article 39.4 lit e, Bihonegn 2015). This way, parliaments of all affected levels of government must be included in the decision-making, in some instances with entrenched majorities. These can counterbalance majorities in other levels of government, for example, in case a minority group demanding secession is a majority in one particular territorial entity. For example, it could be provided that if a subnational parliament adopts a motion for secession with a qualified majority, the national parliament can stop it only by an equally qualified majority.

Similarly, in secession processes also courts are normally involved (Martinico 2017a, b). The role of courts can be merely negative, i.e. affirming that secession of parts of the national territory is simply not

[25]On top of several constitutions establishing time limits for, in particular, constitutional reforms, it is worth mentioning Schedule 1 of the Good Friday/Belfast Agreement of 1998. As to the possibility to call for a referendum on unification of Ireland it states: "1. The Secretary of State may by order direct the holding of a poll for the purposes of section 1 on a date specified in the order. 2. […] a majority of those voting would express a wish that Northern Ireland should cease to be part of the United Kingdom and for part of united Ireland. 3. *The Secretary of State shall not make an order under paragraph 1 earlier than seven years after the holding of a previous poll under this Schedule*" (emphasis added).

admissible. This was the case, inter alia, of the mentioned pivotal US Supreme Court decision in *Texas v. White* (1869),[26] of the ruling of the Italian Constitutional Court in 2015 on the request of the region of Veneto to hold an independence referendum,[27] of the 2016 decision by the German Federal Constitutional Court on the individual complaint of a political group supporting Bavarian independence,[28] of the Iraqi Federal Supreme Court decision in 2017.[29] Courts can, however, also clarify important aspects in terms of procedure and constitutional principles that must guide a request for independence. This notably happened in the case of the Quebec Secession Reference or of the seminal ruling of the Spanish Constitutional Court that clarified the terms for a possible independence claim under the Spanish Constitution, specifying that these had not been met in the case of Catalonia.[30] An early involvement of courts in determining paths and limits of secessionist processes would in any case help clarify the legal contours of requests, the principles to be respected, and the modalities of decision-making. Such an involvement is less unthinkable than was some years ago the inclusion of constitutional/supreme courts in constitution-amending processes, which is now a not uncommon practice (Chen and Poiares Maduro 2013: 103). In some cases, courts can give advisory opinions (as it was the case for the Canadian Reference on the Secession of Quebec), which is an additional way to involve the guardians of the law in these complex processes.

A *fifth* guarantee against plebiscitary abuses in independence processes is the "double-check" by the electorate through elections after a referendum. Elections and referendums are different categories of vote, especially as the latter are mediated by political parties and produce a longer-term effect in shaping the political composition of parliaments. Constitutionalism offers several examples of complex procedures for the total revision of constitutions, which is a similar attempt to regulate regime changes that historically used to take place in revolutionary ways

[26] *Texas v. White*, 74 US 700 (1869).

[27] Ruling no. 118/2015.

[28] BVerfG, 2. Kammer, 2. Senat, decision 16 december 2016—2 BvR 349/16. The decision is as short as 3 sentences. Two of them simply affirm: "in the Fundamental Law there is no place for secession claims of individual *Länder*. These violate the constitutional order".

[29] See footnote 13.

[30] STC 42/2014 and subsequent rulings—see Castellà Andreu (2016).

(see the distinction between "revolutionary" and "institutionalized" constituent power by Burdeau 1985). Such procedures often require dissolution of parliament in order for the total revision of the constitution to be voted (by qualified majority) by two different parliaments and supported by a referendum. Article 168 of the Spanish constitution provides that total or other revisions affecting existential principles of the constitution[31] have to be approved by two thirds of majority in both chambers of parliament; subsequently, parliament is dissolved and the new chambers have to approve the same text by the same majority. After that, the revision is to be ratified by popular referendum. In Switzerland Article 191.3 of the federal constitution provides that "if the people vote for a total revision, new elections shall be held to both Chambers". In Bulgaria, total of structural amendments to the constitution can only be adopted by a special "Grand Assembly" specifically elected for this purpose, by a "majority of two-thirds of the votes of all members, in three ballots on three different days" (Article 161 Bulgarian constitution).

Other procedural guarantees can be imagined and borrowed from other constitutional rules aimed at reducing the potentially distorting impact of one-shot, majority decisions, such as, for instance, federalism and participatory democracy (on this see Fraenkel-Haeberle et al. 2015 as well as Palermo and Alber 2015). Furthermore, it is likely that the debate on sovereignty will cease to be a black-and-white issue in future, especially in some areas, and take some more nuances, such as in the case of de facto states, so that it is plausible that statehood and sovereignty will increasingly be seen as matter of degree rather than of either-or (Harzl 2018). In any case, in a comparative perspective, the trend outlined in the Quebec Secession Reference is being gradually establishing a first set of rules aimed at regulating secession by legal procedures. The embryo of such rules is no doubt the referendum, but additional, more sophisticated and fascinating instruments are being created, sometimes unwittingly, and it is easy to predict that in future there will be significant improvements in this regard.

[31] The Spanish Constitutional Court very convincingly explained the rationale of the total revision. In its ruling 48/2003, it stated that the Spanish constitution does not contain any substantive limitation to the amending power (unlike most other European constitutions) and precisely for that it contains a detailed (and extremely rigid) procedure to legally regulate changes that are so significant to substantially modify the basic traits of the current constitution.

References

Baldacchino, Godfrey and Hepburn, Eve (2012), "A Different Appetite for Sovereignty? Independence Movements in Subnational Island Jurisdictions", in *Commonwealth and Comparative Politics*, 50 (4), 555–568.

Bihonegn, Tesfa (2015), "Federalization with a Constitutional Guarantee to Secession: Controversies, Paradoxes and Imponderables in Ethiopia", in *Regional & Federal Studies*, 25 (1), 45–70.

Bílková, Veronika (2016), "Territorial (Se)cession in Light of Recent Events in Crimea", in Matteo Nicolini, Francesco Palermo and Enrico Milano (eds.), *Law, Territory and Conflict Resolution: Law as a Problem and Law as a Solution*, Brill-Nijhoff, Leiden-Boston, 194–218.

Blokker, Paul ed. (2018), *Constitutional Acceleration within the European Union and Beyond*, Routledge, London.

Bowring, Bill (2015), "From Empire to Multilateral Player: The Deep Roots of Autonomy in Russia", in Tove Malloy and Francesco Palermo (eds.), *Minority Accommodation Through Territorial and Non-territorial Autonomy*, Oxford University Press, Oxford, 133–157.

Burdeau, Georges (1985), *Traité de Science Politique, Tome V, Les régimes politiques*, 3rd ed., Librairie générale de droit et de jurisprudence, Paris.

Castellà Andreu, Josep Maria (2016), "Tribunal constitucional y proceso secesionista catalán: respuestas juriídico-constitucionales a un conflicto político-constitucional", in *Teoría y Realidad Constitucional*, (37), 561–592.

Castellà Andreu, Josep Maria (2017), "Sobre el encaje constitucional del pretendido referéndum de secesión en Cataluña", in Eva Sáenz Royo and Carlos Garrido López (eds.), *La funcionalidad del referéndum en la democracia representativa*, Tirant lo Blanc, Valencia, 129–153.

Chen, Albert HY and Poiares Maduro, Miguel (2013), "The Judiciary and Constitutional Review", in Mark Tushnet, Thomas Fleiner and Cheryl Saunders (eds.), *Routledge Handbook of Constitutional Law*, Routledge, London, 97–109.

Devo Plus Group (2012), *A New Union: Third Report of the Devo Plus Group*, available at http://www.centreonconstitutionalchange.ac.uk/resources/new-union-third-report-devo-plus-group.

Ellis, Andrew (2018), *Research Report "Administration of Referendums": A Comparative Study of Independence Referendums*, National Research Institute, Boroko.

Elster, Jon (1995), "Forces and Mechanisms in the Constitution-Making Process", in *Duke Law Journal*, 45 (2), 364–396.

Elster, Jon (2012), "Constitution-Making and Violence", in *Journal of Legal Analysis*, 4 (1), 7–39.

Ferraiuolo, Gennaro (2016), *Costituzione federalismo secessione. Un itinerario*, ES, Napoli.

Fraenkel-Haeberle, Cristina, Kropp, Sabine, Palermo, Francesco and Sommermann, Karl-Peter eds. (2015), *Citizen Participation in Multi-level Democracies*, Brill-Nijhoff, Leiden-Boston.

Habtu, Alem (2005), "Multiethnic Federalism in Ethiopia: A Study of the Secession Clause in the Constitution", in *Publius*, 35 (2), 313–335.

Haljan, David (2014), *Constitutionalising Secession*, Hart, Oxford.

Harzl, Benedikt (2018), *The Law and Politics of Engaging De Facto States: Injecting New Ideas for an Enhanced EU Role*, Center for Transatlantic Relations, Washington, DC.

Hayek, Friedrich A. (1960), *The Constitution of Liberty*, Chicago University Press, Chicago.

Kössler, Karl (2018), "Territorial Referendums from a Constitutionalist Perspective: Functions, Justifications and Legal Design", in Alberto Lopez Basaguren and Leire Escajedo San Epifanio (eds.), *Claims for Secession and Federalism: A Comparative Study with a Special Focus on Spain*, Springer, Berlin.

Levrat, Nicolas, Antunes, Sandrina, Tusseau, Guillaume and Williams, Paul (2017), *Catalonia's Legitimate Right to Decide. Paths to Self-Determination*, Report Commissioned by the Minister of Foreign Affairs, Institutional Relations and Transparency of the Government of Catalonia, Barcelona.

Leyland, Peter (2016), *The Constitution of the United Kingdom: A Contextual Analysis*, Hart, Oxford.

López-Basaguren, Alberto (2018), "The Secession Issue and Territorial Autonomy in Spain: Bicameralism Revisited", in *Perspectives on Federalism*, 10 (2), E-238–267.

Mancini, Susanna (2012), "Secession and Self-Determination", in Michael Rosenfeld and András Sajó (eds.), *The Oxford Handbook of Comparative Constitutional Law*, Oxford University Press, Oxford, 481–500.

Martinico, Giuseppe (2017a), "Identity Conflicts and Secession Before Courts: Three Case Studies", in *Revista general de derecho público comparado*, (21), 1–30.

Martinico, Giuseppe (2017b), "Considerazioni comparatistiche sul referendum alla luce del caso britannico", in *Diritto Pubblico* (2), 429–467.

Martinico, Giuseppe (2018), *How Can Constitutionalism Deal with Secession in the Age of Populism? The Case of Referendums*, Stals Research Paper 5, http://stals.sssup.it.

Mendez, Fernando and Germann, Micha (2018), "Contested Sovereignty: Mapping Referendums on Sovereignty Over Time and Space", in *British Journal of Political Science*, 48 (1), 141–165.

Mendez, Fernando, Mendez, Mario and Triga, Vasilika (2014), *Referendums and the European Union: A Comparative Inquiry*, Cambridge University Press, Cambridge.

Mitchell, James (2014), *The Scottish Question*, Oxford University Press, Oxford.

Novic, Elisa and Priya, Urs (2016), "Secession", in *Max Planck Encyclopedia of Comparative Constitutional Law*, Oxford University Press, Oxford.

Palermo, Francesco and Alber, Elisabeth eds. (2015), *Federalism as Decision-Making: Changes in Structures, Procedures and Policies*, Brill-Nijhoff, Leiden-Boston.

Poggeschi, Giovanni (2018), *La Catalogna: dalla nazione storica alla repubblica immaginaria*, ES, Napoli.

Qvortrup, Mads (2014), *Referendums and Ethnic Conflict*, University of Pennsylvania Press, Philadelphia.

Regan, Anthony J. (2013), "Autonomy and Conflict Resolution in Bougainville, Papua New Guinea", in Yash Ghai and Sophia Woodman (eds.), *Practising Self-Government: A Comparative Study of Autonomous Regions*, Cambridge University Press, Cambridge, 412–448.

Şen, İlker Gökhan (2015), *Sovereignty Referendums in International and Constitutional Law*, Springer, Berlin.

Sunstein, Cass R. (1991), "Constitutionalism and Secession", in *University of Chicago Law Review*, 58 (2), 633–670.

Tierney, Stephen (2012), *Constitutional Referendums: The Theory and Practice of Republican Deliberation*, Oxford University Press, Oxford.

Tierney, Stephen (2013), "Legal Issues Surrounding the Referendum on Independence for Scotland", in *European Constitutional Law Review*, 9 (3), 359–390.

Venice Commission (2014), Opinion on "Whether the Decision Taken by the Supreme Council of the Autonomous Republic of Crimea in Ukraine to Organise a Referendum on Becoming a Constituent Territory of the Russian Federation or Restoring Crimea's 1992 Constitution Is Compatible with Constitutional Principles", CDL-AD(2014)002-e.

Weinstock, Daniel (2001), "Constitutionalizing the Right to Secede", in *The Journal of Political Philosophy*, 9 (2), 182–203.

Weller, Marc (2008), "Why the Legal Rules on Self-Determination Do Not Resolve Self-Determination Disputes", in Marc Weller and Barbara Metzger (eds.), *Settling Self-Determination Disputes: Complex Power-Sharing in Theory and Practice*, Brill, Leiden-Boston, 17–46.

Index

G. Delledonne and G. Martinico (eds.), *The Canadian Contribution to a Comparative Law of Secession*, https://doi.org/10.1007/978-3-030-03469-6

The manufacturer's authorised representative in the EU is Springer Nature Customer Service Centre GmbH, Europaplatz 3, 69115 Heidelberg, Germany. If you have any concerns regarding our products, please contact ProductSafety@springernature.com

Printed and bound by CPI Group (UK) Ltd, Croydon, CR0 4YY

30/09/2026

02225649-0008